lonely planet

MEXICAN SPANISH

Travel Phrasebook & Dictionary

Credits

Production Editor Ailbhe MacMahon
Language Writers Cecilia Carmona, Rafael Carmona

Thanks

Sofie Andersen, Marc Backwell, Fergal Condon, Gwen Cotter, Kellie Langdon, Liza Prado, Saralinda Turner, Clifton Wilkinson

Published by Lonely Planet Global Limited
CRN 554153

Digital Depot, Roe Lane off Thomas Street, Dublin
D08 TCV4, Ireland (EU authorised representative)

7th Edition – Sep 2026
ISBN 978 1 80653 140 0

Cover Image Saguaro cactus, Mr Doomits/Shutterstock
Printed in China 10 9 8 7 6 5 4 3 2 1

Contact lonelyplanet.com/contact

Look out for the following icons throughout the book:

'Shortcut' Phrase
Easy-to-remember alternative to the full phrase

Q&A Pair
'Question-and-answer' pair – we suggest a response to the question asked

Look for
Phrases you may see on signs, menus etc

Listen for
Phrases you may hear from officials, locals etc

LANGUAGE TIP

An insight into the foreign language

CULTURE TIP

An insight into the local culture

How to read the phrases:

- Coloured words and phrases throughout the book are phonetic guides to help you pronounce the foreign language.
- Lists of phrases with tinted background are options you can choose to complete the phrase above them.

These abbreviations will help you choose the right words and phrases in this book:

f	feminine	m	masculine	sg	singular
inf	informal	pl	plural		
lit	literal	pol	polite		

CONTENTS

INTRO

Mexican Spanish

ESPAÑOL MEXICANO/
ES·PA·NYOL ME·HEE·KAN·O

Who speaks Mexican Spanish?

Why Bother

Even if you can't roll your *r*'s like Speedy Gonzales, communicating with locals is crucial, as Mexicans well know – it was La Malinche, the enslaved Maya mistress of conquistador Hernán Cortés, who ultimately facilitated the Spanish conquest by interpreting for him.

Distinctive Sounds

The strong and rolled r, and kh (as in the Scottish *loch*).

Spanish in the World

Over the last 500 years, Spanish in Mexico has evolved differently to the Spanish spoken in Europe. You'll easily recognise Spaniards by the 'lisp' in their

110 MILLION
speak Mexican Spanish as their first language

speech – ie *cerveza* (beer) is ser·*ve*·sa in Mexico but ther·*ve*·tha in Spain.

Spanish in Mexico

What sets Mexican Spanish apart from other Latin American Spanish varieties is the rich vocabulary. In addition to the influence by indigenous Náhuatl and Maya languages, there's strong impact from US English, especially in the northern border areas.

False Friends

Warning: many Spanish words look like English words but have a different meaning altogether, eg *éxito* *ek*·see·to is 'success', not 'exit' (which is *salida* sa·*lee*·da in Spanish).

Language Family

Romance (developed from Vulgar Latin spoken by Romans during the conquest of the Iberian Peninsula from the 3rd to the 1st century BCE). Close relatives include Portuguese, Italian, French and Romanian.

Must-Know Grammar

Spanish has a formal and informal word for 'you' (*Usted* oos·*ted* and *tú* too respectively). Also, verbs have a different ending for each person, like the English 'I do' vs 'he/she does'.

Donations to English

Numerous. Thanks to Columbus' arrival in the New World in 1492, there's a large corpus of words from indigenous languages that have entered English via Mexican Spanish. You may recognise *avocado, chocolate, coyote, tomato.*

5 Phrases TO LEARN BEFORE YOU GO

01 Where can I buy handicrafts?

¿Dónde se puede comprar artesanías?

don·de se *pwe*·de kom·*prar* ar·te·sa·*nee*·as

Star buys in Mexico are the regional handicrafts produced all over the country, mainly by indigenous people.

02 Which *antojitos* do you have?

¿Qué antojitos tiene? ke an·to·*hee*·tos *tye*·ne

'Little whimsies' (snacks) can encompass anything – have an entire meal of them, eat a few as appetisers, or get one on the street for a quick bite.

03 Not too spicy, please.

No muy picoso, por favor. no mooy pee·*ko*·so por fa·*vor*

Not all food in Mexico is spicy, but beware – many dishes can be fierce indeed, so it may be a good idea to play it safe.

04 Where can I find a *cantina* nearby?

¿Dónde hay una cantina cerca de aquí?

don·de ai *oo*·na kan·*tee*·na *ser*·ka de a·*kee*

Ask locals about the classical Mexican venue for endless snacks – and often dancing as well.

05 How do you say ... in your language?

¿Cómo se dice ... en su lengua?

ko·mo se *dee*·se ... en su *len*·gwa

Numerous indigenous languages are spoken around Mexico, primarily Maya languages and Náhuatl. People will appreciate it if you try to use their local language.

10 Phrases TO SOUND LIKE A LOCAL

Hey!	**¡Oye!/¡Oiga!** inf/pol	o·ye/*oy*·ga
How's things?	**¿Qué tal?**	ke tal
What's new?	**¿Qué onda?**	ke *on*·da
How cool!	**¡Qué chido!**	ke *chee*·do
Sounds good!	**¡Cámara!**	*ka*·ma·ra
Check this out!	**¡Checa ésto!**	*che*·ka *es*·to
Wow, really?	**¡Órale!**	o·ra·le
Are you serious?	**¿Te cae?**	te kai
You must be kidding!	**¡No manches!**	no *man*·ches
Whatever.	**Me vale.**	me *va*·le

MEXICAN SPANISH

Pronunciation

Mexican Spanish pronunciation differs slightly from the Castilian Spanish spoken in Spain. The most obvious difference is the lack of the lisping 'th' sound which is found in Castilian Spanish. With a bit of practice you'll soon get the basics.

VOWEL SOUNDS

SYMBOL	ENGLISH EQUIVALENT	SPANISH EXAMPLE	TRANSLITERATION
a	run	agua	a·gwa
e	red	número	*noo*·me·ro
ee	bee	día	*dee*·a
o	dog	ojo	*o*·ho
oo	book	gusto	*goos*·to

Vowels in Mexican Spanish are quite short and fairly closed. The sound remains level, and each vowel is pronounced as an individual unit. There are a few cases where two vowel sounds become very closely combined (so-called 'diphthongs'):

SYMBOL	ENGLISH EQUIVALENT	SPANISH EXAMPLE	TRANSLITERATION
ai	aisle	bailar	bai·*lar*
ay	say	seis	says
ow	house	autobús	ow·to·*boos*
oy	boy	hoy	oy

CONSONANT SOUNDS

SYMBOL	ENGLISH EQUIVALENT	SPANISH EXAMPLE	TRANSLITERATION
b	big	barco	*bar*·ko
ch	chili	chica	*chee*·ka
d	din	dinero	dee·*ne*·ro
f	fun	fiesta	*fye*·sta
g	go	gato	*ga*·to
h	happy	gente, jardín, México	*hen*·te, har·*deen*, *me*·hee·ko
k	kick	cabeza, queso	ka·*be*·sa, *ke*·so
l	loud	lago	*la*·go
m	man	mañana	ma·*nya*·na
n	no	nuevo	*nwe*·vo
ny	canyon	señora	se·*nyo*·ra
p	pig	padre	*pa*·dre
r	run (but strongly rolled, especially *rr*)	ritmo, mariposa, burro	*reet*·mo, ma·ree·*po*·sa, *boo*·ro
s	so	semana, zarzuela, Xochimilco	se·*ma*·na, sar·*swe*·la, so·chee·*meel*·ko
t	tin	tienda	*tyen*·da
v	a soft 'b' (between 'v' and 'b')	veinte	*vayn*·te
w	win	guardia, Oaxaca	*gwar*·dya, wa·*ha*·ka
y	yes	llave, viaje, ya	*ya*·ve, *vya*·he, ya

WORD STRESS

Words in Spanish have stress, which means you emphasise one syllable over another. Rule of thumb: when a written word ends in *n*, *s* or a vowel, the stress falls on the second-last syllable. Otherwise, the final syllable is stressed. If you see an accent mark over a syllable, it cancels out these rules and you just stress that syllable instead. Don't worry if you can't remember these details – our coloured phonetic guides give you the stressed syllable in italics.

PLUNGE IN

Don't worry too much about pronunciation. Just take your cue from the locals when it comes to the sounds and intonation of Mexican Spanish. The coloured phonetic guides we've provided for every phrase give you all the correct sounds and the stressed syllables. Even if you pronounce them as if they were English, you should be understood just fine.

MEXICAN SPANISH ALPHABET

A a	a	**J j**	*ho*·ta	**R r**	e·re
B b	be *lar*·ga	**K k**	ka	**S s**	e·se
C c	se	**L l**	e·le	**T t**	te
D d	de	**M m**	e·me	**U u**	oo
E e	e	**N n**	e·ne	**V v**	be *kor*·ta
F f	e·fe	**Ñ ñ**	e·nye	**W w**	*do*·ble ve
G g	he	**O o**	o	**X x**	e·kees
H h	a·che	**P p**	pe	**Y y**	ee *grye*·ga
I i	ee la·*tee*·na	**Q q**	koo	**Z z**	se·ta

The letters *ch* and *ll* are no longer officially considered separate letters but they're still sounds in their own right.

SPELLBOUND

The relationship between Mexican Spanish sounds and their spelling is quite straightforward and consistent. Here are the rules:

c	before *e* or *i* pronounced as the 's' in 'so'; before *a*, *o* and *u* pronounced as the 'k' in 'kick'	cerveza, cita, carro, corto, cubo	ser·*ve*·sa, *see*·ta, *ka*·ro, *kor*·to, *koo*·bo
g	before *e* or *i* pronounced as the 'ch' in the Scottish *loch;* before *a*, *o* and *u* pronounced as the 'g' in 'go'	gente, gitano, gato, gordo, guante	*hen*·te, hee·*ta*·no, *ga*·to, *gor*·do, *gwan*·te
gue, gui, güi	as the 'g' in 'go' (*u* is not pronounced unless there are two dots above it)	guerra, Guillermo, güiski	*ge*·ra, gee·*yer*·mo, *gwees*·kee
h	not pronounced	haber	a·*ber*
j	as the 'ch' in the Scottish *loch*	jardín	har·*deen*
ll	as the 'y' in 'yes'	llave	*ya*·ve
ñ	as the 'ny' in 'canyon'	niño	*nee*·nyo
qu	as the 'k' in 'kick' (*u* is not pronounced)	quince	*keen*·se
x	usually as the 'ch' in the Scottish *loch;* as 's' in some place names; as 'ks' in other words	México Xochimilco próximo	*me*·hee·ko so·chee·*meel*·ko *prok*·see·mo
z	as the 's' in 'soup'	zorro	*so*·ro

MEXICAN SPANISH

Grammar

This chapter is designed to explain the main grammatical structures you need in order to make your own sentences. Look under each heading – listed in alphabetical order – for information on functions which these grammatical categories express in a sentence. For example, demonstratives are used for giving instructions, so you'll need them to tell the taxi driver where your hotel is, etc. A glossary of grammatical terms is included at the end of the chapter to help you.

ADJECTIVES & ADVERBS

Describing People/Things • Doing Things

Adjectives in Spanish have different endings depending on whether the noun is masculine or feminine, and singular or plural (see **gender** and **plurals**).

ADJECTIVES

m sg	**fantastic hotel**	hotel fantástico	o·*tel* fan·*tas*·tee·ko
f sg	**fantastic hammock**	hamaca fantástica	a·*ma*·ka fan·*tas*·tee·ka
m pl	**fantastic books**	libros fantásticos	*lee*·bros fan·*tas*·tee·kos
f pl	**fantastic artworks**	obras fantásticas	*ob*·ras fan·*tas*·tee·kas

Adjectives generally come after the noun in Spanish. However, adjectives of quantity (such as 'much', 'a lot', 'little/few', 'too much') and possessive adjectives (eg 'my' and 'your') always precede the noun. See also **demonstratives** (p17) and **possessives** (p22).

many tourists	muchos turistas (lit: many-m-pl tourists)	*moo*·chos too·*rees*·tas
my hat	mi sombrero (lit: my hat)	mee som·*bre*·ro

Most adverbs in Spanish are derived from adjectives by adding the ending *-mente* ·*men*·te to the singular feminine form of the adjective (ie the form ending in *-a*), just like adding '-ly' to adjectives in English. In Spanish, adverbs are generally placed after the verb they refer to.

a slow train	un tren lento (lit: a-m-sg train slow-m-sg)	oon tren *len*·to
to speak slowly	hablar lentamente (lit: to-speak slowly)	ab·*lar* len·ta·*men*·te

ARTICLES

Naming People/Things

Spanish has two words for 'a/an': *un* oon and *una* *oo*·na. The gender of the noun determines which one you use. *Un* and *una* also have plural forms – *unos* *oo*·nos and *unas* *oo*·nas (some).

INDEFINITE ARTICLES

m sg	**a taco**	un taco	oon *ta*·ko
m pl	**some tacos**	unos tacos	*oo*·nos *ta*·kos
f sg	**a house**	una casa	*oo*·na *ka*·sa
f pl	**some houses**	unas casas	*oo*·nas *ka*·sas

The articles *el* el and *la* la both mean 'the'. Whether you use *el* or *la* also depends on the gender of the noun. For the plural, use *los* los and *las* las for masculine and feminine. See also **gender** (p19) and **plurals** (p22).

DEFINITE ARTICLES

m sg	**the donkey**	el burro	el *boo*·ro
m pl	**the donkeys**	los burros	los *boo*·ros
f sg	**the shop**	la tienda	la *tyen*·da
f pl	**the shops**	las tiendas	las *tyen*·das

BE

Describing People/Things • Making Statements

Spanish has two words for the English verb 'be': *ser* ser and *estar* es·*tar*, which are used depending on the context.

USE OF *SER* (TO BE)

permanent characteristics of persons/things	Cecilia is very nice.	Cecilia es muy amable. se·*see*·lya es mooy a·*ma*·ble
occupation or nationality	Marcos is from Mexico.	Marcos es de México. *mar*·kos es de *me*·hee·ko
time or location of events	It's 3 o'clock.	Son las tres. son las tres
possession	Whose backpack is this?	¿De quién es esta mochila? de kyen es *es*·ta mo·*chee*·la

USE OF *ESTAR* (TO BE)

temporary characteristics of persons/things	The food is cold.	La comida está fría. la ko·*mee*·da es·*ta free*·a
time or location of persons/things	We are in Coyoacán.	Estamos en Coyoacán. es·*ta*·mos en ko·yo·a·*kan*
a person's mood	I'm happy.	Estoy contento/a. m/f es·*toy* kon·*ten*·to/a

SER – PRESENT TENSE

I	**am**	yo	soy	yo	soy
you sg inf	**are**	tú	eres	too	e·res
you sg pol	**are**	Usted	es	oos·*ted*	es
he/she	**is**	él/ella	es	el/e·ya	es
we	**are**	nosotros/ nosotras m/f	somos	no·so·tros/ no·so·tras	so·mos
you pl	**are**	Ustedes	son	oos·te·des	son
they	**are**	ellos/ellas m/f	son	e·yos/e·yas	son

ESTAR – PRESENT TENSE

I	**am**	yo	estoy	yo	es·*toy*
you sg inf	**are**	tú	estás	too	es·*tas*
you sg pol	**are**	Usted	está	oos·*ted*	es·*ta*
he/she	**is**	él/ella	está	el/e·ya	es·*ta*
we	**are**	nosotros/ nosotras m/f	estamos	no·so·tros/ no·so·tras	es·*ta*·mos
you pl	**are**	Ustedes	están	oos·te·des	es·*tan*
they	**are**	ellos/ellas m/f	están	e·yos/e·yas	es·*tan*

DEMONSTRATIVES

Giving Instructions • Indicating Location • Pointing Things Out

To point something out the easiest phrases to use are *es* es (it is), or *eso es* e·so es (that is). To say 'this is' use *este es* es·te es if it's a masculine object and *esta es* es·ta es if it's feminine.

Esta es mi licencia. es·ta es mee lee·*sen*·sya
This is my driving licence.
(lit: this-f-sg is my driving-licence)

There are three 'distance words' in Spanish, depending on whether something or someone is close (this), away from you (that), or even further away in time or distance (that over there). See also **gender** and **plurals** (p22).

DEMONSTRATIVES

	m sg		m pl	
this (close)	éste	es·te	éstos	es·tos
that (away)	ése	e·se	ésos	e·sos
that (further away)	aquél	a·*kel*	aquéllos	a·*ke*·yos
	f sg		**f pl**	
this (close)	ésta	es·ta	éstas	es·tas
that (away)	ésa	e·sa	ésas	e·sas
that (further away)	aquélla	a·*ke*·ya	aquéllas	a·*ke*·yas

DIMINUTIVES

Naming People/Things

Mexicans frequently use diminutives, which are nouns whose endings have been altered in order to soften their intensity, emphasise smallness, express endearment or even show politeness. A person's name can be made diminutive as a way of expressing affection, especially towards a child or younger sibling.

Diminutives are created by changing the ending of the noun to *-ito* ·*ee*·to for a masculine noun, or *-ita* ·*ee*·ta for a feminine noun. Less commonly, diminutives may be formed with *-illo* ·*ee*·yo, *-illa* ·*ee*·ya, *-ico* ·*ee*·ko and *-ica* ·*ee*·ka endings.

NOUN	DIMINUTIVE NOUN	USED FOR
un momento oon mo·*men*·to one moment	**un momentito** oon mo·men·*tee*·to just a moment (lit: a-m-sg moment-little-m-sg)	showing politeness
dos semanas dos se·*ma*·nas two weeks	**dos semanitas** dos·se·ma·*nee*·tas just two weeks (lit: two weeks-little-f-pl)	softening intensity
perro *pe*·ro dog	**perrito** pe·*ree*·to doggy (lit: dog-little-m-sg)	emphasising smallness
Pablo *pab*·lo Paul	**Pablito** pab·*lee*·to (dear) Paul (lit: Paul-little-m-sg)	expressing endearment/ affection

GENDER

Naming People/Things

In Spanish, all nouns – words which denote a thing, person or concept – are either masculine or feminine. The dictionary will tell you what gender a noun is, but here are some handy tips to help you determine gender:

- a word is masculine/feminine if referring to a man/woman
- words ending in *-o* or *-or* are often masculine
- words ending in *-a*, *-d*, *-z* or *-ión* are often feminine

In this book, masculine forms appear before the feminine forms. If you see a word ending in *-o/a*, it means the masculine form ends in *-o*, and the feminine form ends in *-a* (ie replace *o* with *-a* to make it feminine). The same goes for the plural endings *-os/as*. If you see an *(a)* between brackets at the end of a word, eg *escritor(a)* es·kree·*tor*/es·kree·*to*·ra, it means you add that ending to make the word feminine. In other cases we spell out the whole word. See also **adjectives**, **articles** (p14) and **possessives** (p22).

HAVE

Possessing

Possession can be indicated in various ways in Spanish (see also **possessives**, p22). The easiest way is by using the verb *tener* te·*ner* (have).

I have two sisters. Tengo dos hermanas.
(lit: I-have two sisters)
ten·go dos er·*ma*·nas

TENER – PRESENT TENSE

I	**have**	yo	tengo	yo	*ten*·go
you sg inf	**have**	tú	tienes	too	*tye*·nes
you sg pol	**have**	Usted	tiene	oos·*ted*	*tye*·ne
he/she	**has**	él/ella	tiene	el/e·ya	*tye*·ne
we	**have**	nosotros/ nosotras m/f	tenemos	no·*so*·tros/ no·*so*·tras	te·*ne*·mos
you pl	**have**	Ustedes	tienen	oos·*te*·des	*tye*·nen
they	**have**	ellos/ellas m/f	tienen	e·yos/e·yas	*tye*·nen

NEGATIVES

Negating

To make a negative statement, just add the word *no* no before the main verb of the sentence:

I don't like cooking. No me gusta cocinar.
(lit: not me it-pleases cooking)
no me *goo*·sta ko·see·*nar*

Contrary to English, double negatives are not only acceptable but necessary in Spanish:

I have nothing to declare.	No tengo nada que declarar. (lit: not I-have nothing to declare) no *ten*·go *na*·da ke dek·la·*rar*

PERSONAL PRONOUNS

Making Statements • Naming People/Things

Personal pronouns ('I', 'you' etc) change form in Spanish depending on whether they're the subject or the object of a sentence. It's the same in English, which has 'I' and 'me' as the subject and object pronouns (eg 'I see her' and 'She sees me'). The subject pronoun is often omitted in Spanish as the subject is understood from the corresponding verb form (see also **verbs**, p25).

I'm a student.	Soy estudiante. (lit: I-am student) soy es·too·*dyan*·te

SUBJECT PRONOUNS

I	yo	yo	**we**	nosotros m nosotras f	no·so·tros no·so·tras
you sg inf **you** sg pol	tú Usted	too oos·*ted*	**you** pl	Ustedes	oos·*te*·des
he/she	él/ella	el/e·ya	**they**	ellos m ellas f	e·yos e·yas

Mexicans use two different words for the singular 'you'. When talking to someone familiar to you or younger than you, it's usual to use the informal form *tú* too, rather than the polite form *Usted* oos·*ted*. The polite form should be used when you're meeting someone for the first time, talking to someone much older than you, or when you're in a formal situation (eg when talking to the police, customs officers etc). In this book we have chosen the appropriate form for the situation. Note that in Mexico you use the word *Ustedes* oos·*te*·des for the plural 'you' – whether or not it's a formal situation.

See also **be** (p16) and **have** (p20).

PLURALS

Naming People/Things

Forming plurals is easy – in general, if the word ends in a vowel, you add *-s* for plural. If the noun ends in a consonant (or *y*), you add *-es*:

SINGULAR			PLURAL		
bed	cama	*ka*·ma	**beds**	camas	*ka*·mas
woman	mujer	moo·*her*	**women**	mujeres	moo·*he*·res

POSSESSIVES

Possessing

A common way of indicating possession is by using possessive adjectives before the noun they describe. As with any other adjective, they always agree with the noun in number (singular or plural) and gender (masculine or feminine). See also **gender** (p19) and **plurals**.

This is our daughter.	Ésta es nuestra hija. (lit: this-f-sg is our-f-sg daughter) *es*·ta es *nwes*·tra *ee*·ha

In the table opposite, the forms separated by a slash are used with a singular/plural noun.

POSSESSIVE ADJECTIVES

my	mi/ mis	mee/ mees	**our**	nuestro/ nuestros m nuestra/ nuestras f	*nwes*·tro/ *nwes*·tros *nwes*·tra/ *nwes*·tras
your sg inf	tu/ tus	too/ toos	**your** pl inf	vuestro/ vuestros m vuestra/ vuestras f	*vwes*·tro/ *vwes*·tros *vwes*·tra/ *vwes*·tras
your sg pol	su/ sus	soo/ soos	**your** pl pol	su/ sus	soo/ soos
his/ her	su/ sus	soo/ soos	**their**	su/ sus	soo/ soos

In Spanish, ownership can also be expressed by using the word *de* de (of).

That's my friend's backpack.	Esa es la mochila de mi amigo. (lit: that-f-sg is the-f-sg back-pack of my friend-m) e·sa es la mo·*chee*·la de mee a·*mee*·go

Alternatively, you can use the verb *tener* (see **have**, p20).

PREPOSITIONS

Giving Instructions • Indicating Location • Pointing Things Out

Like English, Spanish uses prepositions to explain where things are in time or space. Common prepositions are listed in the table below. For more prepositions, see the **dictionary** (p205).

PREPOSITIONS

after	después de	des·*pwes* de	**from**	de	de
at (time)	a	a	**in (place)**	en	en
before	antes de	*an*·tes de	**to**	a	a

QUESTIONS

Asking Questions • Negating

To ask a simple 'yes/no' question, just make a statement but raise your intonation towards the end of the sentence, as you would in English. The inverted question mark in written Spanish prompts you to do this.

Is that the main square?	¿Eso es el zócalo? (lit: that-m-sg is the-m-sg main-square) e·so es el so·ka·lo

It's not impolite to answer questions with a simple *sí* see (yes) or *no* no (no) in Spanish, even when you'd like to say 'Yes it is/does', or 'No, it isn't/doesn't'.

As in English, there are also question words for more specific questions. These words go at the start of a sentence.

QUESTION WORDS

How?	¿Cómo?	*ko*·mo
How many?	¿Cuántos? m pl ¿Cuántas? f pl	*kwan*·tos *kwan*·tas
What?	¿Qué?	ke
When?	¿Cuándo?	*kwan*·do
Where?	¿Dónde?	*don*·de
Which?	¿Cuál? sg ¿Cuáles? pl	kwal *kwa*·les
Who?	¿Quién? sg ¿Quiénes? pl	kyen *kye*·nes
Why?	¿Por qué?	por *ke*

VERBS

Doing Things • Making Statements

There are three verb categories in Spanish, depending on whether the infinitive ends in *-ar*, *-er* or *-ir*, eg *hablar* ab·*lar* (talk), *comer* ko·*mer* (eat), *vivir* vee·*veer* (live). Tenses are formed by adding various endings for each person to the verb stem (after removing *-ar*, *-er* or *-ir* from the infinitive) or to the infinitive, and for most verbs these endings follow regular patterns. The verb endings for the present, past and future tenses are presented in the tables on the following pages. For negative forms of verbs, see **negatives** (p20).

PRESENT TENSE

		hablar	**comer**	**vivir**
I	yo	hablo	como	vivo
you sg inf	tú	hablas	comes	vives
you sg pol	Usted	habla	come	vive
he	él	habla	come	vive
she	ella	habla	come	vive
we	nosotros m nosotras f	hablamos	comemos	vivimos
you pl	Ustedes	hablan	comen	viven
they	ellos m ellas f	hablan	comen	viven

See also **be** (p16) and **have** (p20) for present-tense forms of these verbs.

PAST TENSE

		hablar	comer	vivir
I	yo	hablé	comí	viví
you sg inf	tú	hablaste	comiste	viviste
you sg pol	Usted	habló	comió	vivió
he	él	habló	comió	vivió
she	ella	habló	comió	vivió
we	nosotros m nosotras f	hablamos	comimos	vivimos
you pl	Ustedes	hablaron	comieron	vivieron
they	ellos m ellas f	hablaron	comieron	vivieron

In the future tense, all three verb categories have the same endings added to the infinitive:

FUTURE TENSE

		hablar	comer	vivir
I	yo	hablaré	comeré	viviré
you sg inf	tú	hablarás	comerás	vivirás
you sg pol	Usted	hablará	comerá	vivirá
he	él	hablará	comerá	vivirá
she	ella	hablará	comerá	vivirá
we	nosotros m nosotras f	hablaremos	comeremos	viviremos
you pl	Ustedes	hablarán	comerán	vivirán
they	ellos m ellas f	hablarán	comerán	vivirán

☑ CULTURE TIP: THE MEANING OF 'MÉXICO'

The mysterious origins of the word *México* me·hee·ko have long been the subject of debate. A popular theory is that *México* literally means 'navel of the moon' in the indigenous Náhuatl language, derived from *meztli* mes·tlee (moon) and *xictli* sheek·tlee (navel). Another theory associates the name with the Náhuatl word *metl* metl (maguey plant). In the 15th and 16th centuries some clerics tried vainly to establish a link between *México* and the Hebrew word *Mesi* (Messiah). Other theories include words which mean 'place of springs' and 'that which kills by an obsidian arrow'.

In 1998, a 'Round Table on the True Meaning of the Word México' was convened in an attempt to lay the issue to rest once and for all. The panel agreed unanimously that the Aztecs who founded Mexico City called themselves *mexítin* me·shee·teen (Mexicans) in honour of their leader Mexítli, known affectionately as 'Mexi'. Add the Náhuatl suffix *-co* ·ko (place of) and you get *México*: 'Place of the Mexicans'.

WORD ORDER

Making Statements

Sentences in Spanish have a basic word order of subject–verb–object, just like in English. However, the subject pronoun is generally omitted because the subject is obvious from the corresponding verb form (see **verbs**, p25):

I study business.	Yo estudio comercio. (lit: I I-study business) yo es·*too*·dyo ko·*mer*·syo Estudio comercio. (lit: I-study business) es·*too*·dyo ko·*mer*·syo

See also **negatives** (p20) and **questions** (p24).

GLOSSARY

adjective	a word that describes something – 'he was the **greatest** mariachi of his time'
adverb	a word that explains how an action is done – 'he sang **beautifully**'
article	the words 'a', 'an' and 'the'
demonstrative	a word that means 'this' or 'that'
direct object	the thing or person in the sentence that has the action directed to it – 'and the crowd loved **him**'
gender	classification of nouns into classes (like masculine and feminine), requiring other words (eg adjectives) to belong to the same class
indirect object	the person or thing in the sentence that is the recipient of the action – 'the public yelled to **him**'
infinitive	dictionary form of a verb – 'to **play** more'
noun	a thing, person or idea – 'the **ensemble** was excited'
number	whether a word is singular or plural – 'and they performed more **songs**'
personal pronoun	a word that means 'I', 'you' etc
possessive adjective	a word that means 'my', 'your' etc
possessive pronoun	a word that means 'mine', 'yours' etc
preposition	a word like 'for' or 'before' in English
subject	the thing or person in the sentence that does the action – 'the **musicians** played for hours'
tense	form of a verb that tells you whether the action is in the present, past or future – eg 'run' (present), 'ran' (past), 'will run' (future)
verb	a word that shows an action or a state of being – '**wrote** a letter'
verb stem	part of a verb that doesn't change – eg '**play**' in '**play**ing' and '**play**ed'

BASICS

Understanding

KEY PHRASES

Do you speak English?	¿Habla/Hablas inglés? pol/inf	a·bla/a·blas een·*gles*
I don't understand.	No entiendo.	no en·*tyen*·do
What does ... mean?	¿Qué significa ...?	ke seeg·nee·*fee*·ka ...

Q **Do you speak English?**	¿Habla/Hablas inglés? pol/inf *a*·bla/*a*·blas een·*gles*
Q **Does anyone speak English?**	¿Hay alguien que hable inglés? ai al·*gyen* ke *a*·ble een·*gles*
A **I (don't) speak Spanish.**	(No) Hablo español. (no) *a*·blo es·pa·*nyol*
A **I speak a little.**	Hablo un poquito. *a*·blo oon po·*kee*·to
Q **Do you understand?**	¿Me entiende/entiendes? pol/inf me en·*tyen*·de/en·*tyen*·des
A **I (don't) understand.**	(No) Entiendo. (no) en·*tyen*·do
How do you pronounce this?	¿Cómo se pronuncia ésto? *ko*·mo se pro·*noon*·sya *es*·to
How do you write ...?	¿Cómo se escribe ...? *ko*·mo se es·*kree*·be ...
What does ... mean?	¿Qué significa ...? ke seeg·nee·*fee*·ka ...

Could you please repeat that?	¿Puede repetirlo, por favor? *pwe*·de re·pe·*teer*·lo por fa·*vor*
Could you please speak more slowly?	¿Puede hablar más despacio, por favor? *pwe*·de a·*blar* mas des·*pa*·syo por fa·*vor*
Slowly, please!	¡Despacio, por favor! — des·*pa*·syo por fa·*vor*
Could you please write it down?	¿Puede escribirlo, por favor? *pwe*·de es·kree·*beer*·lo por fa·*vor*
I'd like to learn some of your (indigenous) language.	Me gustaría aprender un poco de su lengua (indígena). me goos·ta·*ree*·a a·pren·*der* oon *po*·ko de soo *len*·gwa (een·*dee*·he·na)

LANGUAGE TIP: FALSE FRIENDS

Beware of words which sound like English words but have a different meaning altogether.

embarazada f — em·ba·ra·sa·da — pregnant
not 'embarrassed', which is *apenado/a* m/f a·pe·*na*·do/a

éxito m — *ek*·see·to — success
not 'exit', which is *salida* sa·*lee*·da

injuria f — een·*hoo*·ree·a — insult
not 'injury', which is *herida* e·*ree*·da

parientes m pl — pa·*ryen*·tes — relatives
not 'parents', which is *padres pa*·dres

Numbers & Amounts

CARDINAL NUMBERS

1	uno	*oo*·no
2	dos	dos
3	tres	tres
4	cuatro	*kwa*·tro
5	cinco	*seen*·ko
6	seis	says
7	siete	*sye*·te
8	ocho	*o*·cho
9	nueve	*nwe*·ve
10	diez	dyes
11	once	*on*·se
12	doce	*do*·se
13	trece	*tre*·se
14	catorce	ka·*tor*·se
15	quince	*keen*·se
16	dieciséis	dye·see·*says*
17	diecisiete	dye·see·*sye*·te
18	dieciocho	dye·see·*o*·cho
19	diecinueve	dye·see·*nwe*·ve
20	veinte	*vayn*·te
21	veintiuno	vayn·tee·*oo*·no
30	treinta	*trayn*·ta
40	cuarenta	kwa·*ren*·ta
50	cincuenta	seen·*kwen*·ta

60	sesenta	se·*sen*·ta
70	setenta	se·*ten*·ta
80	ochenta	o·*chen*·ta
90	noventa	no·*ven*·ta
100	cien	*syen*
200	doscientos	do·*syen*·tos
1000	mil	meel
1,000,000	un millón	oon mee·*yon*

ORDINAL NUMBERS

1st	primero/a m/f	pree·*me*·ro/a
2nd	segundo/a m/f	se·*goon*·do/a
3rd	tercero/a m/f	ter·se·ro/a

USEFUL AMOUNTS

How much?	¿Cuánto/a? m/f	*kwan*·to/a
How many?	¿Cuántos/as? m/f pl	*kwan*·tos/as
a little	un poco	oon *po*·ko
a lot/much	mucho/a m/f	*moo*·cho/a
many	muchos/as m/f pl	*moo*·chos/as
some	algunos/as m/f pl	al·*goo*·nos/as

For other useful amounts, see **self-catering** (p182).

Time & Dates

KEY PHRASES

What time is it?	¿Qué hora es?	ke *o*·ra es
At what time ...?	¿A qué hora ...?	a ke *o*·ra ...
What date?	¿Qué día?	ke *dee*·a

TELLING THE TIME

When telling the time in Mexico, 'It is ...' is expressed by *Son las ...* son las ... followed by a number. The exceptions are *Es la una* es la *oo*·na (It's one o'clock), *Es mediodía* es me·dyo·*dee*·a (It's midday) and *Es medianoche* es me·dya·*no*·che (It's midnight).

Q **What time is it?**	¿Qué hora es? ke *o*·ra es
A **It's one o'clock.**	Es la una. es la *oo*·na
A **It's (10) o'clock.**	Son las (diez). son las (dyes)
A **Quarter past one.**	Es la una y cuarto. es la *oo*·na ee *kwar*·to
A **Twenty past one.**	Es la una y veinte. es la *oo*·na ee *vayn*·te
A **Half past (eight).**	Son las (ocho) y media. son las (*o*·cho) ee *me*·dya
A **Twenty to (eight).**	Son veinte para las (ocho). son *vayn*·te *pa*·ra las (*o*·cho)
A **Quarter to (eight).**	Son cuarto para las (ocho). son *kwar*·to *pa*·ra las (*o*·cho)

Ⓠ **At what time ...?**	¿A qué hora ...? a ke *o*·ra ...	
Ⓐ **At one o'clock.**	A la una. a la *oo*·na	
Ⓐ **At (eight) o'clock.**	A las (ocho). a las (*o*·cho)	
Ⓐ **At (4.40pm).**	A las (cuatro y cuarenta de la tarde). a las (*kwa*·tro ee kwa·*ren*·ta de la *tar*·de)	

in the morning	de la mañana	de la ma·*nya*·na
in the afternoon	de la tarde	de la *tar*·de
in the evening	de la noche	de la *no*·che
sunrise	amanecer m	a·ma·ne·*ser*
dawn	madrugada f	ma·droo·*ga*·da
morning	mañana f	ma·*nya*·na
day	día m	*dee*·a
afternoon	tarde f	*tar*·de
evening	noche f	*no*·che
night	noche f	*no*·che
sunset	atardecer m	a·tar·de·*ser*

THE CALENDAR

Monday	lunes m	*loo*·nes
Tuesday	martes m	*mar*·tes
Wednesday	miércoles m	*myer*·ko·les
Thursday	jueves m	*hwe*·ves
Friday	viernes m	*vyer*·nes
Saturday	sábado m	*sa*·ba·do
Sunday	domingo m	do·*meen*·go

January	enero m	e·*ne*·ro
February	febrero m	fe·*bre*·ro
March	marzo m	*mar*·so
April	abril m	a·*breel*
May	mayo m	*ma*·yo
June	junio m	*hoo*·nyo
July	julio m	*hoo*·lyo
August	agosto m	a·*gos*·to
September	septiembre m	sep·*tyem*·bre
October	octubre m	ok·*too*·bre
November	noviembre m	no·*vyem*·bre
December	diciembre m	dee·*syem*·bre
Q **What date?**	¿Qué día?	ke *dee*·a
Q **What's today's date?**	¿Qué día es hoy?	ke *dee*·a es oy
A **It's (17 November).**	Es el (diecisiete de noviembre).	es el (dye·see·*sye*·te de no·*vyem*·bre)
summer	verano m	ve·*ra*·no
autumn	otoño m	o·*to*·nyo
winter	invierno m	een·*vyer*·no
spring	primavera f	pree·ma·*ve*·ra

PRESENT

now	ahora	a·*o*·ra
right now	ahora mismo	a·*o*·ra *mees*·mo
today	hoy	oy
tonight	esta noche	*es*·ta *no*·che

LANGUAGE TIP: MULTIPLE MEANINGS

It's worth remembering that the word *mañana* ma·*nya*·na means 'tomorrow', but *la mañana* la ma·*nya*·na means 'morning'. More rarely, *mañana* can mean 'later on' (especially in bureaucratic situations). Also, *la madrugada* la ma·droo·*ga*·da can mean 'daybreak' or 'the small hours of the morning', depending on the context.

this morning	esta mañana	es·ta ma·*nya*·na
this afternoon	esta tarde	es·ta *tar*·de
this week	esta semana	es·ta se·*ma*·na
this month	este mes	es·te mes
this year	este año	es·te a·nyo

PAST

yesterday	ayer	a·*yer*
yesterday morning	ayer en la mañana	a·*yer* en la ma·*nya*·na
yesterday afternoon	ayer en la tarde	a·*yer* en la *tar*·de
yesterday evening	ayer en la noche	a·*yer* en la *no*·che
day before yesterday	antier	an·*tyer*
(three days) ago	hace (tres días)	a·se (tres *dee*·as)
since (May)	desde (mayo)	*des*·de (*ma*·yo)
last night	anoche	a·*no*·che
last week	la semana pasada	la se·*ma*·na pa·*sa*·da
last month	el mes pasado	el mes pa·*sa*·do
last year	el año pasado	el a·nyo pa·*sa*·do

☑ CULTURE TIP: MEETING ETIQUETTE

Being late for an appointment isn't the end of the world in Mexico. In situations where punctuality is important, make sure you add *a la hora europea* a la *o*·ra e·oo·ro·*pe*·a (meaning 'exactly') after arranging a time to meet. Family obligations always take precedence over social or business meetings, and if you're invited to a party it's expected that you'll arrive between 30 minutes to an hour later than the specified time.

FUTURE

tomorrow	mañana	ma·*nya*·na
tomorrow morning	mañana en la mañana	ma·*nya*·na en la ma·*nya*·na
tomorrow afternoon	mañana en la tarde	ma·*nya*·na en la *tar*·de
tomorrow evening	mañana en la noche	ma·*nya*·na en la *no*·che
day after tomorrow	pasado mañana	pa·*sa*·do ma·*nya*·na
in (six) days	en (seis) días	en (says) *dee*·as
until (June)	hasta (junio)	*as*·ta (*hoo*·nyo)
next week	la próxima semana	la *prok*·see·ma se·*ma*·na
next month	el mes que viene	el mes ke *vye*·ne
next year	el año que viene	el *a*·nyo ke *vye*·ne

PRACTICAL

Transport

KEY PHRASES

When's the next bus?	¿A qué hora sale el próximo camión?	a ke *o*·ra *sa*·le el *prok*·see·mo ka·*myon*
A ticket to ..., please.	Un boleto a ..., por favor.	oon bo·*le*·to a ... por fa·*vor*
Can you tell me when we get to ...?	¿Me puede avisar cuando lleguemos a ...?	me *pwe*·de a·vee·*sar kwan*·do ye·*ge*·mos a ...
Please take me to this address.	Por favor, lléveme a esta dirección.	por fa·*vor* *ye*·ve·me a es·ta dee·rek·*syon*
I'd like to hire a car.	Quisiera rentar un coche.	kee·*sye*·ra ren·*tar* oon *ko*·che

GETTING AROUND

Can we get there by public transport?	¿Podemos llegar en transporte público? po·*de*·mos ye·*gar* en trans·*por*·te *poo*·blee·ko
Can we get there by bicycle?	¿Podemos llegar en bicicleta? po·*de*·mos ye·*gar* en bee·see·*kle*·ta
I'd prefer to walk there.	Prefiero ir caminando. pre·*fye*·ro eer ka·mee·*nan*·do

What time does the ... leave?	¿A qué hora sale el ...?	a ke *o*·ra *sa*·le el ...

boat	barco	*bar*·ko
bus (city)	autobús	ow·to·*boos*
bus (intercity)	camión	ka·*myon*
metro	metro	*me*·tro
minibus	microbús	mee·kro·*boos*
plane	avión	a·*vyon*
train	tren	tren
trolleybus	trolebús	tro·le·*boos*

What time's the first bus?	¿A qué hora sale el primer autobús? a ke *o*·ra *sa*·le el pree·*mer* ow·to·*boos*
What time's the last bus?	¿A qué hora sale el último autobús? a ke *o*·ra *sa*·le el *ool*·tee·mo ow·to·*boos*
What time's the next bus?	¿A qué hora sale el próximo autobús? a ke *o*·ra *sa*·le el *prok*·see·mo ow·to·*boos*
Can I have a lift in your ...?	¿Me puede dar un aventón en su ...? me *pwe*·de dar oon a·ven·*ton* en soo ...

trailer	trailer	*trai*·ler
truck	camión	ka·*myon*
ute/pick-up	camioneta	ka·myo·*ne*·ta
van	vagoneta	va·go·*ne*·ta

LISTEN FOR

Está cancelado.	es·*ta* kan·se·*la*·do	It's cancelled.
Está lleno.	es·*ta* *ye*·no	It's full.
Está retrasado.	es·*ta* re·tra·*sa*·do	It's delayed.

That's my seat.
Ése es mi asiento.
e·se es mee a·*syen*·to

Is this seat free?
¿Está libre este asiento?
es·*ta* *lee*·bre *es*·te a·*syen*·to

✂ **Is it free?** ¿Está libre? es·*ta* *lee*·bre

How long will it be delayed?
¿Cuánto tiempo será el retraso?
kwan·to *tyem*·po se·*ra* el re·*tra*·so

When's the next flight to (Mexico City)?
¿Cuándo sale el próximo vuelo para (México)?
kwan·do *sa*·le el *prok*·see·mo *vwe*·lo *pa*·ra (*me*·hee·ko)

Can you tell me when we get to (Puerto Vallarta)?
¿Me puede avisar cuando lleguemos a (Puerto Vallarta)?
me *pwe*·de a·vee·*sar* *kwan*·do ye·*ge*·mos a (*pwer*·to va·*yar*·ta)

I want to get off here.
¡Aquí me bajo!
a·*kee* me *ba*·ho

✂ **Getting off!** ¡Bajan! *ba*·han

BUYING TICKETS

Where can I buy a ticket?	¿Dónde puedo comprar un boleto? *don*·de pwe·do kom·*prar* oon bo·*le*·to
Do I need to book?	¿Tengo que reservar? *ten*·go ke re·ser·*var*
Can I get a stand-by ticket?	¿Puede ponerme en la lista de espera? *pwe*·de po·*ner*·me en la *lees*·ta de es·*pe*·ra
I'd like to ... my ticket, please.	Me gustaría ... mi boleto, por favor. me goos·ta·*ree*·a ... mee bo·*le*·to por fa·*vor*

cancel	cancelar	kan·se·*lar*
change	cambiar	kam·*byar*
collect	recoger	re·ko·*her*
confirm	confirmar	kon·feer·*mar*

A ... ticket (to Oaxaca), please.	Un boleto ... (a Oaxaca), por favor. oon bo·*le*·to ... (a wa·*ha*·ka) por fa·*vor*

1st-/2nd-class	de primera/ segunda clase	de pree·*me*·ra/ se·*goon*·da *kla*·se
child's	infantil	een·fan·*teel*
one-way	de viaje sencillo	de *vya*·he sen·*see*·yo
return	redondo	re·*don*·do
student's	de estudiante	de es·too·*dyan*·te

I'd like an aisle seat.	Quisiera un asiento de pasillo. kee·*sye*·ra oon a·*syen*·to de pa·*see*·yo
I'd like a window seat.	Quisiera un asiento de ventanilla. kee·*sye*·ra oon a·*syen*·to de ven·ta·*nee*·ya
I'd like a (non-)smoking seat.	Quisiera un asiento en la sección de (no) fumar. kee·*sye*·ra oon a·*syen*·to en la sek·*syon* de (no) foo·*mar*
Is there (a) ...?	¿Hay ...? ai ...

air-conditioning	aire acondicionado	*ai*·re a·kon·dee·syo·*na*·do
blanket	una cobija	*oo*·na ko·*bee*·ha
toilet	sanitario	sa·nee·*ta*·ryo
video	video	vee·*de*·o

How long does the trip take?	¿Cuánto dura el viaje? *kwan*·to *doo*·ra el *vya*·he
Is it a direct route?	¿Es un viaje directo? es oon *vya*·he dee·*rek*·to
What time do I have to check in?	¿A qué hora tengo que documentar? a ke *o*·ra *ten*·go ke do·koo·men·*tar*

For phrases about entering and leaving countries, see **border crossing** (p54).

LUGGAGE

My luggage has been damaged.	Se dañaron mis maletas. se da·*nya*·ron mees ma·*le*·tas

Buying a Ticket

WHAT TIME IS THE NEXT ...?
¿A qué hora sale el próximo ...?
a ke *o*·ra *sa*·le el *prok*·see·mo ...

BOAT
barco
bar·ko

BUS
camión
ka·*myon*

TRAIN
tren
tren

ONE ... TICKET, PLEASE.
Un boleto ..., por favor.
oon bo·*le*·to ... por fa·*vor*

ONE-WAY
de viaje sencillo
de *vya*·he sen·*see*·yo

RETURN
redondo
re·*don*·do

I'D LIKE A/AN ... SEAT.
Quisiera un asiento ...
kee·*sye*·ra oon a·*syen*·to ...

AISLE
de pasillo
de pa·*see*·yo

WINDOW
de ventanilla
de ven·ta·*nee*·ya

WHICH PLATFORM DOES IT DEPART FROM?
¿De cuál andén sale?
de kwal an·*den* *sa*·le

My luggage has been lost.	Se perdieron mis maletas. se per·*dye*·ron mees ma·*le*·tas
My luggage has been stolen.	Se robaron mis maletas. se ro·*ba*·ron mees ma·*le*·tas
My luggage hasn't arrived.	Mis maletas no han llegado. mees ma·*le*·tas no an ye·*ga*·do
I'd like a luggage locker.	Quisiera un casillero. kee·*sye*·ra oon ka·see·*ye*·ro
I'd like some coins/tokens.	Quisiera unas monedas/fichas. kee·*sye*·ra *oo*·nas mo·*ne*·das/*fee*·chas

BUS, TROLLEYBUS & METRO

In Mexico City, you'll probably use the *Metrobús* me·tro·*boos,* a bus line with stations (like a train) that criss-crosses the city and links up to the metro system.

Which city/intercity bus goes to ...?	¿Qué autobús/camión va a ...? ke ow·to·*boos*/ka·*myon* va a ...
How many stops (to the market)?	¿Cuántas paradas son (al mercado)? *kwan*·tas pa·*ra*·das son (al mer·*ka*·do)
Please take me to the bus terminal.	Por favor, lléveme a la central (de autobuses). por fa·*vor ye*·ve·me a la sen·*tral* (de ow·to·*boo*·ses)
This/That one.	Éste./Ése. *es*·te/*e*·se
Bus/Trolleybus number (11).	El autobús/trolebús número (once). el ow·to·*boos*/tro·le·*boos noo*·me·ro (*on*·se)

CULTURE TIP: MEXICO CITY

Mexico City is called 'México' if you're travelling there from anywhere else in the country. It is also very often called *DF* de·*e*·fe (short for *Distrito Federal* dis·*tree*·to fe·de·*ral*), a special administrative district around the national capital. Throughout the country, it's also spoken of as *la Ciudad de México* la syu·*dad* de *me*·hee·ko.

TRAIN

What station is this?	¿Cuál es esta estación? kwal es *es*·ta es·ta·*syon*
What's the next station?	¿Cuál es la próxima estación? kwal es la *prok*·see·ma es·ta·*syon*
Does this train stop at (Chihuahua)?	¿Para el tren en (Chihuahua)? *pa*·ra el tren en (chee·*wa*·wa)
Do I need to change trains?	¿Tengo que cambiar de tren? *ten*·go ke kam·*byar* de tren
Which is the dining car?	¿Cuál es el vagón comedor? kwal es el va·*gon* ko·me·*dor*
Which carriage is 1st class?	¿Cuál es el vagón de primera clase? kwal es el va·*gon* de pree·*me*·ra *kla*·se
Which carriage is for (Querétaro)?	¿Cuál es el vagón para (Querétaro)? kwal es el va·*gon* *pa*·ra (ke·*re*·ta·ro)

CULTURE TIP: BUSSING IT

Originally, a small bus was simply called a *colectivo* ko·*lek*·tee·vo but in the '70s, small public transport vehicles (including cars and vans) in Mexico City and surrounding areas came to be classified as *peseros* pe·*se*·ros – so called because the trip then cost one peso. During the '80s, the government began introducing new minibuses known as *microbuses* mee·kro·*boo*·ses or just *micros* *mee*·kros.

There are also different terms for intercity minibuses and open-backed trucks, depending on the route and city: *combi* *kom*·bee, *rédila* *re*·dee·la, *suburban* soo·*boor*·ban etc. The general word in Mexico City is still *pesero*, whereas in the rest of the country, *colectivo*, *combi*, *microbús* and *suburban* are commonly used. To keep it simple, you can just use the word *transporte* trans·*por*·te.

TAXI

I'd like a taxi now/ tomorrow.	Quisiera un taxi ahora/ mañana. kee·*sye*·ra oon *tak*·see a·*o*·ra/ ma·*nya*·na
I'd like a taxi at (9am).	Quisiera un taxi a las (nueve de la mañana). kee·*sye*·ra oon *tak*·see a las (*nwe*·ve de la ma·*nya*·na)
Is this taxi free?	¿Está libre este taxi? es·*ta* *lee*·bre es·te *tak*·see

Is it free? ¿Está libre? es·*ta* *lee*·bre

How much is it to ...?	¿Cuánto cuesta ir a ...? *kwan*·to *kwes*·ta eer a ...

Please put the meter on.	Por favor, ponga el taxímetro. por fa·*vor pon*·ga el tak·*see*·me·tro
Please take me to (this address).	Por favor, lléveme a (esta dirección). por fa·*vor ye*·ve·me a (*es*·ta dee·rek·*syon*)
To ...	A ... a ...
Please slow down.	Por favor vaya más despacio. por fa·*vor va*·ya mas des·*pa*·syo
Please wait here.	Por favor espere aquí. por fa·*vor* es·*pe*·re a·*kee*
Stop at the corner.	Pare en la esquina. *pa*·re en la es·*kee*·na
Stop here.	Pare aquí. *pa*·re a·*kee*

¿Por aquí se va a ...?

por a·*kee* se va a ...

Is this the road to ...?

CAR & MOTORBIKE

I'd like to hire a/an ... Quisiera rentar ... *kee·sye·ra ren·tar ...*

4WD	un cuatro por cuatro	oon *kwa*·tro por *kwa*·tro
automatic (car)	un (coche) automático	oon (*ko*·che) ow·to·*ma*·tee·ko
manual (car)	un (coche) manual	oon (*ko*·che) man·*wal*
motorbike	una moto	*oo*·na *mo*·to

with (air-conditioning) con (aire acondicionado) kon (*ai*·re a·kon·dee·syo·*na*·do)

without (a driver) sin (chofer) seen (cho·*fer*)

How much for hourly hire? ¿Cuánto cuesta la renta por hora? *kwan*·to *kwes*·ta la *ren*·ta por *o*·ra

How much for daily hire? ¿Cuánto cuesta la renta diaria? *kwan*·to *kwes*·ta la *ren*·ta *dya*·rya

LISTEN FOR

diesel	*dee*·sel	diesel
gasolina	ga·so·*lee*·na	gas/petrol
Magna	*mag*·na	regular unleaded
Premium	*pre*·mee·oom	premium unleaded
sin plomo	seen *plo*·mo	unleaded

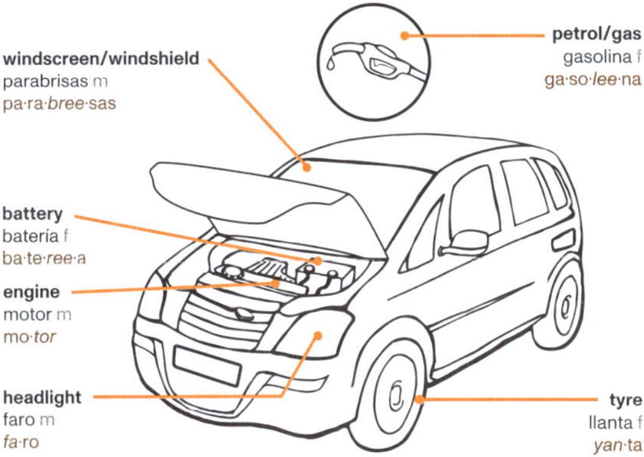

How much for weekly hire?	¿Cuánto cuesta la renta semanal? *kwan*·to *kwes*·ta la *ren*·ta se·ma·*nal*
What's the speed limit in town?	¿Cuál es el límite de velocidad en la ciudad? kwal es el *lee*·mee·te de ve·lo·see·*dad* en la see·*u*·dad
What's the speed limit on the highway?	¿Cuál es el límite de velocidad en la carretera? kwal es el *lee*·mee·te de ve·lo·see·*dad* en las ka·re·*te*·ras
Is this the road to (Palenque)?	¿Por aquí se va a (Palenque)? por a·*kee* se va a (pa·*len*·ke)

LOOK FOR

Alto	*al*·to	Stop
Ceda el Paso	*se*·da el *pa*·so	Give Way
Cuota	*kwo*·ta	Toll
Entrada	en·*tra*·da	Entrance
Estacionamiento	es·ta·syo·na·*myen*·to	Parking
Peligro	pe·*lee*·gro	Danger
Prohibido el Paso	pro·ee·*bee*·do el *pa*·so	No Entry
Prohibido Estacionar	pro·ee·*bee*·do es·ta·syo·*nar*	No Parking
Salida	sa·*lee*·da	Exit
Una Vía	*oo*·na *vee*·a	One Way

Where's a gas/petrol station?	¿Dónde hay una gasolinera? *don*·de ai *oo*·na ga·so·lee·*ne*·ra
Please fill it up.	Lleno, por favor. *ye*·no por fa·*vor*
I'd like (100) pesos' worth.	Quiero (cien) pesos. *kye*·ro (syen) *pe*·sos
Please check the oil/water.	Por favor, revise el nivel del aceite/agua. por fa·*vor* re·*vee*·se el nee·*vel* del a·*say*·te/*a*·gwa
Please check the tyre pressure.	Por favor, revise la presión de las llantas. por fa·*vor* re·*vee*·se la pre·*syon* de las *yan*·tas
(How long) Can I park here?	¿(Por cuánto tiempo) Puedo estacionarme aquí? (por *kwan*·to *tyem*·po) *pwe*·do es·ta·syo·*nar*·me a·*kee*

Where do I pay?
¿Dónde se paga?
don·de se *pa*·ga

I need a mechanic.
Necesito un mecánico.
ne·se·*see*·to oon me·*ka*·nee·ko

The car has broken down (at the intersection).
El coche se descompuso (en la intersección).
el *ko*·che se des·kom·*poo*·so (en la een·ter·sek·*syon*)

I had an accident.
Tuve un accidente.
too·ve oon ak·see·*den*·te

BICYCLE

I have a puncture.
Se me ponchó una llanta.
se me pon·*cho* *oo*·na *yan*·ta

Where can I buy a second-hand bike?
¿Dónde puedo comprar una bicicleta usada?
don·de *pwe*·do kom·*prar* *oo*·na bee·see·*kle*·ta oo·*sa*·da

Where can I hire a bicycle?
¿Dónde puedo rentar una bicicleta?
don·de *pwe*·do ren·*tar* *oo*·na bee·see·*kle*·ta

How much is it per hour?
¿Cuánto cuesta por hora?
kwan·to *kwes*·ta por *o*·ra

How much is it per day?
¿Cuánto cuesta por día?
kwan·to *kwes*·ta por *dee*·a

Border Crossing

KEY PHRASES

I'm here for ... days.	Voy a estar ... días.	voy a es·*tar* ... *dee*·as
I'm staying at ...	Me estoy quedando en ...	me es·*toy* ke·*dan*·do en ...
I have nothing to declare.	No tengo nada que declarar.	no *ten*·go *na*·da ke de·kla·*rar*

BORDER CROSSING

I'm here ... Estoy aquí ... es·*toy* a·*kee* ...

in transit	en tránsito	en *tran*·see·to
on business	de negocios	de ne·*go*·syos
on holiday	de vacaciones	de va·ka·*syo*·nes
to study	estudiando	es·too·*dyan*·do
to visit family	visitando a mi familia	vee·see·*tan*·do a mee fa·*mee*·lya

LOOK FOR

Aduana	a·*dwa*·na	Customs
Artículos Libres de Impuestos	ar·*tee*·koo·los *lee*·bres de eem·*pwes*·tos	Duty-Free Goods
Control de Pasaportes	kon·*trol* de pa·sa·*por*·tes	Passport Control

LISTEN FOR

Su pasaporte, por favor.	*soo pa·sa·por·te por fa·vor* Your passport, please.
Su tarjeta de turista, por favor.	*soo tar·he·ta de too·rees·ta por fa·vor* Your tourist card, please.
¿Está viajando en grupo?	*es·ta vya·han·do en groo·po* Are you travelling in a group?
¿Está viajando solo/a? m/f	*es·ta vya·han·do so·lo/a* Are you travelling on your own?

I'm here for (10) days.	Voy a estar (diez) días. *voy a es·tar (dyes) dee·as*
I'm here for (two) months.	Voy a estar (dos) meses. *voy a es·tar (dos) me·ses*
I'm here for (three) weeks.	Voy a estar (tres) semanas. *voy a es·tar (tres) se·ma·nas*
I'm staying at (the) ...	Me estoy quedando en (el) ... *me es·toy ke·dan·do en (el) ...*

For phrases about payment, see **money & banking** (p90).

AT CUSTOMS

I have nothing to declare.	No tengo nada que declarar. *no ten·go na·da ke de·kla·rar*
I have something to declare.	Quisiera declarar algo. *kee·sye·ra de·kla·rar al·go*
I didn't know I had to declare it.	No sabía que tenía que declararlo. *no sa·bee·a ke te·nee·a ke de·kla·rar·lo*
Do you have this form in (English)?	¿Tiene este formato en (inglés)? *tye·ne es·te for·ma·to en (een·gles)*

Directions

KEY PHRASES

Where's ...?	¿Dónde queda ...?	*don*·de *ke*·da ...
What's the address?	¿Cuál es la dirección?	kwal es la dee·rek·*syon*
How far is it?	¿A qué distancia está?	a ke dees·*tan*·sya es·*ta*

I'm looking for (the cathedral).	Busco (la catedral). *boos*·ko (la ka·te·*dral*)
Which way's (the main square)?	¿Cómo se llega (al zócalo)? *ko*·mo se *ye*·ga (al *so*·ka·lo)
How do I get to ...?	¿Cómo llego a ...? *ko*·mo *ye*·go a ...
What's the address?	¿Cuál es la dirección? kwal es la dee·rek·*syon*
How far is it?	¿A qué distancia está? a ke dees·*tan*·sya es·*ta*
Can you show me (on the map)?	¿Me lo puede señalar (en el mapa)? me lo *pwe*·de se·nya·*lar* (en el *ma*·pa)
Q **Where's (the bank)?**	¿Dónde queda (el banco)? *don*·de *ke*·da (el *ban*·ko)
A **It's ...**	Está ... es·*ta* ...
Turn left/right.	Dé vuelta a la izquierda/ derecha. de *vwel*·ta a la ees·*kyer*·da/ de·*re*·cha

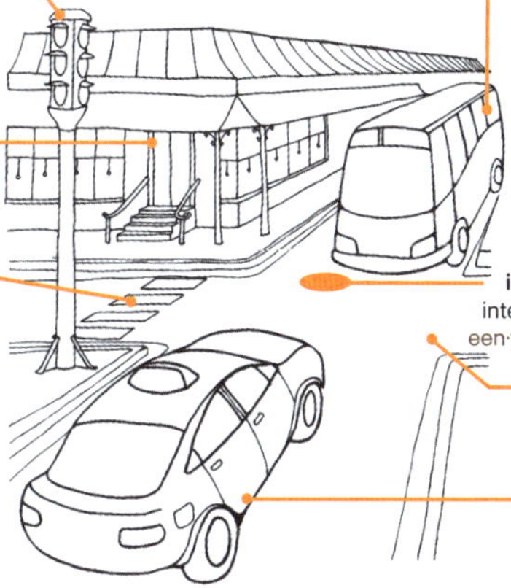

Turn at the corner.	Dé vuelta en la esquina. de *vwel*·ta en la es·*kee*·na
Turn at the traffic lights.	Dé vuelta en el semáforo. de *vwel*·ta en el se·*ma*·fo·ro
It's (100) metres away.	Está a (cien) metros. es·*ta* a (syen) *me*·tros
It's (two) kilometres away.	Está a (dos) kilómetros. es·*ta* a (dos) kee·*lo*·me·tros
It's (30) minutes away.	Está a (treinta) minutos. es·*ta* a (*trayn*·ta) mee·*noo*·tos

LISTEN FOR

a (tres) cuadras	a (tres) *kwa*·dras	(three) blocks away
a la derecha	a la de·*re*·cha	to the right
a la izquierda	a la ees·*kyer*·da	to the left
a una cuadra	a *oo*·na *kwa*·dra	one block away
ahí	a·*ee*	there
al lado de ...	al *la*·do de ...	next to ...
aquí	a·*kee*	here
cerca (de ...)	*ser*·ka (de ...)	near (to ...)
detrás de ...	de·*tras* de ...	behind ...
en frente de ...	en *fren*·te de ...	in front of ...
en la esquina	en la es·*kee*·na	on the corner
frente a ...	*fren*·te a ...	opposite ...
lejos	*le*·hos	far away
todo derecho	*to*·do de·*re*·cho	straight ahead
todo recto	*to*·do *rek*·to	straight ahead

by bus (city)	en autobús en ow·to·*boos*
by car	en coche en *ko*·che
by metro	en metro en *me*·tro
by minibus	en microbús en mee·kro·*boos*
by taxi	en taxi en *tak*·see
by train	en tren en tren
on foot	a pie a pye

Accommodation

KEY PHRASES

Where's a hotel?	¿Dónde hay un hotel?	*don*·de ai oon o·*tel*
Do you have a double room?	¿Tiene una habitación doble?	*tye*·ne *oo*·na a·bee·ta·*syon* *do*·ble
How much is it per night?	¿Cuánto cuesta por noche?	*kwan*·to *kwes*·ta por *no*·che
Is breakfast included?	¿Está incluido el desayuno?	es·*ta* een·kloo·*ee*·do el de·sa·*yoo*·no
What time is checkout?	¿A qué hora es la salida?	a ke *o*·ra es la sal·*ee*·da

FINDING ACCOMMODATION

Where's a ...? ¿Dónde hay ...?
don·de ai ...

campsite	un área para acampar	oon *a*·re·a *pa*·ra a·kam·*par*
guesthouse	una pensión	*oo*·na pen·*syon*
hotel	un hotel	oon o·*tel*
lodging house	casa de huéspedes	*ka*·sa de *wes*·pe·des
room	una habitación	*oo*·na a·bee·ta·*syon*
small inn	una posada	*oo*·na po·*sa*·da
youth hostel	un albergue juvenil	oon al·*ber*·ge hoo·ve·*neel*

Can you recommend somewhere ...?

¿Puede recomendarme alojamiento ...?
pwe·de re·ko·men·*dar*·me a·lo·ha·*myen*·to ...

cheap	barato	ba·*ra*·to
good	bueno	*bwe*·no
luxurious	lujoso	loo·*ho*·so
nearby	cercano	ser·*ka*·no
romantic	romántico	ro·*man*·tee·ko

BOOKING AHEAD & CHECKING IN

I'd like to book a room, please.

Quisiera reservar una habitación.
kee·*sye*·ra re·ser·*var oo*·na a·bee·ta·*syon*

Are there rooms?	¿Hay disponibilidad?	ai dees·pon·ee·bee·lee·*dad*

Do I need to pay upfront?

¿Necesito pagar por adelantado?
ne·se·*see*·to pa·*gar* por a·de·lan·*ta*·do

Do you have a ... room?

¿Tiene una habitación ...?
tye·ne *oo*·na a·bee·ta·*syon* ...

single	sencilla	sen·*see*·ya
double	doble	*do*·ble
twin	con dos camas	kon dos *ka*·mas
triple	triple	*tree*·ple

LISTEN FOR

Lo siento, no hay disponibilidad.	lo *syen*·to no ai dees·pon·ee·bee·lee·*dad* I'm sorry, we're full.
¿Por cuántas noches?	por *kwan*·tas *no*·ches For how many nights?
Su pasaporte, por favor.	soo pa·sa·*por*·te por fa·*vor* Your passport, please.

with/without (a) ... — con/sin ... *kon/seen ...*

air-conditioning	aire acondicionado	*ai*·re a·kon·dee·syo·*na*·do
bathroom	baño	*ba*·nyo
fan	ventilador	ven·tee·la·*dor*
sea view	vista al mar	*vees*·ta al mar
street view	vista a la calle	*vees*·ta a la *ka*·ye
TV	televisión	te·le·vee·*syon*

How much is it per person?	¿Cuánto cuesta por persona? *kwan*·to *kwes*·ta por per·*so*·na
How much is it per night?	¿Cuánto cuesta por noche? *kwan*·to *kwes*·ta por *no*·che
How much is it per week?	¿Cuánto cuesta por semana? *kwan*·to *kwes*·ta por se·*ma*·na
Is breakfast included?	¿Está incluido el desayuno? es·*ta* een·kloo·ee·do el de·sa·*yoo*·no
I have a reservation.	Tengo una reservación. *ten*·go *oo*·na re·ser·va·*syon*
For (three) nights/weeks.	Por (tres) noches/semanas. por (tres) *no*·ches/se·*ma*·nas

From (30 July) to (4 August).	Del (treinta de julio) al (cuatro de agosto). del (*trayn*·ta de *hoo*·lyo) al (*kwa*·tro de a·*gos*·to)
Can I see it?	¿Puedo verla? *pwe*·do *ver*·la
It's fine, I'll take it.	Está bien, la tomo. es·*ta* byen la *to*·mo

For phrases on payment, see **money & banking** (p90).

REQUESTS & QUERIES

When/Where is breakfast served?	¿Cuándo/Dónde se sirve el desayuno? *kwan*·do/*don*·de se *seer*·ve el de·sa·*yoo*·no
Do you have room service?	¿Tiene servicio al cuarto? *tye*·ne ser·*vee*·syo al *kwar*·to
Please wake me at (seven).	Despiérteme a las (siete) por favor. des·*pyer*·te·me a las (*sye*·te) por fa·*vor*
Can I get (another towel)?	¿Me da (otra toalla)? me da (*o*·tra to·*a*·ya)
Can I use the kitchen?	¿Puedo usar la cocina? *pwe*·do oo·*sar* la ko·*see*·na
Can I use the laundry?	¿Puedo usar la lavandería? *pwe*·do oo·*sar* la la·van·de·*ree*·a
Can I use the telephone?	¿Puedo usar el teléfono? *pwe*·do oo·*sar* el te·*le*·fo·no
There's no need to change my sheets.	No es necesario que cambie mis sábanas. no es ne·se·*sa*·ryo ke *kam*·bye mees *sa*·ba·nas

Finding a Room

DO YOU HAVE A ... ROOM?
¿Tiene una habitación ...?
tye·ne *oo*·na a·bee·ta·*syon* ...

DOUBLE
doble
do·ble

SINGLE
sencilla
sen·*see*·ya

HOW MUCH IS IT PER ...?
¿Cuánto cuesta por ...?
kwan·to *kwes*·ta por ...

NIGHT
noche
no·che

PERSON
persona
per·*so*·na

IS BREAKFAST INCLUDED?
¿Está incluido el desayuno?
es·*ta* een·kloo·*ee*·do el de·sa·*yoo*·no

CAN I SEE THE ROOM?
¿Puedo ver la habitación?
pwe·do ver la a·bee·ta·*syon*

I'LL TAKE IT.
La tomo.
la *to*·mo

I WON'T TAKE IT.
No la tomo.
no la *to*·mo

Do you have (a/an) ...?	¿Hay ...? *ai ...*	
dry-cleaning service	servicio de tintorería	ser·*vee*·syo de teen·to·re·*ree*·a
elevator/lift	elevador	e·le·va·*dor*
gym	gimnasio	heem·*na*·syo
internet	internet	een·ter·*net*
laundry service	servicio de lavandería	ser·*vee*·syo de la·van·de·*ree*·a
message board	pizarrón de anuncios	pee·sa·*ron* de a·*noon*·syos
safe	caja fuerte	*ka*·ha *fwer*·te
swimming pool	alberca	al·*ber*·ka

Do you arrange tours here?	¿Aquí organizan tours? a·*kee* or·ga·*nee*·san toors
Do you change money here?	¿Aquí cambian dinero? a·*kee* *kam*·byan dee·*ne*·ro
Can I leave a message for someone?	¿Puedo dejar un mensaje para alguien? *pwe*·do de·*har* oon men·*sa*·he pa·ra *al*·gyen
Is there a message for me?	¿Hay algún mensaje para mí? ai al·*goon* men·*sa*·he *pa*·ra mee
I'm locked out of my room.	Me quedé fuera de mi habitación. me ke·*de* *fue*·ra de mi a·bee·ta·*syon*
The (bathroom) door is locked.	La puerta (del baño) está cerrada con llave. la *pwer*·ta (del *ba*·nyo) es·*ta* se·*ra*·da kon *ya*·ve

LISTEN FOR

lugar de mala muerte	loo·*gar* de *ma*·la *mwer*·te	dive
lugar de moda	loo·*gar* de *mo*·da	top spot
plagado de ratas	pla·*ga*·do de *ra*·tas	rat-infested

COMPLAINTS

The room is too ...	La habitación es demasiado ... la a·bee·ta·*syon* es de·ma·*sya*·do ...

cold	fría	*free*·a
dark	oscura	os·*koo*·ra
light/bright	iluminada	ee·loo·mee·*na*·da
noisy	ruidosa	rwee·*do*·sa
small	pequeña	pe·*ke*·nya

The (air-conditioning) doesn't work.	No funciona (el aire acondicionado). no foon·*syo*·na (el *ai*·re a·kon·dee·syo·*na*·do)
This (blanket) isn't clean.	Esta (cobija) no está limpia. *es*·ta (ko·*bee*·ha) no es·*ta* *leem*·pya

For more things you might want in your room, see the **dictionary** (p205).

ANSWERING THE DOOR

Who is it?	¿Quién es? *kyen* es
Just a moment.	Un momentito. oon mo·men·*tee*·to

Come in.	Pase. *pa*·se
Come back later, please.	Por favor, regrese más tarde. por fa·*vor* re·*gre*·se mas *tar*·de

CHECKING OUT

What time is checkout?	¿A qué hora es la salida? a ke *o*·ra es la sal·*ee*·da
Can I have a late checkout?	¿Me puede dar salida más tarde? me *pwe*·de dar sa·*lee*·da mas *tar*·de
How much extra to stay until (six o'clock)?	¿Cuánto cuesta quedarse hasta (las seis)? *kwan*·to *kwes*·ta ke·*dar*·se *as*·ta (las says)
Can I leave my luggage here?	¿Puedo dejar mis maletas aquí? *pwe*·do de·*har* mees ma·*le*·tas a·*kee*
Can you call a taxi for me (for 11 o'clock)?	¿Me puede pedir un taxi (para las once)? me *pwe*·de pe·*deer* oon *tak*·see (*pa*·ra las *on*·se)
I'm leaving now.	Me voy ahora. me voy a·*o*·ra
Could I have my deposit, please?	¿Me devuelve mi depósito, por favor? me de·*bwehl*·veh mee de·*po*·see·to por fa·*vor*

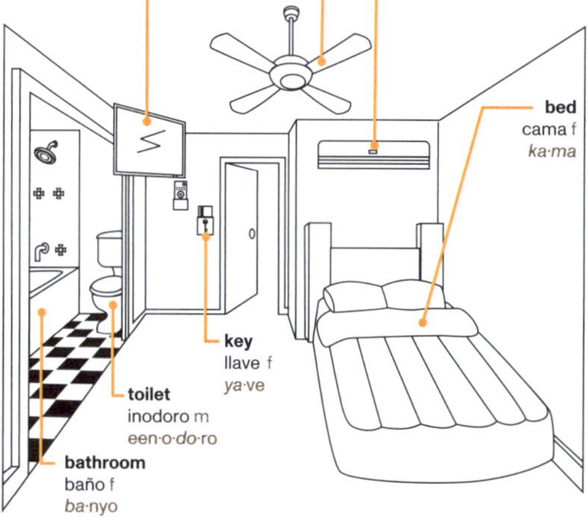

Could I have my passport, please?	¿Me da mi pasaporte, por favor? me da mee pa·sa·*por*·te por fa·*vor*
Could I have my valuables, please?	¿Me da mis objetos de valor, por favor? me da mees ob·*he*·tos de va·*lor* por fa·*vor*
I'll be back in (three) days.	Volveré en (tres) días. vol·ve·*re* en (tres) *dee*·as
I'll be back on (Tuesday).	Volveré el (martes). vol·ve·*re* el (*mar*·tes)
There's a mistake in the bill.	Hay un error en la cuenta. ai oon e·*ror* en la *kwen*·ta

LISTEN FOR

La llave está en la recepción.	la *ya*·ve es·*ta* en la re·sep·*syon* The key is at reception.
¿Consumió algo del mini-bar?	kon·soo·*myo al*·go del mee·nee·*bar* Did you use the mini-bar?

I had a great stay, thank you.	Tuve una estancia muy agradable, gracias. *too*·ve *oo*·na es·*tan*·sya mooy a·gra·*da*·ble *gra*·syas
You've been terrific.	Han sido estupendos. pl an *see*·do es·too·*pen*·dos
I'll recommend it to my friends.	Se lo recomendaré a mis amigos. se lo re·ko·men·da·*re* a mees a·*mee*·gos

CAMPING

Where's the nearest campsite?	¿Dónde está el área para acampar más cercana? *don*·de es·*ta* el *a*·re·a *pa*·ra a·kam·*par* mas ser·*ka*·na
Who do I ask to stay here?	¿Con quién debo hablar para quedarme aquí? kon kyen *de*·bo a·*blar pa*·ra ke·*dar*·me a·*kee*
Can I camp here?	¿Se puede acampar aquí? se *pwe*·de a·kam·*par* a·*kee*
Can I park next to my tent?	¿Se puede estacionar al lado de la tienda? se *pwe*·de es·ta·syo·*nar* al *la*·do de la *tyen*·da

Do you have ...?	¿Tiene ...? *tye*·ne ...	
a site	un lugar de acampado	oon *loo*·gar de a·*kam*·pa·do
electricity	electricidad	e·lek·tree·see·*dad*
shower facilities	regaderas	re·ga·*de*·ras
tents for hire	tiendas de campaña en renta	*tyen*·das de kam·*pa*·nya en *ren*·ta

How much is it per tent?	¿Cuánto es por tienda? *kwan*·to es por *tyen*·da
How much is it per vehicle?	¿Cuánto es por vehículo? *kwan*·to es por ve·*ee*·koo·lo
Could I borrow (a mallet)?	¿Me presta (un martillo)? me *pres*·ta (oon mar·*tee*·yo)
Where's the nearest shop?	¿Dónde está la tienda más cercana? *don*·de es·*ta* la *tyen*·da mas ser·*ka*·na
Where's the toilet block?	¿Dónde están los sanitarios? *don*·de es·*tan* los sa·nee·*ta*·ryos
Is it coin-operated?	¿Funciona con monedas? foon·*syo*·na kon mo·*ne*·das
Is the water drinkable?	¿El agua es potable? el *a*·gwa es po·*ta*·ble

For more words related to camping, see the **dictionary** (p205).

RENTING

I'm here about the ... for rent.	Vengo por el/la ... en renta. m/f *ven*·go por el/la ... en *ren*·ta
Do you have a/an ... for rent?	¿Tiene ... en renta? *tye*·ne ... en *ren*·ta

apartment	un departamento	oon de·par·ta·*men*·to
bungalow	un búngalow	oon *boon*·ga·lo
cabin	una cabaña	*oo*·na ka·*ba*·nya
house	una casa	*oo*·na *ka*·sa
room	un cuarto	oon *kwar*·to
villa	una villa	*oo*·na *vee*·ya

(partly) furnished	(parcialmente) amueblado/a m/f (par·*syal*·men·te) a·mwe·*bla*·do/a
unfurnished	sin amueblar seen a·mwe·*blar*
How much is it for (one) week?	¿Cuánto cuesta por (una) semana? *kwan*·to *kwes*·ta por (*oo*·na) se·*ma*·na
How much is it for (two) months?	¿Cuánto cuesta por (dos) meses? *kwan*·to *kwes*·ta por (dos) *me*·ses
Are bills extra?	¿Los servicios se pagan aparte? los ser·*vee*·syos se *pa*·gan a·*par*·te

¿Se puede acampar aquí?

se *pwe*·de a·kam·*par* a·*kee*

Can I camp here?

STAYING WITH LOCALS

Can I stay at your place?	¿Me puedo quedar en su/tu casa? pol/inf me *pwe*·do ke·*dar* en soo/too *ka*·sa
Thanks for your hospitality.	Gracias por su/tu hospitalidad. pol/inf *gra*·syas por soo/too os·pee·ta·lee·*dad*
Is there anything I can do to help?	¿Puedo ayudar en algo? *pwe*·do a·*yoo*·dar en *al*·go
I have my own hammock.	Tengo mi propia hamaca. *ten*·go mee *pro*·pya a·*ma*·ka
I have my own mattress.	Tengo mi propio colchón. *ten*·go mee *pro*·pyo kol·*chon*

CULTURE TIP: BODY LANGUAGE

Be aware of sending the wrong signals with your body language. In Mexico, women are expected to initiate handshakes with men, but will greet other women or male friends with a kiss on the cheek or a pat on the forearm. Conversations take place at a close physical distance and male acquaintances often hug each other when meeting.

I have my own sleeping bag.	Tengo mi propia bolsa de dormir. *ten*·go mee *pro*·pya *bol*·sa de dor·*meer*
Can I ...?	¿Puedo ...? *pwe*·do ...

bring anything for the meal	traer algo para la comida	tra·*er al*·go *pa*·ra la ko·*mee*·da
do the dishes	lavar los platos	la·*var* los *pla*·tos
set/clear the table	poner/recoger la mesa	po·*ner*/re·ko·*hehr* la *me*·sa
take out the rubbish	sacar la basura	sa·*kar* la ba·*soo*·ra

If you're dining with your hosts, see **eating out** (p174) for additional phrases.

Shopping

KEY PHRASES

I'd like to buy ...	Quisiera comprar ...	kee·*sye*·ra kom·*prar* ...
Can I look at it?	¿Puedo verlo?	*pwe*·do *ver*·lo
Can I try it on?	¿Me lo puedo probar?	me lo *pwe*·do *pro*·bar
How much is this?	¿Cuánto cuesta esto?	*kwan*·to *kwes*·ta *es*·to
That's too expensive.	Es demasiado caro/a. m/f	es de·ma·*sya*·do *ka*·ro/a

LOOKING FOR ...

Where's (a supermarket)?	¿Dónde hay (un supermercado)? *don*·de ai (oon soo·per·mer·*ka*·do)
Where can I buy (locally produced) goods/souvenirs?	¿Dónde puedo comprar productos/recuerdos (locales)? *don*·de *pwe*·do kom·*prar* pro·*dook*·tos/re·*kwer*·dos (lo·*ka*·les)
What is typical of the region?	¿Qué es lo típico de la región? ke es lo *tee*·pee·ko de la re·*hyon*

For more items and shopping locations, see the **dictionary** (p205). Want to know how to get there? See **directions** (p56).

MAKING A PURCHASE

I'm just looking.	Sólo estoy mirando. *so*·lo es·*toy* mee·*ran*·do
I'd like to buy ...	Quisiera comprar ... kee·*sye*·ra kom·*prar* ...
How much is this?	¿Cuánto cuesta esto? *kwan*·to *kwes*·ta *es*·to

How much? ¿Cuánto cuesta? *kwan*·to *kwes*·ta

Can you write down the price?	¿Me anota el precio? me a·*no*·ta el *pre*·syo
Can I look at it?	¿Puedo verlo? *pwe*·do *ver*·lo
I don't like it.	No me gusta. no me *goos*·ta
It's faulty/broken.	Está defectuoso/roto. es·*ta* de·fek·*two*·so/*ro*·to
Do you have any others?	¿Tiene otros? *tye*·ne *o*·tros
Does it have a guarantee?	¿Tiene garantía? *tye*·ne ga·ran·*tee*·a
Could I have it wrapped?	¿Me lo podría envolver? me lo po·*dree*·a en·vol·*ver*
Could I have a bag/box, please?	¿Me da una bolsa/caja, por favor? me da *oo*·na *bol*·sa/*ka*·ha por fa·*vor*
I don't need a bag, thanks.	No necesito bolsa, gracias. no ne·se·*see*·to *bol*·sa *gra*·syas

For phrases about payment, see **money & banking** (p90).

Making a Purchase

I'D LIKE TO BUY ...
Quisiera comprar ...
kee·*sye*·ra kom·*prar* ...

HOW MUCH IS THIS?
¿Cuánto cuesta esto?
kwan·to *kwes*·ta *es*·to

OR

CAN YOU WRITE DOWN THE PRICE?
¿Me anota el precio?
me a·*no*·ta el *pre*·syo

DO YOU ACCEPT CREDIT CARDS?
¿Aceptan tarjetas de crédito?
a·*sep*·tan tar·*he*·tas de *kre*·dee·to

COULD I HAVE A ..., PLEASE?
¿Me da ..., por favor?
me da ... por fa·*vor*

RECEIPT
un recibo
oon re·see·bo

BAG
una bolsa
oo·na *bol*·sa

SHOPPING PRACTICAL

Could I have a receipt, please?	¿Me da un recibo, por favor? me da *oon* re·*see*·bo por fa·*vor*

Receipt, please.	El recibo, por favor.	el re·*see*·bo por fa·*vor*

I'd like my change, please.	Quisiera mi cambio, por favor. kee·*sye*·ra mee *kam*·byo por fa·*vor*
I'd like to return this, please.	Quisiera devolver esto, por favor. kee·*sye*·ra de·vol·*ver* *es*·to por fa·*vor*
I'd like my money back, please.	Quisiera que me devuelva mi dinero, por favor. kee·*sye*·ra ke me de·*vwel*·va mi dee·*ne*·ro por fa·*vor*

BARGAINING

That's too expensive.	Es demasiado caro/a. m/f es de·ma·*sya*·do *ka*·ro/a
Can you lower the price?	¿Me lo deja más barato? me lo *de*·ha mas ba·*ra*·to
Do you have something cheaper?	¿Tiene algo más barato? *tye*·ne *al*·go mas ba·*ra*·to
I'll give you ...	Le doy ... le doy ...
What's your final price?	¿Cuánto es lo menos? *kwan*·to es lo *me*·nos

LISTEN FOR

cazador/cazadora de ofertas m/f	ka·sa·*dor*/ka·sa·*do*·ra de o·*fer*·tas	bargain hunter
estafa f	es·*ta*·fa	rip-off
ganga f	*gan*·ga	bargain
promociones f pl	pro·mo·*syon*·es	specials
venta f	*ven*·ta	sale

BOOKS & READING

Is there an English-language bookshop/ section?	¿Hay alguna libreria/sección con material en inglés? ai al·*goo*·na lee·bre·*ree*·a/ sek·*syon* kon ma·te·*ryal* en een·*gles*
Do you have a book by (Rosario Castellanos)?	¿Tiene algún libro de (Rosario Castellanos)? *tye*·ne al·*goon* *lee*·bro de (ro·sa·ree·o kas·te·*ya*·nos)
Can you recommend a book for me?	¿Me puede recomendar algún libro? me *pwe*·de re·ko·men·*dar* al·*goon* *lee*·bro
I'd like a ...	Quisiera ... kee·*sye*·ra ...

dictionary	un diccionario	oon deek·syo·*na*·ryo
guidebook	una guía turística	*oo*·na *gee*·a too·*rees*·tee·ka
magazine	una revista	*oo*·na re·*vees*·ta
map	un mapa	oon *ma*·pa
newspaper (in English)	un periódico (en inglés)	oon pe·*ryo*·dee·ko (en een·*gles*)

CLOTHES

Can I try it on?	¿Me lo puedo probar? me lo *pwe*·do *pro*·bar
It doesn't fit.	No me queda. no me *ke*·da
It's too (big).	Es demasiado (grande). es de·ma·*sya*·do (*gran*·de)
My size is ...	Soy talla ... soy *ta*·ya ...

(40)	(cuarenta)	(kwa·*ren*·ta)
small	chica	*chee*·ka
medium	mediana	me·*dya*·na
large	grande	*gran*·de

For different types of clothes, see the **dictionary** (p205).

MUSIC

I'd like headphones.	Quisiera unos audífonos. kee·*sye*·ra *oo*·nos ow·*dee*·fo·nos
I heard a band called (Maná).	Escuché a un grupo que se llama (Maná). es·koo·*che* a oon *groo*·po ke se *ya*·ma (ma·*na*)
I heard a singer called ...	Escuché a un/una cantante que se llama ... m/f es·koo·*che* a oon/*oo*·na kan·*tan*·te ke se *ya*·ma ...

LANGUAGE TIP: HOW MUCH?

In Mexican Spanish, there are three ways to ask about the cost of something – and therefore three possible replies. The first two options below are equally common in Mexico.

Q How much is it?	¿Cuánto cuesta? ¿Cuánto sale? ¿Cuánto vale?	*kwan*·to *kwes*·ta *kwan*·to *sa*·le *kwan*·to *va*·le
A It is ...	Cuesta ... Sale ... Vale ...	*kwes*·ta ... *sa*·le ... *va*·le ...

What's his/her best recording?	¿Cuál es su mejor grabación? kwal es soo me·*hor* gra·ba·*syon*
Can I listen to this?	¿Puedo escucharlo? *pwe*·do es·koo·*char*·lo

PHOTOGRAPHY

I need passport photos taken.	Necesito fotos tamaño pasaporte. ne·se·*see*·to *fo*·tos ta·*ma*·nyo pa·sa·*por*·te
Can you print digital photos?	¿Se puede imprimir fotos digitales? se *pwe*·de eem·pree·*meer fo*·tos dee·hee·*ta*·les
Can you recharge the battery?	¿Se puede recargar la pila? se *pwe*·de re·kar·*gar* la *pee*·la

LISTEN FOR

¿En qué le puedo servir?	en ke le *pwe*·do ser·*veer* Can I help you?
¿Qué desea?	ke de·*se*·a What would you like?
No, no tenemos.	no no te·*ne*·mos No, we don't have any.

Do you have batteries for this camera?	¿Tiene pilas para esta cámara? *tye*·ne *pee*·las *pa*·ra *es*·ta *ka*·ma·ra
Do you have a memory card for this camera?	¿Tiene una tarjeta de memoria para esta cámara? *tye*·ne *oo*·na tar·*he*·ta de me·*mo*·rya *pa*·ra *es*·ta *ka*·ma·ra

¿Me lo puedo probar?
me lo *pwe*·do pro·*bar*
Can I try it on?

I'm (not) happy with these photos.	(No) Estoy satisfecho/a con estas fotos. m/f (no) es·*toy* sa·tee·*fe*·cho/a kon es·tas *fo*·tos

For more photographic equipment, see the **dictionary** (p205).

REPAIRS

Can I have my backpack/ camera repaired here?	¿Puede reparar mi mochila/cámara aquí? *pwe*·de re·pa·*rar* mee mo·*chee*·la/*ka*·ma·ra a·*kee*
When will it be ready?	¿Cuándo estará listo? *kwan*·do es·ta·*ra* *lees*·to

CULTURE TIP: SOUVENIRS

alebrijes m pl — a·le·*bree*·hes
wood carvings of mythical creatures, crafted in Oaxaca

hamacas f pl — a·*ma*·kas
hammocks, usually of cotton or nylon

huaraches m pl — wa·*ra*·ches
leather sandals, available all over Mexico

huipiles m pl — wee·*pee*·les
traditional women's tunics, worn mostly in the south

jipijapas m pl — hee·pee·*ha*·pas
Panama-style hats, sold in Mérida and Campeche

papel amate m — pa·*pel* a·*ma*·te
decorated bark paper, made in central Mexico

piñatas f pl — pee·*nya*·tas
traditional festive dolls filled with candy

Communications

KEY PHRASES

I'd like to check my email.	Quisiera revisar mi correo electrónico.	kee·*sye*·ra re·vee·*sar* mee ko·*re*·o e·lek·*tro*·nee·ko
I want to send a parcel.	Quisiera enviar un paquete.	kee·*sye*·ra en·*vyar* oon pa·*ke*·te
I want to make a call to ...	Quiero hacer una llamada a ...	*kye*·ro a·*ser* *oo*·na ya·*ma*·da a ...
I'd like a SIM card.	Quiero un chip.	*kye*·ro oon cheep

THE INTERNET

Is there internet access here?	¿Hay acceso al internet aquí? ai ak·*se*·so al een·ter·*net* a·*kee*
Is there wireless internet access here?	¿Tienen wifi aquí? *tyen*·en *wee*·fee a·*kee*
Can I connect my laptop here?	¿Se puede conectar mi laptop aquí? se *pwe*·de ko·nek·*tar* mee *lap*·top a·*kee*
Do you have a Zip drive?	¿Tiene una unidad Zip? *tye*·ne *oo*·na oo·nee·*dad* seep
Do you have Macs/PCs?	¿Tiene Macs/PCs? *tye*·ne maks/*pe*·ses

I'd like to ... Quisiera ...
kee·sye·ra ...

check my email	revisar mi correo electrónico	re·vee·*sar* mee ko·*re*·o e·lek·*tro*·nee·ko
download my photos	descargar mis fotos	des·kar·*gar* mees *fo*·tos
get internet access	usar el internet	oo·*sar* el een·ter·*net*
use a printer	usar una impresora	oo·sar *oo*·na eem·pre·*so*·ra
use a scanner	usar un escáner	oo·*sar* oon es·*ka*·ner

How much per ...? ¿Cuánto cuesta por ...?
kwan·to *kwes*·ta por ...

hour	hora	*o*·ra
(five) minutes	(cinco) minutos	(*seen*·ko) mee·*noo*·tos
page	hoja	*o*·ha

Do you have headphones (with a microphone)? ¿Tiene audífonos (con micrófono)?
tye·ne ow·*dee*·fo·nos (kon mee·*kro*·fo·no)

I need help with the computer. Necesito ayuda con la computadora.
ne·se·*see*·to a·*yoo*·da kon la kom·poo·ta·*do*·ra

How do I log on? ¿Cómo entro al sistema?
ko·mo *en*·tro al sees·*te*·ma

How do I log off?
¿Cómo salgo del sistema?
ko·mo *sal*·go del sees·*te*·ma

It's crashed.
Se trabó.
se tra·*bo*

I've finished.
Ya terminé.
ya ter·mee·*ne*

MOBILE/CELL PHONE

I'd like a/an ...
Quisiera ...
kee·*sye*·ra ...

adaptor plug	un adaptador	oon a·dap·ta·*dor*
charger for my phone	un cargador para mi celular	oon kar·ga·*dor* *pa*·ra mee se·loo·*lar*
SIM card for your network	una chip para su red	oon cheep *pa*·ra soo red

What are the rates?
¿Cuáles son las tarifas?
kwa·les son las ta·*ree*·fas

PHONE

Q **What's your phone number?**
¿Cuál es su número de teléfono?
kwal es soo *noo*·me·ro de te·*le*·fo·no

A **The number is ...**
El número es ...
el *noo*·me·ro es ...

I want to make a call to ...
Quiero hacer una llamada a ...
kye·ro a·*ser* *oo*·na ya·*ma*·da a ...

LISTEN FOR

(Cinco pesos) por minuto.	(*seen*·ko *pe*·sos) por mee·*noo*·to (Five pesos) per minute.

What's the area/country code for ...?	¿Cuál es la clave Lada de ...? kwal es la *kla*·ve *la*·da de ...
It's engaged.	Está llamando. es·*ta* ya·*man*·do
I've been cut off.	Se cortó la línea. se kor·*to* la *lee*·ne·a
The connection's bad.	La conexión es mala. la ko·nek·*syon* es *ma*·la
Hello. (when making a call)	¡Hola! *o*·la
It's ... (when introducing yourself)	Habla ... *a*·bla ...
Can I speak to ..., please?	¿Me comunica con..., por favor? me ko·moo·*nee*·ka kon ... por fa·*vor*
Can I leave a message?	¿Puedo dejar un mensaje? *pwe*·do de·*har* oon men·*sa*·he
Please tell him/her I called.	Por favor, dile que le llamé. por fa·*vor* *dee*·le ke le ya·*me*
I'll call back (later).	Llamaré (más tarde). ya·ma·*re* (mas *tar*·de)

¿Hay acceso al internet aquí?
ai ak·*se*·so al een·ter·*net* a·*kee*
Is there internet access here?

What time should I call?	¿A qué hora debería llamar? a ke *o*·ra de·be·*ree*·a ya·*mar*
I don't have a contact number.	No tengo número. no *ten*·go *noo*·mer·o
My number is ...	Mi número es ... mee *noo*·me·ro es ...

LISTEN FOR

¿Bueno?	*bwe*·no Hello? (answering a call)
¿De parte de quién?	de *par*·te de kyen Who's calling?
¿Con quién quiere hablar?	kon kyen *kye*·re a·*blar* Who do you want to speak to?
Ahorita no está.	a·o·*ree*·ta no es·*ta* He's/she's not here right now.
Sí, aquí está.	see a·*kee* es·*ta* Yes, he's/she's here.
Habla con él/ella. m/f	*ah*·blah kon el/*e*·ya You're speaking to him/her.
No puedo oírte.	no *pwe*·do o·*eer*·te I can't hear you.
Tiene el número equivocado.	*tye*·ne el *noo*·me·ro e·kee·vo·*ka*·do You have the wrong number.

POST OFFICE

I want to buy an envelope.	Quisiera comprar un sobre. kee·*sye*·ra kom·*prar* oon *so*·bre
I want to buy some stamps.	Quisiera comprar unas estampillas. kee·*sye*·ra kom·*prar* *oo*·nas es·tam·*pee*·yas

I want to send a ... | Quisiera enviar ... *kee·sye·ra en·vyar ...*

letter	una carta	*oo·na kar·ta*
money order	un giro	*oon hee·ro*
parcel	un paquete	*oon pa·ke·te*
postcard	una postal	*oo·na pos·tal*

Please send it by air/ regular mail to (France).
Por favor, mándelo por vía aérea/correo ordinario a (Francia).
por fa·vor man·de·lo por vee·a a·e·re·a/ko·re·o or·dee·na·ryo a (fran·sya)

It contains ...
Contiene ...
kon·tye·ne ...

LISTEN FOR

correo m **aéreo**	*ko·re·o a·e·re·o*	airmail
correo m **certificado**	*ko·re·o ser·tee·fee·ka·do*	registered mail
correo m **expreso**	*ko·re·o ek·spre·so*	express mail
correo m **ordinario**	*ko·re·o or·dee·na·ryo*	regular mail
declaración f **de aduana**	*de·kla·ra·syon de a·dwa·na*	customs declaration

Money & Banking

KEY PHRASES

How much is it?	¿Cuánto cuesta esto?	*kwan*·to *kwes*·ta *es*·to
What's the exchange rate?	¿Cuál es el tipo de cambio?	kwal es el *tee*·po de *kam*·byo
Where's the nearest ATM?	¿Dónde está el cajero automático más cercano?	*don*·de es·*ta* el ka·*he*·ro ow·to·*ma*·tee·ko mas ser·*ka*·no
I'd like to change money.	Me gustaría cambiar dinero.	me goos·ta·*ree*·a kam·*byar* dee·*ne*·ro
Can I have smaller notes?	¿Me lo puede dar en billetes más pequeños?	me lo *pwe*·de dar en bee·*ye*·tes mas pe·*ke*·nyos

PAYING THE BILL

Q **How much is this?**	¿Cuánto cuesta esto? *kwan*·to *kwes*·ta *es*·to
A **It's free.**	Es gratis. es *gra*·tees
A **It's (10) pesos.**	Cuesta (diez) pesos. *kwes*·ta (dyes) *pe*·sos
Can you write down the price?	¿Me anota el precio? me a·*no*·ta el *pre*·syo
Can I pay cash?	¿Puedo pagar en efectivo? *pwe*·do pa·*gar* en e·fek·*tee*·vo

Do you accept credit cards?	¿Aceptan tarjetas de crédito? a·*sep*·tan tar·*he*·tas de *kre*·dee·to
Do you accept debit cards?	¿Aceptan tarjetas de débito? a·*sep*·tan tar·*he*·tas de *de*·bee·to
Do I need to pay upfront?	¿Necesito pagar por adelantado? ne·se·*see*·to pa·*gar* por a·de·lan·*ta*·do
I'd like a receipt, please.	Quisiera un recibo, por favor. kee·*sye*·ra oon re·*see*·bo por fa·*vor*
I'd like my change, please.	Quisiera mi cambio, por favor. kee·*sye*·ra mee *kam*·byo por fa·*vor*
There's a mistake in the bill.	Hay un error en la cuenta. ai oon e·*ror* en la *kwen*·ta

BANKING

Where's the nearest ATM?	¿Dónde está el cajero automático más cercano? *don*·de es·*ta* el ka·*he*·ro ow·to·*ma*·tee·ko mas ser·*ka*·no
Where's the nearest foreign exchange office?	¿Dónde está la casa de cambio más cercana? *don*·de es·*ta* la *ka*·sa de *kam*·byo mas ser·*ka*·na

PRACTICAL MONEY & BANKING

What time does the bank open?	¿A qué hora abre el banco? a ke *o*·ra *a*·bre el *ban*·ko
I'd like to ...	Me gustaría ... me goos·ta·*ree*·a ...

arrange a transfer	hacer una transferencia	a·ser *oo*·na trans·fe·*ren*·sya
change money	cambiar dinero	kam·*byar* dee·*ne*·ro
get a cash advance	obtener un adelanto	ob·te·*ner* oon a·de·*lan*·to
use internet banking	usar la banca por internet	oo·*sar* la *ban*·ka por een·ter·*net*
withdraw money	sacar dinero	sa·*kar* dee·*ne*·ro

Do you change money here?	¿Se cambia dinero aquí? se *kam*·bya dee·*ne*·ro a·*kee*
The ATM took my card.	El cajero automático se tragó mi tarjeta. el ka·*he*·ro ow·to·*ma*·tee·ko se tra·*go* mee tar·*he*·ta
I've forgotten my PIN.	Se me olvidó mi NIP. se me ol·vee·*do* mee neep
Can I use my credit card to withdraw money?	¿Puedo usar mi tarjeta de crédito para sacar dinero? *pwe*·do oo·*sar* mee tar·*he*·ta de *kre*·dee·to *pa*·ra sa·*kar* dee·*ne*·ro
What's the exchange rate?	¿Cuál es el tipo de cambio? kwal es el *tee*·po de *kam*·byo
What's the commission?	¿Cuál es la comisión? kwal es la ko·mee·*syon*

LISTEN FOR

¿Me lo anota?	me lo a·*no*·ta Can you write it down?
Su identificación.	soo ee·den·tee·fee·ka·*syon* Your ID.
Firme aquí.	*feer*·me a·*kee* Sign here.
En (cinco) días hábiles.	en (*seen*·ko) *dee*·as a·bee·les In (five) working days.
En (dos) semanas.	en (dos) se·*ma*·nas In (two) weeks.
Hay un problema con su cuenta.	ai oon pro·*ble*·ma kon soo *kwen*·ta There's a problem with your account.
No podemos hacer eso.	no po·*de*·mos a·*ser* e·so We can't do that.

What's the charge for that?	¿Cuánto hay que pagar por éso? *kwan*·to ai ke pa·*gar* por e·so
Can I have smaller notes?	¿Me lo puede dar en billetes más pequeños? me lo *pwe*·de dar en bee·*ye*·tes mas pe·*ke*·nyos
Where do I sign?	¿Dónde firmo? *don*·de *feer*·mo

Business

KEY PHRASES

I'm attending a conference.	Estoy asistiendo a un congreso.	es·*toy* a·sees·*tyen*·do a oon kon·*gre*·so
I have an appointment with ...	Tengo una cita con ...	*ten*·go *oo*·na *see*·ta kon ...
Can I have your business card?	¿Me da su tarjeta de presentación?	me da soo tar·*he*·ta de pre·sen·ta·*syon*

Where's the business centre? ¿Dónde está el centro de conferencias?
don·de es·*ta* el *sen*·tro de kon·fe·*ren*·syas

I'm attending a/an ... Estoy asistiendo a ...
es·*toy* a·sees·*tyen*·do a ...

conference	un congreso	oon kon·*gre*·so
convention	una convención	*oo*·na kon·ven·*syon*
course	un curso	oon koor·*so*
exhibition	una exhibición	*oo*·na ek·see·bee·*syon*
meeting	una reunión	*oo*·na re·oo·*nyon*
trade fair	una feria de negocios	*oo*·na *fe*·rya de ne·*go*·syos

I'm with my company. Estoy con mi compañía.
es·*toy* kon mee kom·pa·*nyee*·a

I'm with my colleague(s).	Estoy con mi(s) colega(s). es·*toy* kon mee(s) ko·*le*·ga(s)
I'm alone.	Estoy solo/a. m/f es·*toy* *so*·lo/a
I have an appointment with ...	Tengo una cita con ... *ten*·go *oo*·na *see*·ta kon ...
Let me introduce my colleague.	Le/Te presento a mi colega. pol/inf le/te pre·*sen*·to a mee ko·*le*·ga
Q **Can I have your business card?**	¿Me da su tarjeta de presentación? me da soo tar·*he*·ta de pre·sen·ta·*syon*
A **Here's my business card.**	Aquí tiene mi tarjeta de presentación. a·*kee* *tye*·ne mee tar·*he*·ta de pre·sen·ta·*syon*
I'm expecting a call.	Estoy esperando una llamada. es·*toy* es·pe·*ran*·do *oo*·na ya·*ma*·da
I need ...	Necesito ... ne·se·*see*·to ...

an internet connection	una conexión al internet	*oo*·na ko·nek·*syon* al een·ter·*net*
an interpreter	un/una intérprete m/f	oon/*oo*·na een·*ter*·pre·te
to make photocopies	sacar fotocopias	sa·*kar* fo·to·*ko*·pyas
to use a computer	usar una computadora	oo·*sar* *oo*·na kom·poo·ta·*do*·ra

For equipment you might need at a conference, see the **dictionary** (p205).

Sightseeing

KEY PHRASES

I'd like a guide.	Quisiera un guía.	kee·*sye*·ra oon *gee*·a
Can I take a photo?	¿Puedo tomar una foto?	*pwe*·do to·*mar* *oo*·na *fo*·to
When's the museum open?	¿A qué hora abre el museo?	a ke *o*·ra *a*·bre el moo·*se*·o
I'm interested in ...	Me interesa ...	me een·te·*re*·sa ...
When's the next tour?	¿Cuándo es el próximo tour?	*kwan*·do es el *prok*·see·mo toor

I'd like a/an ... Quisiera ... kee·*sye*·ra ...

audio set	una audioguía	*oo*·na ow·dyo·*gee*·a
catalogue	un catálogo	oon ka·*ta*·lo·go
guide (person)	un guía	oon *gee*·a
guidebook (in English)	una guía turística (en inglés)	*oo*·na *gee*·a too·*rees*·tee·ka (en een·*gles*)
(local) map	un mapa (de la zona)	oon *ma*·pa (de la *so*·na)

I'd like to see ... Me gustaría ver ... me goos·ta·*ree*·a ver ...

Do you have information on ... sights?	¿Tiene información sobre atracciones ... *tye*·ne een·for·ma·*syon* *so*·bre a·trak·*syo*·nes ...

cultural	culturales	kool·too·*ra*·les
local	locales	lo·*ka*·les
religious	religiosas	re·lee·*hyo*·sas
historic	históricas	ees·*to*·ree·kas

What's that?	¿Qué es eso? ke es *e*·so
Who made it?	¿Quién lo hizo? kyen lo *ee*·so
How old is it?	¿Cuántos años tiene? *kwan*·tos *ayn*·os tee·*eh*·ne
Could you take a photograph of me?	¿Me puede tomar una foto? me *pwe*·de to·*mar* *oo*·na *fo*·to
Can I take a photograph (of you)?	¿Puedo tomar(le) una foto? *pwe*·do to·*mar*(le) *oo*·na *fo*·to

GETTING IN

What time does it open/close?	¿A qué hora abren/cierran? a ke *o*·ra *a*·bren/*sye*·ran
What's the admission charge?	¿Cuánto cuesta la entrada? *kwan*·to *kwes*·ta la en·*tra*·da
Is there a discount for ...?	¿Hay descuento para ...? ai des·*kwen*·to *pa*·ra ...

children	niños	*nee*·nyos
groups	grupos	*groo*·pos
retirees	jubilados	hoo·bee·*la*·dos
students	estudiantes	es·too·*dyan*·tes

MUSEUMS & GALLERIES

When does the (museum) open?	¿A qué hora abre el (museo)? a ke *o*·ra *a*·bre el (moo·*se*·o)
When does the (gallery) close?	¿A qué hora cierra la (galería)? a ke *o*·ra *sye*·ra la (ga·le·*ree*·a)
Q **What kind of art are you interested in?**	¿Qué tipo de arte le/te interesa? pol/inf ke *tee*·po de *ar*·te le/te een·te·*re*·sa
A **I'm interested in (Mexican muralism).**	Me interesa (el muralismo mexicano). me een·te·*re*·sa (el moo·ra·*lees*·mo me·hee·*ka*·no)
A **I like the works of ...**	Me gustan las obras de ... me *goos*·tan las *o*·bras de ...
Q **What's in the collection?**	¿Qué hay en la colección? ke ai en la ko·lek·*syon*
A **It's a (cartoon) exhibition.**	Hay una exposición de (caricaturas). ai *oo*·na ek·spo·see·*syon* de (kar·i·ka·*too*·ras)
What do you think of ...?	¿Qué piensa/piensas de ...? pol/inf ke *pyen*·sa/pyen·sas de ...
... art	arte m ... *ar*·te ...

Aztec	azteca	as·*te*·ka
Maya	maya	*ma*·ya
prehispanic	prehispánico	pre·ees·*pa*·nee·ko
revolutionary	revolucionario	re·vo·loo·syo·*na*·ryo

¿Qué es eso?
ke es *e*·so
What's that?

TOURS

Can you recommend a boat trip?	¿Puede recomendar algún paseo en lancha? *pwe*·de re·ko·men·*dar* al·*goon* pa·*se*·o en *lan*·cha
Can you recommend a tour?	¿Puede recomendar algún tour? *pwe*·de re·ko·men·*dar* al·*goon* toor
When's the next tour?	¿Cuándo es el próximo tour? *kwan*·do es el *prok*·see·mo toor
When's the next day trip?	¿Cuando es la próxima excursión de un día? *kwan*·do es la *prok*·see·ma ek·skoor·*syon* de oon *dee*·a

LISTEN FOR

(No) Hay demasiados turistas.	(no) ai de·ma·*sya*·dos too·*rees*·tas There are (not) too many tourists.
(No) Hay mucho que ver.	(no) ai *moo*·cho ke ver There's (not) a lot to see.
La mejor época para ir es ...	la me·*hor* e·po·ka *pa*·ra eer es ... The best time to go is ...
Hay una muy buena vida nocturna.	ai *oo*·na mooy bwe·na *vee*·da nok·*toor*·na There's fabulous nightlife.

Is accommodation/ transport included?	¿Incluye alojamiento/ transporte? een·*kloo*·ye a·lo·ha·*myen*·to/ trans·*por*·te
Do I need to take food?	¿Necesito llevar comida? ne·se·*see*·to ye·*var* ko·*mee*·da
Can we hire a (local) guide?	¿Podemos contratar un guía (local)? po·*de*·mos kon·tra·*tar* oon *gee*·a (lo·*kal*)
How long is the tour?	¿Cuánto dura el tour? *kwan*·to *doo*·ra el toor
What time should I be back?	¿A qué hora tengo que regresar? a ke *o*·ra *ten*·go ke re·gre·*sar*
I'm with them.	Estoy con ellos. es·*toy* kon *e*·yos
I've lost my group.	Perdí a mi grupo. per·*dee* a mee *groo*·po

Seniors & Travellers with Disabilities

KEY PHRASES

I need assistance.	Necesito ayuda.	ne·se·*see*·to a·*yoo*·da
Is there wheelchair access?	¿Hay acceso para silla de ruedas?	ai ak·*se*·so *pa*·ra *see*·ya de *rwe*·das
Are there toilets for people with a disability?	¿Hay baños para discapacitados?	ai *ba*·nyos *pa*·ra dees·ka·pa·see·*ta*·dos

I need assistance.	Necesito ayuda. ne·se·*see*·to a·*yoo*·da
I have a disability.	Soy discapacitado/a. m/f soy dees·ka·pa·see·*ta*·do/a
What services do you have for people with a disability?	¿Qué servicios tienen para discapacitados? ke ser·*vee*·syos *tye*·nen *pa*·ra dees·ka·pa·see·*ta*·dos
Are guide dogs permitted?	¿Se permiten perros guía? se per·*mee*·ten *pe*·ros *gee*·a
Is there wheelchair access?	¿Hay acceso para silla de ruedas? ai ak·*se*·so *pa*·ra *see*·ya de *rwe*·das

How wide is the entrance?	¿Qué tan ancha es la entrada? ke tan *an*·cha es la en·*tra*·da
Is there a lift/elevator?	¿Hay elevador? ai e·le·va·*dor*
How many steps are there?	¿Cuántos escalones hay? *kwan*·tos es·ka·*lo*·nes ai
Is there somewhere I can sit down?	¿Hay algún lugar donde me pueda sentar? ai al·*goon* loo·*gar don*·de me *pwe*·da sen·*tar*
Are there toilets for people with a disability?	¿Hay baños para discapacitados? ai *ba*·nyos *pa*·ra dees·ka·pa·see·*ta*·dos
Could you call me a taxi for the disabled, please?	¿Podría llamarme un taxi para discapacitados? po·*dree*·a ya·*mar*·me oon *tak*·see *pa*·ra dees·ka·pa·see·*ta*·dos
Could you help me cross this street?	¿Podría ayudarme a cruzar la calle? po·*dree*·a a·yoo·*dar*·me a kroo·*sar* la *ka*·ye
access for the disabled	acceso m para discapacitados ak·*se*·so *pa*·ra dees·ka·pa·see·*ta*·dos
guide dog	perro m guía *pe*·ro *gee*·a
person with a disability	persona f discapacitada per·*so*·na dees·ka·pa·see·*ta*·da
ramps	rampas f pl *ram*·pas
wheelchair	silla f de ruedas *see*·ya de *rwe*·das

Travel with Children

KEY PHRASES

Are children allowed?	¿Se permiten niños?	se per·*mee*·ten nee·*nyos*
Is there a family discount?	¿Hay descuento familiar?	ai des·*kwen*·to fa·mee·*lyar*
Is there a baby change room?	¿Hay un cambiador de bebés?'	ai oon kam·*bya*·dor de be·*bes*

I need (a) ... Necesito ... ne·se·*see*·to ...

baby seat	un asiento de seguridad para bebé	oon a·*syen*·to de se·goo·ree·*dad* *pa*·ra be·*be*
booster seat	un asiento de seguridad para niños	oon a·*syen*·to de se·goo·ree·*dad* *pa*·ra *nee*·nyos
bottle	una mamila	*oo*·na ma·*mee*·la
crib	una cuna	*oo*·na *koo*·na
diapers/ nappies	unos pañales	*oo*·nos pa·*nya*·les
dummy/pacifier	un chupón	oon choo·*pon*
potty	una bacinica	*oo*·na ba·see·*nee*·ka
stroller	una carreola	*oo*·na ka·re·*o*·la

Is there a/an ...? ¿Hay ...?
ai ...

baby change room	un cambiador de bebés	oon kam·*bya*·dor de be·*bes*
child-minding service	servicio de niñera	ser·*vee*·cyo de nee·*nye*·ra
children's menu	menú infantil	me·*noo* een·fan·*teel*
creche	guardería	gwar·de·*ree*·a
(English-speaking) babysitter	niñera (que hable inglés)	nee·*nye*·ra (ke *a*·ble een·*gles*)
family discount	descuento familiar	des·*kwen*·to fa·mee·*lyar*
highchair	periquera	pe·ree·*ke*·ra
park	un parque	oon *par*·ke
playground nearby	un parque infantíl cercano	oon *par*·ke een·fan·*teel* ser·*ka*·no
theme park	un parque de diversiones	oon *par*·ke de dee·ver·*syon*·es
toyshop	una juguetería	*oo*·na joo·ge·te·*ree*·a

Do you mind if I breastfeed here?	¿Le molesta si doy pecho aquí? le mo·*les*·ta see doi *pe*·cho a·*kee*
Are children allowed?	¿Se permiten niños? se per·*mee*·ten nee·*nyos*
Is this suitable for (four)-year-old children?	¿Es apto para niños de (cuatro) años? es *ap*·to *pa*·ra *nee*·nyos de (*kwa*·tro) a·nyos

If your child is sick, see **health** (p158).

SOCIAL

Meeting People

KEY PHRASES

My name is ...	Me llamo ...	me *ya*·mo ...
I'm from ...	Soy de ...	soy de ...
I work in ...	Trabajo en ...	tra·*ba*·ho en ...
I'm ... years old.	Tengo ... años.	*ten*·go ... a·nyos
And you?	¿Y Usted? pol ¿Y tú? inf	ee oos·*ted* ee too

BASICS

Yes.	Sí. see
No.	No. no
Please.	Por favor. por fa·*vor*
Thank you (very much).	(Muchas) Gracias. (*moo*·chas) *gra*·syas
You're welcome.	De nada. de *na*·da No hay de qué. no ai de ke
Sorry. (regret)	Lo siento. lo *syen*·to
Sorry. (apology)	Perdón. per·*don*
Excuse me. (attention, apology)	Disculpe. dees·*kool*·pe

Pardon? (misunderstanding)	¿Mande? *man*·de

GREETINGS

Hi.	¡Hola! *o*·la
Hello./Good day.	Buen día. bwen *dee*·a ¡Buenas! inf *bwe*·nas
Good morning.	Buenos días. *bwe*·nos *dee*·as
Good afternoon.	Buenas tardes. *bwe*·nas *tar*·des
Good evening/night.	Buenas noches. *bwe*·nas *no*·ches
See you later.	Hasta luego. *as*·ta *lwe*·go
Goodbye.	Adiós. a·*dyos*
Q **How are you?**	¿Cómo está? sg pol *ko*·mo es·*ta* ¿Cómo estás? sg inf *ko*·mo es·*tas* ¿Cómo están? pl *ko*·mo es·*tan*
A **Fine, thanks. And you?**	Bien, gracias. ¿Y Usted/tú? pol/inf byen *gra*·syas ee oos·*ted*/too
Q **What's your name?**	¿Cómo se llama Usted? pol *ko*·mo se *ya*·ma oos·*ted* ¿Cómo te llamas? inf *ko*·mo te *ya*·mas

My name is ...	Me llamo ... me *ya*·mo ...
I'm pleased to meet you.	Mucho gusto. *moo*·cho *goos*·to
I'd like to introduce you to ...	Le/Te presento a ... pol/inf le/te pre·*sen*·to a ...

This is ...	Éste/Ésta es ... m/f	*es*·te/*es*·ta es ...

TITLES & ADDRESSING PEOPLE

The terms *Don* don (Sir) and *Doña do*·nya (Madam) are sometimes used to address older men and women in rural areas or local neighbourhoods, but are rare elsewhere. Use the word *Señor* se·*nyor* to show politeness towards a man and *Señora* se·*nyo*·ra towards a woman. You might also hear children address their godfather as *padrino* pa·*dree*·no and godmother as *madrina* ma·*dree*·na.

Mr	Señor se·*nyor*
young man	jóven *ho*·ven
Mrs	Señora se·*nyo*·ra
Miss/Ms	Señorita se·nyo·*ree*·ta
Doctor	Doctor(a) m/f dok·*tor*/dok·*to*·ra

MAKING CONVERSATION

Do you live here?	¿Vive/Vives aquí? pol/inf *vee*·ve/*vee*·ves a·*kee*
Where are you going?	¿A dónde va/vas? pol/inf a *don*·de va/vas
What are you doing?	¿Qué hace/haces? pol/inf ke *a*·se/*a*·ses

LANGUAGE TIP: POLITE & INFORMAL

Remember that there are two ways of saying 'you'. When addressing a stranger, an older person or someone in a position of authority, use the polite form *Usted* oos·*ted*. When talking to children or people who are familiar to you, use the informal form *tú* too. In this book we have used the most appropriate form for each phrase, but where you see pol/inf you have both options.

Are you waiting (for a bus)? ¿Está/Estás esperando (el autobús)? pol/inf
es·*ta*/es·*tas* es·pe·*ran*·do (el ow·to·*boos*)

Can I have a light? ¿Me da/das fuego? pol/inf
me da/das *fweh*·go

What's this called? ¿Cómo se llama ésto?
ko·mo se *ya*·ma *es*·to

What a beautiful baby! ¡Qué bebé tan hermoso/a! m/f
ke be·*be* tan er·*mo*·so/a

I'm here ... Estoy aquí ...
es·*toy* a·*kee* ...

with my family	con mi familia	kon mee fa·*mee*·lya
with my friends	con mis amigos/as m/f	kon mees a·*mee*·gos/as
with my partner	con mi pareja m&f	kon mee pa·*re*·ha

CULTURE TIP: CHICANISMOS

Americans with a Mexican background often identify themselves as *chicanos/as* chee·*ka*·nos/chee·*ka*·nas **m/f**, a label derived from the word *mexicano* (formerly pronounced me·shee·*ka*·no). Though originally a derogatory term, it now denotes an empowered Mexican-American cultural identity, which has also led to a greater recognition of Chicano Spanish. Chicanos may use older words that have disappeared from 'standard' Spanish, eg *semos* *se*·mos for *somos* *so*·mos (we are), or new words influenced by English, eg *cookiar* koo·kee·*ar* (cook). Here are some other common *chicanismos* (with their standard Spanish equivalents given in the third column):

ansina an·see·na	like this	*así* a·see
dispués dees·*pwes*	after	*después* des·*pwes*
leyer le·*yer*	read	*leer* le·*er*
muncho *moon*·cho	much/a lot	*mucho* *moo*·cho
naiden *nai*·den	nobody	*nadie* *na*·dye
nejecitar ne·he·see·*tar*	need	*necesitar* ne·se·see·*tar*
ónde *on*·de	where	*dónde* *don*·de
parkiar par·*kyar*	park	*estacionar* es·ta·syo·*nar*
pos pos	since	*pués* pwes
prebar pre·*bar*	try	*probar* pro·*bar*
watchar wa·*char*	watch	*mirar* mee·*rar*

Q	**How long are you here for?**	¿Cuánto tiempo va/vas a estar aquí? pol/inf *kwan*·to *tyem*·po va/vas a es·*tar* a·*kee*
A	**I'm here for ... weeks/ days.**	Voy a estar ... semanas/ días. voy a es·*tar* ... se·*ma*·nas/ *dee*·as
Q	**Do you like it here?**	¿Le/Te gusta este lugar? pol/inf le/te *goos*·ta *es*·te loo·*gar*
A	**I love it here.**	Me encanta este lugar. me en·*kan*·ta *es*·te loo·*gar*
	I'm here for a holiday.	Estoy aquí de vacaciones. es·*toy* a·*kee* de va·ka·*syo*·nes
	I'm here on business.	Estoy aquí por negocios. es·*toy* a·*kee* en por ne·*go*·syos

NATIONALITIES

Q	**Where are you from?**	¿De dónde es/eres? pol/inf de *don*·de es/*e*·res
A	**I'm from (Japan).**	Soy de (Japón). soy de (ha·*pon*)

For more countries, see the **dictionary** (p205).

AGE

Q	**How old are you?**	¿Cuántos años tiene/ tienes? pol/inf *kwan*·tos *a*·nyos *tye*·ne/*tye*·nes

LISTEN FOR

¡De ninguna manera!	de neen·*goo*·na ma·*ne*·ra	No way!
Está bien.	es·*ta* byen	It's OK.
Estoy bien.	es·*toy* byen	I'm OK.
No hay problema.	no ai pro·*ble*·ma	No problem.
¡Padrísimo!	pa·*dree*·see·mo	Great!
¡Qué chido!	ke *chee*·do	How cool!
¿Qué hubo?	*kyoo*·bo	What's up?
Seguro.	se·*goo*·ro	Sure.
Tal vez.	tal ves	Maybe.

(A) **I'm ... years old.**	Tengo ... años. *ten*·go ... *a*·nyos
(Q) **How old is your daughter?**	¿Cuántos años tiene su/tu hija? **pol/inf** *kwan*·tos *a*·nyos *tye*·ne soo/too *ee*·ha
(Q) **How old is your son?**	¿Cuántos años tiene su/tu hijo? **pol/inf** *kwan*·tos *a*·nyos *tye*·ne soo/too *ee*·ho
(A) **He/She is ... years old.**	Tiene ... años. *tye*·ne ... *a*·nyos
Too old!	¡Demasiados! de·ma·*sya*·dos
I'm younger than I look.	Soy más joven de lo que parezco. soy mas *ho*·ven de lo ke pa·*res*·ko

For your age, see **numbers & amounts** (p32).

OCCUPATIONS & STUDIES

Q **What's your occupation?**	¿A qué se dedica? pol a ke se de·*dee*·ka ¿A qué te dedicas? inf a ke te de·*dee*·kas
A **I'm a (teacher).**	Soy (maestro/a). m/f soy (ma·*es*·tro/a)
A **I work in communications.**	Trabajo en comunicaciones. tra·*ba*·ho en ko·moo·nee·ka·*syo*·nes
A **I work in education.**	Trabajo en educación. tra·*ba*·ho en e·doo·ka·*syon*
A **I work in hospitality.**	Trabajo en hotelería. tra·*ba*·ho en o·te·le·*ree*·a
A **I'm retired.**	Estoy jubilado/a. m/f es·*toy* hoo·bee·*la*·do/a
A **I'm unemployed.**	Estoy desempleado/a. m/f es·*toy* des·em·ple·a·do/a

CULTURE TIP: GRINGO LINGO

So are you a *gringo green*·go? In Mexico the word *gringo/a green*·go/*green*·ga m/f generally describes an English-speaking Anglo-American. Travellers needn't be offended by the term, which is rarely derogatory. It can be used to describe anything that has come from over the northern border, be it people, cars or films.

A popular myth is that the term originated during the war between Mexico and the USA (1846–48). American soldiers, who wore green uniforms, were supposedly taunted with the slogan 'Green, go home!'. The most likely theory, though, is that *gringo* is derived from the Spanish *griego grye*·go (meaning 'Greek').

LANGUAGE TIP: ADDRESSING FRIENDS

The most common word for friend is *amigo/a* a·*mee*·go/a·*mee*·ga m/f, but Mexican Spanish has an abundance of fun alternatives. You may hear people call each other *mano* m *ma*·no or *mana* f *ma*·na, an abbreviation of *hermano/a* er·*ma*·no/a (brother/sister). Young people may call each other *güey* gway (buddy), while in the north friends sometimes address each other as *batos* *ba*·tos (youngsters). Here are some other colloquial Mexican words for 'friend':

cuate m&f	*kwa*·te	(from 'twin' in Náhuatl)
chavo/a m/f	*cha*·vo/a	(lit: kid)
maestro/a m/f	ma·*es*·tro/a	(lit: teacher)

A **I'm self-employed.**	Trabajo por mi cuenta. tra·*ba*·ho por mee *kwen*·ta
Q **What are you studying?**	¿Qué estudia/estudias? pol/inf ke es·*too*·dya/es·*too*·dyas
A **I'm studying economics.**	Estudio economía. es·*too*·dyo e·ko·no·*mee*·a
A **I'm studying history.**	Estudio historia. es·*too*·dyo ees·*to*·rya
A **I'm studying languages.**	Estudio idiomas. es·*too*·dyo ee·*dyo*·mas

For more occupations and studies, see the **dictionary** (p205).

FAMILY

Q **Do you have (children)?**	¿Tiene/Tienes (hijos)? pol/inf *tye*·ne/*tye*·nes (*ee*·hos)
A **I have (a partner).**	Tengo (pareja). *ten*·go (pa·*re*·ha)

Q **Do you live with (your family)?**	¿Vive/Vives con (su/tu familia)? pol/inf *vee*·ve/*vee*·ves kon (soo/too fa·*mee*·lya)
A **I live with (my parents).**	Vivo con (mis papás). *vee*·vo kon (mees pa·*pas*)
Q **Are you married?**	¿Está casado/a? m/f pol es·*ta* ka·*sa*·do/a ¿Estás casado/a? m/f inf es·*tas* ka·*sa*·do/a
A **I'm married.**	Soy casado/a. m/f soy ka·*sa*·do/a
A **I live with someone.**	Vivo con alguien. *vee*·vo kon *al*·gyen
A **I'm separated.**	Soy separado/a. m/f soy se·pa·*ra*·do/a
A **I'm single.**	Soy soltero/a. m/f soy sol·*te*·ro/a

For more kinship terms, see the **dictionary** (p205).

TALKING WITH CHILDREN

When's your birthday?	¿Cuándo es tu cumpleaños? *kwan*·do es too koom·ple·*a*·nyos
Do you go to school?	¿Vas a la escuela? vas a la es·*kwe*·la
What grade are you in?	¿En qué año estás? en ke *a*·nyo es·*tas*
Do you like school?	¿Te gusta la escuela? te *goos*·ta la es·*kwe*·la
Do you like sport?	¿Te gusta el deporte? te *goos*·ta el de·*por*·te

Do you learn (English)?	¿Aprendes (inglés)? a·*pren*·des (een·*gles*)
What do you do after school?	¿Qué haces después de la escuela? ke *a*·ses des·*pwes* de la es·*kwe*·la
Show me how to play.	Enseñame cómo se juega. en·se·nyah·me *ko*·mo se *hwe*·ga
Well done!	¡Muy bien! mooy byen

FAREWELLS

Tomorrow is my last day here.	Mañana es mi último día aquí. ma·*nya*·na es mee *ool*·tee·mo *dee*·a a·*kee*
Q **What's your ...?**	¿Cuál es tu ...? kwal es too ...
A **Here's my ...**	Éste/a es mi ... m/f es·te/a es mee ...

address	dirección f	dee·rek·*syon*
email address	correo electrónico	ko·*re*·o e·lek·*tro*·nee·ko
mobile/cell phone number	número m de celular	*noo*·me·ro de se·loo·*lar*
work number	número m de trabajo	*noo*·me·ro de tra·*ba*·ho

If you ever visit (the United States), come and visit us.	Si algún día visitas (los Estados Unidos), ven a visitarnos. see al·*goon dee*·a vee·*see*·tas (los es·*ta*·dos oo·*nee*·dos) ven a vee·see·*tar*·nos

LANGUAGE TIP: PRONOUNCING THE LETTER 'X'

Beware of the letter *x* in Mexican Spanish, as it can be pronounced in four different ways. In words such as *México* *me*·hee·ko it's pronounced kh (as in the Scottish 'loch') and in words like *exacto* ek·*sak*·to it's pronounced ks. In some words of indigenous origin, such as *mixiotes* mee·*shyo*·tes and *xcatic* shka·*teek* (types of food) it sounds like sh, but in place names like *Xóchitl* *so*·cheel and *Xochicalco* so·chee·*kal*·ko it's pronounced s. Don't get too confused by this – just check our coloured phonetic guides for the correct pronunciation, and, of course, listen to Mexicans!

See also **pronunciation** (p11).

If you ever visit (Australia), you can stay with me.	Si algún día visitas (Australia), te puedes quedar conmigo. see al·*goon dee*·a vee·*see*·tas (ow·*stra*·lya) te *pwe*·des ke·*dar* kon·*mee*·go
I'll send you copies of the photos.	Te mandaré copias de las fotos. te *man*·da·re *ko*·pyas de las *fo*·tos
Keep in touch!	¡Mantente en contacto! man·*ten*·te en kon·*tak*·to
It's been great meeting you.	Ha sido un placer conocerte. a *see*·do oon pla·*ser* ko·no·*ser*·te
I'm going to miss you!	¡Te voy a extrañar! te voy a ek·stra·*nyar*

For addresses, see also **directions** (p56).

Interests

KEY PHRASES

What do you do in your spare time?	¿Qué te gusta hacer en tu tiempo libre?	ke te *goos*·ta a·*ser* en too *tyem*·po *lee*·bre
Do you like ...?	¿Te gusta ...? sg ¿Te gustan ...? pl	te *goos*·ta ... te *goos*·tan ...
I (don't) like ...	(No) Me gusta ... sg (No) Me gustan ... pl	(no) me *goos*·ta ... (no) me *goos*·tan ...

COMMON INTERESTS

What do you do in your spare time?	¿Qué te gusta hacer en tu tiempo libre? ke te *goos*·ta a·*ser* en too *tyem*·po *lee*·bre
Q **Do you like ...?**	¿Te gusta/gustan ...? sg/pl te *goos*·ta/*goos*·tan ...
A **I (don't) like ...**	(No) Me gusta ... sg (no) me *goos*·ta ... (No) Me gustan ... pl (no) me *goos*·tan ...

cooking	cocinar sg	ko·see·*nar*
dancing	bailar sg	bai·*lar*
gardening	la jardinería sg	la har·dee·ne·*ree*·a
sport	los deportes pl	los de·*por*·tes
travelling	viajar sg	vya·*har*

For more hobbies and types of sports, see **sports** (p140), and the **dictionary** (p205).

MUSIC

Do you like to ...?	Te gusta ...?	te *goos*·ta ...
dance	bailar	bai·*lar*
go to concerts	ir a conciertos	eer a kon·*syer*·tos
listen to music	escuchar música	es·koo·*char* *moo*·see·ka
play an instrument	tocar un instrumento	to·*kar* oon een·stroo·*men*·to
sing	cantar	kan·*tar*

Which bands do you like?	¿Qué grupos te gustan? ke *groo*·pos te *goos*·tan
What music do you like?	¿Qué música te gusta? ke *moo*·see·ka te *goos*·ta
... music	música ... *moo*·see·ka ...

electronic	electrónica	e·lek·*tro*·nee·ka
Spanish-language	en español	en es·pa·*nyol*
traditional	tradicional	tra·dee·syo·*nal*
world	folklórica	fol·*klo*·ree·ka

Planning to go to a concert? See **buying tickets** (p43), and **going out** (p129).

CINEMA & THEATRE

I feel like going to a movie.	Tengo ganas de ir al cine. *ten*·go *ga*·nas de eer al *see*·neh

☑ CULTURE TIP: MEXICAN MUSIC STYLES

From Latin rhythms blaring from bus stereos to wandering mariachis and live salsa bands, music is absolutely everywhere in Mexico. Here are some unique styles to listen for:

corridos m pl — ko·*ree*·dos
narrative ballads influenced by polka and waltz styles

huapango m — wa·*pan*·go
a fast, indigenous dance-song from the Huastec region

música f **tropical** — *moo*·see·ka tro·pee·*kal*
slow-paced rhythmic music of Caribbean origin including *danzón* (Cuba) and *cumbia* (Colombia)

norteña f — nor·*te*·nya
country ballad and dance music from northern Mexico

ranchera f — ran·*che*·ra
very popular, country-style big-band music

son m — son
a folk fusion of African, Spanish and indigenous music styles, combining guitar, violin and voice

trova f — *tro*·va
poetic troubadour-style folk music

I feel like going to a play.	Tengo ganas de ir al teatro. *ten*·go *ga*·nas de eer al te·*a*·tro
What's showing at the cinema/theatre tonight?	¿Qué hay en el cine/teatro esta noche? ke ai en el *see*·ne/te·*a*·tro es·ta *no*·che

Is it in English/Spanish?	¿Es en inglés/español? es en een·*gles*/es·pa·*nyol*
Does it have subtitles?	¿Tiene subtítulos? *tye*·ne soob·*tee*·too·los
Have you seen ...?	¿Has visto ...? as *vees*·to ...
Q **Who's in it?**	¿Quién actúa? kyen ak·*too*·a
A **It stars ...**	Actúa(n) ... sg/pl ak·*too*·a(n) ...
Q **Did you like (the film)?**	¿Te gustó (la película)? te goos·*to* (la pe·*lee*·koo·la)
A **I thought it was ...**	Pienso que fue ... *pyen*·so ke fwe ...

excellent	excelente	ek·se·*len*·te
long	largo/a m/f	*lar*·go/a
OK	regular	re·goo·*lar*
very bad	malísimo/a m/f	ma·*lee*·see·mo/a

animated films	películas animadas f pl pe·*lee*·koo·las a·nee·*ma*·das
(Mexican) cinema	cine m (mexicano) *see*·ne (me·hee·*ka*·no)
documentaries	documentales m pl do·koo·men·*ta*·les
film noir	cine m negro *see*·ne *ne*·gro
horror movies	películas f pl de terror pe·*lee*·koo·las de te·*ror*
sci-fi	películas f pl de ciencia ficción pe·*lee*·koo·las de *syen*·sya feek·*syon*

short films	cortos m pl *kor*·tos
thrillers	películas f pl de suspenso pe·*lee*·koo·las de soos·*pen*·so

BOOKS & READING

Q **What kind of books do you read?**	¿Qué tipo de libros lees? ke *tee*·po de *lee*·bros *le*·es
Q **Have you read ...?**	¿Has leído ...? as le·*ee*·do ...
Q **On this trip I'm reading...**	En este viaje estoy leyendo ... en *es*·te *vya*·he es·*toy* le·*yen*·do ...
A **I normally read ...**	Suelo leer ... *swe*·lo le·*er* ...
Q **Which (Mexican) author do you recommend?**	¿Qué autor (mexicano) me recomiendas? ke ow·*tor* (me·hee·*ka*·no) me re·ko·*myen*·das
A **I recommend ...**	Te recomiendo a ... te re·ko·*myen*·do a ...

☑ CULTURE TIP: MEXICAN LITERATURE

Mexico has a very lively literary scene. Much of the activity centres on Mexico City, though Latin America's most prestigious book fair, *La Feria Internacional del Libro* (International Book Fair) is held in Guadalajara in late November each year. Good city bookshops will stock English translations of famous authors such as Carlos Fuentes, Rosario Castellanos, Mariano Azuela, Elena Poniatowska and Nobel Prize winner Octavio Paz. Newer Mexican writers to look out for include Jorge Volpi, Pedro Ángel Palou and Ignacio Padilla.

LANGUAGE TIP: LIKES & DISLIKES

In Spanish, in order to say you like something, you say *me gusta* me *goos*·ta (lit: me it-pleases). If it's a plural noun, use *me gustan* me *goos*·tan (lit: me they-please). If you're referring to an activity, eg cooking or travelling, use *me gusta* followed by the verb. You can negate any of these sentences by adding *no* no (not) to the beginning of a phrase.

I like this song.	Me gusta esta canción. me *goos*·ta *es*·ta kan·*syon*
I like tacos.	Me gustan los tacos. me *goos*·tan los *ta*·kos
I like singing.	Me gusta cantar. me *goos*·ta kan·*tar*
I don't like dancing.	No me gusta bailar. no me *goos*·ta bai·*lar*

Where can I exchange books?	¿Dónde puedo intercambiar libros? *don*·de *pwe*·do een·ter·kam·*byar lee*·bros

VOLUNTEERING

I'd like to volunteer my skills.	Me gustaría ser voluntario. me goos·ta·*ree*·a ser vo·loon·*ta*·ryo
Are there any volunteer programmes available in the area?	¿Hay algún programa de voluntariado en esta rogión? ai al·*goon* pro·*gra*·ma de vo·loon·ta·*rya*·do en *es*·ta re·*hyon*

Feelings & Opinions

KEY PHRASES

Are you ...?	¿Está ...? pol ¿Estás ...? inf ¿Tiene ...? pol ¿Tienes ...? inf	es·*ta* ... es·*tas* ... *tye*·ne ... *tye*·nes ...
I'm (not) ...	(No) Estoy ... (No) Tengo ...	(no) es·*toy* ... (no) *ten*·go ...
What did you think of it?	¿Qué pensó/ pensaste de eso? pol/inf	ke pen·*so*/ pen·*sas*·te de e·so
I thought it was OK.	Pienso que fue regular.	*pyen*·so ke fwe re·goo·*lar*
How do people feel about ...?	¿Cómo se siente la gente acerca de ...?	*ko*·mo se *syen*·te la *hen*·te a·*ser*·ka de ...

FEELINGS

Feelings are described with either nouns or adjectives: the nouns use the verb *tener* te·*ner* (have) – eg 'I have hunger' – and the adjectives use the verbs *ser* ser or *estar* es·*tar* (be), like in English.

Q **Are you (happy)?**	¿Está/Estás (feliz)? pol/inf es·*ta*/es·*tas* (fe·*lees*)
A **I'm (sick).**	Estoy (enfermo/a). m/f es·*toy* (en·*fer*·mo/a)
A **I'm not (bored).**	No estoy (aburrido/a). m/f no es·*toy* (a·boo·*ree*·do/a)
Q **Are you ...?**	¿Tiene/Tienes ...? pol/inf *tye*·ne/*tye*·nes ...

I'm (not) ... (No) Tengo ... *(no) ten·go ...*

cold	frío	*free·o*
hungry	hambre	*am·bre*
sleepy	sueño	*swe·nyo*
thirsty	sed	*sed*

I'm a little (sad). Estoy un poco (triste). *es·toy oon po·ko (trees·te)*

I'm quite (disappointed). Estoy bastante (decepcionado/a). m/f *es·toy bas·tan·te (de·sep·syo·na·do/a)*

I'm very (happy). Estoy muy (feliz). *es·toy mooy (fe·lees)*

For more feelings, see the **dictionary** (p205).

OPINIONS

Did you like it? ¿Le/Te gustó? pol/inf *le/te goos·to*

What did you think of it? ¿Qué pensó/pensaste de eso? pol/inf *ke pen·so/pen·sas·te de e·so*

I thought it was ... Pienso que fue ... *pyen·so ke fwe ...*

It's ... Es ... *es ...*

beautiful	hermoso/a m/f	*er·mo·so/a*
crazy	loco/a m/f	*lo·ko/a*
excellent	excelente	*ek·se·len·te*
horrible	horrible	*o·ree·ble*

POLITICS & SOCIAL ISSUES

While Mexicans are very critical of their leaders, they can be fiercely patriotic at the same time. Visitors should try to gauge the mood, and ask questions before offering opinions. Mexican history, art and culture are fruitful subjects of conversation. As a rule, avoid topics such as the Mexican-American war and undocumented migration.

Q **Who do you vote for?**	¿Por quién vota/votas? pol/inf por kyen *vo*·ta/*vo*·tas
A **I support the ... party.**	Apoyo al partido ... a·*po*·yo al par·*tee*·do ...
A **I'm a member of the ... party.**	Soy miembro del partido ... soy *myem*·bro del par·*tee*·do ...

communist	comunista	ko·moo·*nees*·ta
conservative	conservador	kon·ser·va·*dor*
green	verde	*ver*·de
labour	laborista	la·bo·*rees*·ta
liberal (progressive)	progresista	pro·gre·*sees*·ta
social democratic	social-demócrata	so·syal·de·*mo*·kra·ta
socialist	socialista	so·sya·*lees*·ta

Q **Are you against ...?**	¿Está/Estás en contra de ...? pol/inf es·*ta*/es·*tas* en *kon*·tra de ...
Q **Are you in favour of ...?**	¿Está/Estás a favor de ...? pol/inf es·*ta*/es·*tas* a fa·*vor* de ...
A **I (don't) agree with ...**	(No) estoy de acuerdo con ... (no) es·*toy* de a·*kwer*·do kon ...

Es hermoso.
es er·*mo*·so
It's beautiful.

How do people feel about ...?	¿Cómo se siente la gente acerca de ...? *ko*·mo se *syen*·te la *hen*·te a·*ser*·ka de ...
In my country we are concerned about ...	En mi país nos preocupamos por ... en mi pa·*ees* nos pre·o·koo·*pa*·mos por ...

organised crime	crimen m organizado	*kree*·men or·ga·nee·*sa*·do
the economy	la economía f	la e·ko·no·*mee*·a
the environment	el medio m ambiente	el *me*·dyo am·*byen*·te
the war in ...	la guerra f en ...	la *ge*·ra en ...

LISTEN FOR

¿De veras?	de *ve*·ras	Really?
¡Es increíble!	es een·kre·*ee*·ble	That's incredible!
¡Escucha (esto)!	es·*koo*·cha (*es*·to)	Listen (to this)!
¡Mira!	*mee*·ra	Look!
¡No me digas!	no me *dee*·gas	You don't say!
¡Por supuesto!	por soo·*pwes*·to	Of course!
¡Ya lo creo!	ya lo *kre*·o	You bet!

THE ENVIRONMENT

Is there a/an (environmental) problem here?	¿Aquí hay algún problema con (el medio ambiente)? a·*kee* ai al·*goon* pro·*ble*·ma kon (el *me*·dyo am·*byen*·te)
Where can I recycle this?	¿Dónde puedo reciclar ésto? *don*·de *pwe*·do re·see·*klar* *es*·to
climate change	cambio m climático *kam*·byo klee·*ma*·tee·ko
pollution	contaminación f kon·ta·mee·na·*syon*
recycling programmes	programas m pl de reciclaje pro·*gra*·mas de re·see·*kla*·he
Is this forest/park protected?	¿Está protegido este bosque/parque? es·*ta* pro·te·*hee*·do *es*·te *bos*·ke/*par*·ke
Is this species protected?	¿Está protegida esta especie? es·*ta* pro·te·*hee*·da *es*·ta es·*pe*·sye

Going Out

KEY PHRASES

What's on tonight?	¿Qué hay esta noche?	ke ai *es*·ta *no*·che
Where are the clubs?	¿Dónde hay antros?	*don*·de ai *an*·tros
Would you like to go for a coffee?	¿Te gustaría tomar un café?	te goos·ta·*ree*·a to·*mar* oon ka·*fe*
What time shall we meet?	¿A qué hora nos vemos?	a ke *o*·ra nos *ve*·mos
Where will we meet?	¿Dónde nos vemos?	*don*·de nos *ve*·mos

WHERE TO GO

What's there to do in the evenings?	¿Qué hay para hacer en las noches? ke ai *pa*·ra a·*ser* en las *no*·ches
What's on ...?	¿Qué hay ...? ke ai ...

locally	en la zona	en la *so*·na
today	hoy	oy
tonight	esta noche	*es*·ta *no*·che
this weekend	este fin de semana	*es*·te feen de se·*ma*·na

Is there a local ... guide?
¿Hay una guía de ... de la zona?
ai *oo*·na *gee*·a de ... de la *so*·na

entertainment	entretenimiento	en·tre·te·nee·*myen*·to
film	cines	*see*·nes
LGBTIQ+	los lugares LGBTI+/gay	los loo·*ga*·res eh·leh·heh·beh·teh·ee·*mas*/gay
music	de música	de *moo*·see·ka

Where are the ...?
¿Dónde hay ...?
don·de ai ...

bars	bares	*ba*·res
cafes	cafeterías	ka·fe·te·*ree*·as
clubs	antros	*an*·tros
gay venues	lugares gay	loo·*ga*·res gay
LGBTIQ+ venues	lugares LGBTI+/gay	loo·*ga*·res eh·leh·heh·beh·teh·ee·*mas*/gay
places to eat	lugares para comer	loo·*ga*·res *pa*·ra ko·*mer*

I feel like going to ...
Tengo ganas de ir ...
ten·go *ga*·nas de eer ...

a cafe	a una cafetería	a *oo*·na ka·fe·te·*ree*·a
a concert	a un concierto	a oon kon·*syer*·to
a party	a una fiesta	a *oo*·na *fyes*·ta
a restaurant	a un restaurante	a oon res·tow·*ran*·te
the movies	al cine	al *see*·ne
the theatre	al teatro	al te·*a*·tro

Do you know a good restaurant?	¿Conoces algún buen restaurante? ko·*no*·ses al·*goon* bwen res·tow·*ran*·te
Where can we go (salsa) dancing?	¿Dónde podemos bailar (salsa)? *don*·de po·*de*·mos bai·*lar* (*sal*·sa)
What's the cover charge?	¿Cuánto cuesta el cover? *kwan*·to *kwes*·ta el *ko*·ver

INVITATIONS

What are you doing ...?	¿Qué vas a hacer ...? ke vas a a·*ser* ...

right now	ahorita	a·o·*ree*·ta
this evening	esta noche	es·ta *no*·che
tomorrow	mañana	ma·*nya*·na
this weekend	este fin de semana	es·te feen de se·*ma*·na

Would you like to go (out somewhere)?	¿Te gustaría salir (a algún lado)? te goos·ta·*ree*·a sa·*leer* (a al·*goon* *la*·do)
I feel like going for a ...	Me gustaría ir a ... me goos·ta·*ree*·a eer a ...

coffee	tomar un café	to·*mar* oon ka·*fe*
dance	bailar	bai·*lar*
drink	tomar algo	to·*mar* *al*·go
meal	comer	ko·*mer*
walk	caminar	ka·mee·*nar*

CULTURE TIP: MEXICAN BARS

From rowdy rum-soaked saloons to cosy, romantic lounge-bars, Mexico has it all.

antro m *an*·tro
bar or nightclub – word formerly used to describe a dive

bar m bar
a place for drinking and talking, rather than dancing or listening to live music

cantina f kan·*tee*·na
a uniquely Mexican establishment, where tequila, mezcal, beer, rum and brandy are the order of the day; some *cantinas* are men-only zones, but most others are more relaxed

peña f *pe*·nya
a place to go for either a drink or a meal, usually with live romantic Mexican music

My round.	Yo invito. yo een·*vee*·to
We're having a party.	Vamos a hacer una fiesta. *va*·mos a a·*ser oo*·na *fyes*·ta
You should come.	¿Por qué no vienes? por ke no *vye*·nes

RESPONDING TO INVITATIONS

Sure!	¡Claro que sí! *kla*·ro ke see
Yes, I'd love to.	Sí, me encantaría. see me en·kan·ta·*ree*·a
Where shall we go?	¿Adónde vamos? a·*don*·de *va*·mos

Thanks, but I'm afraid I can't.	Gracias, pero no puedo. *gra*·syas *pe*·ro no *pwe*·do
What about tomorrow?	¿Qué tal mañana? ke tal ma·*nya*·na
Sorry, I can't sing/dance.	Perdón, no sé cantar/bailar. per·*don* no se kan·*tar*/bai·*lar*

ARRANGING TO MEET

Q **What time shall we meet?**	¿A qué hora nos vemos? a ke *o*·ra nos *ve*·mos
A **Let's meet at (eight o'clock).**	Nos vemos a (las ocho). nos *ve*·mos a (las *o*·cho)
Q **Where will we meet?**	¿Dónde nos vemos? *don*·de nos *ve*·mos
A **Let's meet at (the entrance).**	Nos vemos en (la entrada). nos *ve*·mos en (la en·*tra*·da)
I'll pick you up.	Paso por tí. *pa*·so por *tee*
I'll be coming later.	Te alcanzo más tarde. te al·*kan*·so mas *tar*·de
I'll see you then.	Nos vemos. nos *ve*·mos
I'm looking forward to it.	Tengo muchas ganas de ir. *ten*·go *moo*·chas *ga*·nas de eer

DRUGS

I don't take drugs.	No consumo drogas. no kon·*soo*·mo *dro*·gas
I have ... occasionally.	Consumo ... de vez en cuando. kon·*soo*·mo ... de ves en *kwan*·do
Do you want to have a smoke?	¿Nos fumamos un churro? nos foo·*ma*·mos oon *choo*·ro

Romance

KEY PHRASES

Would you like to do something?	¿Quieres hacer algo?	*kye*·res a·*ser al*·go
I love you.	Te quiero.	te *kye*·ro
Leave me alone.	Déjame en paz.	*de*·ha·me en pas

ASKING SOMEONE OUT

Q **Would you like to do something (tonight)?**	¿Quieres salir conmigo (esta noche)? *kye*·res sa·*leer* con·*mi*·go (*es*·ta *no*·che)
A **Yes, I'd love to.**	Sí, me encantaría. see me en·kan·ta·*ree*·a
A **No, I'm afraid I can't.**	Gracias, pero no puedo. *gra*·syas *pe*·ro no *pwe*·do

PICK-UP LINES

Would you like a drink?	¿Te invito una copa? te een·*vee*·to *oo*·na *ko*·pa
Do you have a light?	¿Tienes fuego? *tye*·nes *fweh*·go
What star sign are you?	¿De qué signo eres? de ke *seeg*·no *e*·res
Shall we get some fresh air?	¿Vamos afuera? *va*·mos a·*fwe*·ra

You have (a) beautiful ...	Tienes ... *tye*·nes ...	
body	un muy buen cuerpo	oon mooy bwen *kwer*·po
eyes	unos ojos preciosos	*oo*·nos *o*·hos pre·*syo*·sos
laugh	una risa preciosa	*oo*·na *ree*·sa pre·*syo*·sa
personality	una gran personalidad	*oo*·na gran per·so·na·lee·*dad*

REJECTIONS

I'm here with my boyfriend/girlfriend.	Vine con mi novio/a. *vee*·ne kon mee *no*·vyo/a
I have a boyfriend/ girlfriend.	Tengo novio/a. *ten*·go *no*·vyo/a
Excuse me, I have to go now.	Lo siento, pero me tengo que ir. lo *syen*·to *pe*·ro me *ten*·go ke eer
I'm not interested.	No estoy interesado/a. m/f no es·*toy* een·te·re·*sa*·do/a
Leave me alone!	Déjame en paz. *de*·ha·me en pas

GETTING CLOSER

You're very nice.	Eres muy simpático/a. m/f *e*·res mooy seem·*pa*·tee·ko/a

You're very attractive.	Eres muy atractivo/a. m/f e·res mooy a·trak·*tee*·vo/a
Do you like me?	¿Te caigo bien? te *kai*·go byen
I like you very much.	Me gustas mucho. me *goos*·tas *moo*·cho
Can I kiss you?	¿Te puedo besar? te *pwe*·do be·*sar*
Will you take me home?	¿Te puedo acompañar a tu casa? te *pwe*·do a·kom·*pa*·nyar a too *ka*·sa
Do you want to come inside for a while?	¿Quieres pasar un rato? *kye*·res pa·*sar* oon *ra*·to

SEX

I want to make love to you.	Quiero hacerte el amor. *kye*·ro a·*ser*·te el a·*mor*
I won't do it without protection.	No lo haré sin protección. no lo a·*re* seen pro·tek·*syon*
Let's use a condom.	Usemos condón. oo·se·mos kon·*don*
I think we should stop now.	Creo que deberíamos parar. *kre*·o ke de·be·*ree*·a·mos pa·*rar*
Let's go to bed!	¡Vamos a la cama! *va*·mos a la *ka*·ma
Kiss me!	¡Bésame! *be*·sa·me
I want you.	Te deseo. te de·se·o

Take this off.	Quítate ésto. *kee*·ta·te *es*·to
(Q) **Do you like this?**	¿Te gusta ésto? te *goos*·ta *es*·to
(A) **I (don't) like that.**	Eso (no) me gusta. *eh*·so (no) me *goos*·ta
Touch me here.	Tócame aquí. *to*·ka·me a·*kee*
That's great.	Eso es genial. *e*·so es he·*nyal*
Please stop!	¡Para, por favor! *pa*·ra por fa·*vor*
Please don't stop!	¡Por favor, no pares! por fa·*vor* no *pa*·res
That was amazing.	Eso fue increíble. *e*·so fwe een·kre·*ee*·ble
Can I stay over?	¿Puedo quedarme? *pwe*·do ke·*dar*·me
When can I see you again?	¿Cuándo nos vemos de nuevo? *kwan*·do nos *ve*·mos de *nwe*·vo

LOVE

I'm in love with you.	Estoy enamorado/a de tí. m/f es·*toy* e·na·mo·*ra*·do/a de tee
(Q) **Do you love me?**	¿Me quieres? me *kye*·res
(A) **I love you.**	Te quiero. te *kye*·ro
I think we're good together.	Creo que hacemos buena pareja. *kre*·o ke a·*se*·mos *bwe*·na pa·*re*·ha

SOCIAL ROMANCE

Beliefs & Culture

KEY PHRASES

What's your religion?	¿Cuál es su/tu religión? pol/inf	kwal es soo/too re·lee·*hyon*
I'm ...	Soy ...	soy ...
I'm sorry, it's against my beliefs.	Lo siento, pero eso va en contra de mis creencias.	lo *syen*·to *pe*·ro e·so va en *kon*·tra de mees kre·*en*·syas

RELIGION

Q **What's your religion?**
¿Cuál es su/tu religión? pol/inf
kwal es soo/too re·lee·*hyon*

A **I'm (not) ...**
(No) Soy ...
(no) soy ...

agnostic	agnóstico/a m/f	ag·*nos*·tee·ko/a
atheist	ateo/a m/f	a·*te*·o/a
Buddhist	budista m&f	boo·*dees*·ta
Catholic	católico/a m/f	ka·*to*·lee·ko/a
Christian	cristiano/a m/f	krees·*tya*·no/a
Hindu	hindú m&f	een·*doo*
Jewish	judío/a m/f	hoo·*dee*·o/a
Muslim	musulmán m musulmana f	moo·sool·*man* moo·sool·*ma*·na
practising	practicante m&f	prak·tee·*kan*·te
Protestant	protestante m&f	pro·tes·*tan*·te

I'd like to go to (the) ...	Me gustaría ir a ... me goos·ta·*ree*·a ...

church	la iglesia	la ee·*gle*·sya
mosque	la mezquita	la mes·*kee*·ta
synagogue	la sinagoga	la see·na·*go*·ga
temple	el templo	el *tem*·plo

Can I (pray) here?	¿Puedo (rezar) aquí? *pwe*·do (re·*sar*) a·*kee*
Where can I (attend mass)?	¿Dónde puedo (ir a misa)? *don*·de *pwe*·do (eer a *mee*·sa)

CULTURAL DIFFERENCES

Is this a local custom?	¿Es una costumbre local? es *oo*·na kos·*toom*·bre lo·*kal*
I'm not used to this.	No estoy acostumbrado/a a ésto. m/f no es·*toy* a·kos·toom·*bra*·do/a a *es*·to
Sorry, I didn't mean to say/do something wrong.	Perdón, lo dije/hice sin querer. per·*don* lo *dee*·he/*ee*·se seen ke·*rer*
I'm sorry, it's against my beliefs.	Lo siento, pero eso va en contra de mis creencias. lo *syen*·to *pe*·ro *e*·so va en *kon*·tra de mees kre·*en*·syas
I don't mind watching, but I'd rather not join in.	No me molesta ver, pero prefiero no participar. no me mol·*es*·ta ver *pe*·ro pre·*fye*·ro no par·tee·see·*par*

Sports

KEY PHRASES

Which sport do you play?	¿Qué deporte practicas?	ke de·*por*·te prak·*tee*·kas
Who's your favourite team?	¿Cuál es tu equipo favorito?	kwal es too e·*kee*·po fa·vo·*ree*·to
What's the score?	¿Cómo van?	*ko*·mo van

SPORTING INTERESTS

Q **Do you like (tennis)?**	¿Te gusta (el tenis)? te *goos*·ta (el *te*·nees)
A **Yes, very much.**	Sí, mucho. see *moo*·cho
A **Not really.**	En realidad, no mucho. en re·a·lee·*dad* no *moo*·cho
A **I like watching it.**	Me gusta ver. me *goos*·ta ver
Q **Which sport do you play?**	¿Qué deporte practicas? ke de·*por*·te prak·*tee*·kas
A **I play (basketball).**	Juego (básquet). *hwe*·go *bas*·ket
Q **Which sport do you follow?**	¿Qué deporte sigues? ke de·*por*·te *see*·ghes
A **I follow (football/ soccer).**	Sigo al (fútbol). *see*·go al (*foot*·bol)

Who's your favourite sportsman/woman?	¿Quién es tu deportista favorito/a? m/f kyen es too de·por·*tees*·ta fa·vo·*ree*·to/a
What's your favourite team?	¿Cuál es tu equipo favorito? kwal es too e·*kee*·po fa·vo·*ree*·to

For more sports, see the **dictionary** (p205).

GOING TO A GAME

Would you like to go to a match?	¿Te gustaría ir a un partido? te goos·ta·*ree*·a eer a oon par·*tee*·do
Who's playing?	¿Quién juega? kyen *hwe*·ga
Who are you supporting?	¿A qué equipo le vas? a ke e·*kee*·po le vas
Who's winning?	¿Quién va ganando? kyen va ga·*nan*·do
What's the score?	¿Cómo van? *ko*·mo van
How much time is left?	¿Cuánto tiempo queda (en el partido)? *kwan*·to *tyem*·po *ke*·da (en el par·*tee*·do)
Q **What was the final score?**	¿Cómo quedó el partido? *ko*·mo ke·*do* el par·*tee*·do
A **It was a draw.**	Fue un empate. fwe oon em·*pa*·te
That was a boring game!	¡Fue un partido aburridísimo! fwe oon par·*tee*·do a·boo·ree·*dee*·see·mo

CULTURE TIP: TRADITIONAL SPORTS

Bullfighting and cockfighting are both popular in Mexico. You might see posters advertising the following:

corridas f pl **de toros** — *ko·ree·das de to·ros*
bullfighting, especially popular in major towns

lucha f **libre** — *loo·cha lee·bre*
theatrical free-style Mexican wrestling in which competitors are masked

peleas f pl **de gallos** — *pe·le·as de ga·yos*
cockfights – two roosters fight to the death using blades attached to their feet

pelota f **mixteca** — *pe·lo·ta mee·ste·ka*
a five-a-side ball game reconstructed from a pre-Hispanic version that often ended with human sacrifice

That was a bad game!	¡Fue un pésimo partido! fwe oon *peh*·see·mo par·*tee*·do
That was a great game!	¡Fue un partido buenísimo! fwe oon par·*tee*·do bwe·*nee*·see·mo
What a ...!	¡Qué ...! ke ...

goal	gol	gol
hit	tiro	*tee*·ro
kick	chute	*choo*·te
pass	pase	*pa*·se

PLAYING SPORT

Do you want to play?	¿Quieres jugar? *kye*·res hoo·*gar*
Can I join in?	¿Puedo jugar? *pwe*·do hoo·*gar*
Yes, that'd be great.	Sí, me encantaría. see me en·kan·ta·*ree*·a
Not at the moment, thanks.	Ahorita no, gracias. a·o·*ree*·ta no *gra*·syas
I have an injury.	Tengo una lesión. *ten*·go *oo*·na le·*syon*
Where's the nearest ...?	¿Dónde queda ...? *don*·de *ke*·da ...

gym	el gimnasio más cercano	el heem·*na*·syo mas ser·*ka*·no
park	el parque más cercano	el *par*·ke mas ser·*ka*·no
sports club	el club deportivo más cercano	el kloob de·por·*tee*·vo mas ser·*ka*·no
swimming pool	la alberca más cercana	la al·*ber*·ka mas ser·*ka*·na
tennis court	la cancha de tenis más cercana	la *kan*·cha de *te*·nees mas ser·*ka*·na

Where's the best place to jog around here?	¿Cuál es el mejor sitio para correr por aquí cerca? kwal es el me·*hor see*·tyo *pa*·ra ko·*rer* por a·*kee ser*·ka
Can I hire a ball?	¿Puedo rentar una pelota? *pwe*·do ren·*tar oo*·na pe·*lo*·ta

Can I hire a court?	¿Puedo rentar una cancha? *pwe*·do ren·*tar* *oo*·na *kan*·cha
Can I hire a racquet?	¿Puedo rentar una raqueta? *pwe*·do ren·*tar* *oo*·na ra·*ke*·ta
What's the charge per ...?	¿Cúanto cobran por ...? *kwan*·to *ko*·bran por ...

day	día	*dee*·a
game	juego	*hwe*·go
hour	hora	*o*·ra
visit	visita	vee·*see*·ta

LISTEN FOR

delantero m	de·lan·*te*·ro	striker
gol m	gol	goal (scored)
fuera de lugar	*fwe*·ra de loo·*gar*	offside
medio-campista m	me·dyo·kam·*pees*·ta	mid-fielder
pelota f	pe·*lo*·ta	ball
penalty m	*pe*·nal·tee	penalty
portería f	por·te·*ree*·a	goal (place)
portero m	por·*te*·ro	goalkeeper
tarjeta f **amarilla**	tar·*he*·ta a·ma·*ree*·ya	yellow card
tarjeta f **roja**	tar·*he*·ta *ro*·ha	red card
tiro m **de esquina**	*tee*·ro de es·*kee*·na	corner (kick)
tiro m **libre**	*tee*·ro *lee*·bre	free kick

Do I have to be a member to attend?	¿Hay que ser socio/a para entrar? m/f ai ke ser *so*·syo/a *pa*·ra en·*trar*
Is there a women-only pool?	¿Hay alguna alberca sólo para mujeres? ai al·*goo*·na al·*ber*·ka *so*·lo *pa*·ra moo·*khe*·res
Where are the changing rooms?	¿Dónde están los vestidores? *don*·de es·*tan* los ves·tee·*do*·res
Can I have a locker?	¿Puedo usar un casillero? *pwe*·do oo·*sar* oon ka·see·*ye*·ro

FOOTBALL/SOCCER

Who plays for (the Pumas)?	¿Quién juega en (los Pumas)? kyen *hwe*·ga en (los *poo*·mas)
He's a great (player).	Es un gran (jugador). es oon gran (hoo·ga·*dor*)
Which team is at the top of the league?	¿Qué equipo va de líder de la liga? ke e·*kee*·po va de *lee*·der de la *lee*·ga
He/She played brilliantly in the match against (Venezuela).	Jugó excelente en el partido contra (Venezuela). hoo·*go* ek·se·*len*·te en el par·*tee*·do *kon*·tra (ve·ne·*swe*·la)
What a terrible team!	¡Qué pésimo equipo! ke *pe*·see·mo e·*kee*·po

Off to see a match? Check out **buying tickets** (p43), and **going to a game** (p141).

Outdoors

KEY PHRASES

Where can I buy supplies?	¿Dónde puedo comprar provisiones?	*don*·de *pwe*·do kom·*prar* pro·vee·*syo*·nes
Do we need a guide?	¿Necesitamos un guía?	ne·se·see·*ta*·mos oon *gee*·a
Is it safe?	¿Es seguro?	es se·*goo*·ro
I'm lost.	Estoy perdido/a. m/f	es·*toy* per·*dee*·do/a
What's the weather like?	¿Cómo está el clima?	*ko*·mo es·*ta* el *klee*·ma

HIKING

Where can I ...? ¿Dónde puedo ...? *don*·de *pwe*·do ...

buy supplies	comprar provisiones	kom·*prar* pro·vee·*syo*·nes
find someone who knows the area	encontrar a alguien que conozca la zona	en·kon·*trar* a *al*·gyen ke ko·*nos*·ka la *so*·na
get a map	obtener un mapa	ob·te·*ner* oon *ma*·pa
hire hiking gear	rentar equipo de senderismo	ren·*tar* e·*kee*·po de sen·der·*ees*·mo

Do we need to take bedding?	¿Necesitamos llevar cobijas/un sleeping? ne·se·see·*ta*·mos ye·*var* ko·*bee*·has/oon *sleep*·ing
Do we need to take food/water?	¿Necesitamos llevar comida/agua? ne·se·see·*ta*·mos ye·*var* ko·*mee*·da/*a*·gwa
Which is the easiest route?	¿Cuál es la ruta más fácil? kwal es la *roo*·ta mas *fa*·seel
Which is the shortest/longest route?	¿Cuál es la ruta más corta/larga? kwal es la *roo*·ta mas *kor*·ta/*lar*·ga
Is the track (well-)marked?	¿El sendero está (bien) marcado? el sen·*de*·ro es·*ta* (byen) mar·*ka*·do
Is the track open?	¿El sendero está abierto? el sen·*de*·ro es·*ta* a·*byer*·to
Is the track scenic?	¿Es escénico el sendero? es e·se·*nee*·ko el sen·*de*·ro
How high is the climb?	¿A qué altura se escala? a ke al·*too*·ra se es·*ka*·la
How long is the trail?	¿Qué tan larga es la ruta? ke tan *lar*·ga es la *roo*·ta
How long does the hike take?	¿Cuánto dura la caminata? *kwan*·to *doo*·ra la ka·mee·*na*·ta
Do we need a guide?	¿Necesitamos un guía? ne·se·see·*ta*·mos oon *gee*·a
Are there guided treks?	¿Hay caminatas guiadas? ai kam·*een*·a·tas gee·*a*·das

Is it safe?	¿Es seguro? es se·*goo*·ro
Is there a hut?	¿Hay alguna cabaña? ai al·*goo*·na ka·*ba*·nya
When does it get dark?	¿A qué hora oscurece? a ke *o*·ra os·koo·*re*·se
Where have you come from?	¿De dónde vienes/ vienen? sg inf/pl de *don*·de *vye*·nes/ *vye*·nen
How long did it take?	¿Cuánto tardaste? *kwan*·to tar·*das*·te
Does this path go to (Morelia)?	¿Este camino va a (Morelia)? es·te ka·*mee*·no va a (mo·*re*·lya)
Can we go through here?	¿Podemos atravesar por aquí? po·*de*·mos a·tra·ve·*sar* por a·*kee*
Is the water OK to drink?	¿Se puede tomar el agua? se *pwe*·de to·*mar* el *a*·gwa
Where's the nearest village?	¿Dónde está pueblo más cercano? *don*·de es·*ta* el *pwe*·blo mas ser·*ka*·no
Where's a campsite?	¿Dónde hay un lugar para acampar? *don*·de ai oon loo·*gar* *pa*·ra a·kam·*par*

LOOK FOR

Prohibido Nadar	pro·ee·*bee*·do na·*dar*	No Swimming

¿Es seguro?
es se·*goo*·ro
Is it safe?

Where are the showers/ toilets?	¿Dónde hay regaderas/ sanitarios? *don*·de ai re·ga·*de*·ras/ sa·nee·*ta*·ryos
I'm lost.	Estoy perdido/a. m/f es·*toy* per·*dee*·do/a

BEACH

Where's the best beach?	¿Dónde está la mejor playa? *don*·de es·*ta* la me·*hor* *pla*·ya
Where's the nearest beach?	¿Dónde esta la playa más cercana? *don*·de es·*ta* la *pla*·ya mas ser·*ka*·na

Where's the nudist beach?	¿Dónde está la playa nudista? *don*·de es·*ta* la *pla*·ya noo·*dees*·ta
Is it safe to dive here?	¿Es seguro echarse clavados aquí? es se·*goo*·ro e·*char*·se kla·va·*dos* a·*kee*
Is it safe to scuba dive here?	¿Es seguro bucear aquí? es se·*goo*·ro boo·se·ar a·*kee*
Is it safe to swim here?	¿Es seguro nadar aquí? es se·*goo*·ro na·*dar* a·*kee*
What time is high/low tide?	¿A qué hora es la marea alta/baja? a ke *o*·ra es la ma·*re*·a *al*·ta/*ba*·ha
How much for a chair/hut?	¿Cuánto cuesta rentar una silla/palapa? *kwan*·to *kwes*·ta ren·*tar oo*·na *see*·ya/pa·*la*·pa
How much for an umbrella (for sun)?	¿Cuánto cuesta rentar una sombrilla? *kwan*·to *kwes*·ta ren·*tar oo*·na som·*bree*·ya
Are there any reefs?	¿Hay arrecifes? ai a·re·*see*·fes

LISTEN FOR

Cuidado con la resaca.	kwee·*da*·do kon la re·*sa*·ka Be careful of the undertow.
¡Es peligroso!	es pe·lee·*gro*·so It's dangerous!

Are there any rips?	¿Hay corrientes? ai ko·*ryen*·tes
Are there any water hazards?	¿Hay peligros en el agua? ai pe·*lee*·gros en el *a*·gwa

WEATHER

Q **What's the weather like?**	¿Cómo está el clima? *ko*·mo es·*ta* el *klee*·ma
A **It's raining.**	Llueve. *ywe*·ve
A **It's (cold).**	Hace (frío). *a*·se (*free*·o)
Q **Will it be (hot) tomorrow?**	Mañana hará (calor)? ma·*nya*·na a·*ra* (ka·*lor*)
A **Tomorrow it will be raining.**	Mañana lloverá. ma·*nya*·na yo·ve·*ra*
Q **Will it be ... tomorrow?**	¿Estará ... mañana? es·ta·*ra* ... (ma·*nya*·na)
A **It's ...**	Está ... es·*ta* ...

cloudy	nublado	noo·*bla*·do
sunny	soleado	so·le·*a*·do
warm	cálido	*ka*·lee·do
windy	ventoso	ven·*to*·so

Where can I buy an umbrella (for rain)?	¿Dónde puedo comprar un paraguras? *don*·de *pwe*·do kom·*prar* oon pa·*ra*·gwas
Where can I buy a rain jacket?	¿Dónde puedo comprar un impermeable? *don*·de *pwe*·do kom·*prar* oon eem·per·me·*a*·ble

dry season	temporada f seca tem·po·*ra*·da *se*·ka
hail	granizo m gra·*nee*·so
rainy season	temporada f de lluvias tem·po·*ra*·da de *yoo*·vyas
storm	tormenta f tor·*men*·ta

FLORA & FAUNA

What ... is that?	¿Qué ... es ése/a? m/f ke ... es *e*·se/a

animal	animal m	a·nee·*mal*
flower	flor f	flor
plant	planta f	*plan*·ta
tree	árbol m	*ar*·bol

What's it used for?	¿Para qué se usa? *pa*·ra ke se *oo*·sa
Can you eat it?	¿Se puede comer? se *pwe*·de ko·*mer*
Is it ...?	¿Es ...? es ...

common	común	ko·*moon*
dangerous	peligroso/a m/f	pe·lee·*gro*·so/a
endangered	en peligro de extinción	en pe·*lee*·gro de ek·steen·*syon*
poisonous	venenoso/a m/f	ve·ne·*no*·so/a
protected	protegido/a m/f	pro·te·*hee*·do/a

For names of plants and animals, see the **dictionary** (p205).

SAFE TRAVEL

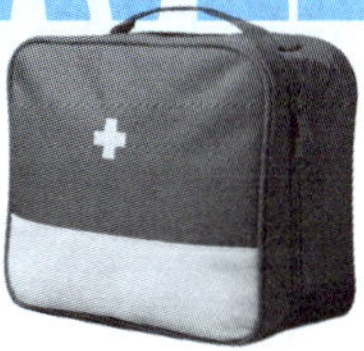

Emergencies

KEY PHRASES

Help!	¡Socorro!	so·*ko*·ro
There's been an accident.	Hubo un accidente.	*oo*·bo oon ak·see·*den*·te
It's an emergency.	Es una emergencia.	es *oo*·na e·mer·*hen*·sya

Help!	¡Socorro! so·*ko*·ro
Stop!	¡Pare! *pa*·re
Go away!	¡Váyase! *va*·ya·se
Thief!	¡Ladrón! la·*dron*
Fire!	¡Fuego! *fwe*·go
Watch out!	¡Cuidado! kwee·*da*·do
Call the police!	¡Llame a la policía! *ya*·me a la po·lee·*see*·a
Call a doctor!	¡Llame a un médico! *ya*·me a oon *me*·dee·ko
Call an ambulance!	¡Llame a una ambulancia! *ya*·me a *oo*·na am·boo·*lan*·sya
It's an emergency.	Es una emergencia. es *oo*·na e·mer·*hen*·sya

Could you help me, please?	¿Me puede ayudar, por favor? *me pwe·de a·yoo·dar por fa·vor*
I have to use the telephone.	Necesito usar el teléfono. *ne·se·see·to oo·sar el te·le·fo·no*
We've had a (traffic) accident.	Tuvimos un accidente (de coche). *too·vee·mos oon ak·see·den·te (de ko·che)*
There's been an accident.	Hubo un accidente. *oo·bo oon ak·see·den·te*
I'm lost.	Estoy perdido/a. m/f *es·toy per·dee·do/a*
Where are the toilets?	¿Dónde están los baños? *don·de es·tan los ba·nyos*
Is it safe ...?	¿Es seguro ...? *es se·goo·ro ...*

at night	de noche	*de no·che*
for foreigners	para los extranjeros	*pa·ra los ek·stran·he·ros*
for LGBTIQ+ travellers	para viajeros LGBTI+/gay	*pa·ra vya·he·ros eh·leh·heh·beh·teh·ee·mas/gay*
for women travellers	para viajeras	*pa·ra vya·he·ras*
to go alone	ir solo/a m/f	*eer so·lo/a*
to hitchhike	pedir aventón	*pe·deer a·ven·ton*

Police

KEY PHRASES

Where's the police station?	¿Dónde está la estación de policía?	*don*·de es·*ta* la es·ta·*syon* de po·lee·*see*·a
I want to contact my consulate/embassy.	Quiero contactar mi consulado/embajada.	*kye*·ro kon·*tak*·tar mee kon·soo·*la*·do/em·ba·*ha*·da
My bag was stolen.	Me robaron mi bolsa.	me ro·*ba*·ron la *bol*·sa

Where's the police station?	¿Dónde está la estación de policía? *don*·de es·*ta* la es·ta·*syon* de po·lee·*see*·a
I want to report an offence.	Quiero denunciar un delito. *kye*·ro de·noon·*syar* oon de·*lee*·to
I've lost (my wallet).	Perdí (mi billetera). per·*dee* (mee bee·ye·*te*·ra)
My bag was stolen.	Me robaron mi bolsa. me ro·*ba*·ron la *bol*·sa
My money was stolen.	Me robaron mi dinero. me ro·*ba*·ron mee dee·*ne*·ro
I've been robbed.	Me han robado. me an ro·*ba*·do
I've been raped.	Me violaron. me vyo·*la*·ron

LISTEN FOR

agresión f	*a·gre·syon* assault
alterar el orden público	*al·te·rar el or·den poo·blee·ko* disturbing the peace
exceso m **de velocidad**	*ek·se·so de ve·lo·see·dad* speeding
faltas f pl **a la moral**	*fal·tas a la mo·ral* indecent behaviour
robo m	*ro·bo* theft

I want to contact my consulate/embassy.	Quiero contactar mi consulado/embajada. *kye·ro kon·tak·tar mee kon·soo·la·do/em·ba·ha·da*
Can I call someone?	¿Puedo llamar a alguien? *pwe·do ya·mar a al·gyen*
Can I have a lawyer (who speaks English)?	Quisiera un abogado (que hable inglés). *kee·sye·ra oon a·bo·ga·do (ke a·ble een·gles)*
I have a prescription for this drug.	Tengo receta para esta medicina. *ten·go re·se·ta pa·ra es·ta me·dee·see·na*
What am I accused of?	¿De qué me acusan? *de ke me a·koo·san*
I'm innocent.	Soy inocente. *soy ee·no·sen·te*
I didn't do it.	No lo hice. *no lo ee·se*

Health

KEY PHRASES

Where's the nearest hospital?	¿Dónde está el hospital más cercano?	*don*·de es·*ta* el os·pee·*tal* mas ser·*ka*·no
I'm sick.	Estoy enfermo/a. m/f	es·*toy* en·*fer*·mo/a
I need a doctor.	Necesito un doctor.	ne·se·see·to oon dok·*tor*
I'm on medication for ...	Tomo medicamento para ...	*to*·mo me·dee·ka·*men*·to *pa*·ra ...
I'm allergic to ...	Soy alérgico/a a ... m/f	soy a·*ler*·hee·ko/a a ...

DOCTOR

Where's the nearest ...? ¿Dónde está ... más cercano/a? m/f
don·de es·*ta* ... mas ser·*ka*·no/a

(night) chemist/ pharmacy	la farmacia f (de guardia)	la far·*ma*·sya (de *gwar*·dya)
dentist	el dentista m	el den·*tees*·ta
doctor	el médico m	el *me*·dee·ko
hospital	el hospital m	el os·pee·*tal*
medical centre	la clínica f	la *klee*·nee·ka
optometrist	el optometrista m	el op·to·me·*trees*·ta

I need a doctor (who speaks English).
Necesito un doctor (que hable inglés).
ne·se·*see*·to oon dok·*tor* (ke *a*·ble een·*gles*)

Could I see a female doctor?
¿Podría atenderme una doctora?
po·*dree*·a a·ten·*der*·me *oo*·na dok·*to*·ra

Can the doctor come here?
¿Podría visitarme el doctor aquí?
po·*dree*·a vee·see·*tar*·me el dok·*tor* a·*kee*

I've been vaccinated against ...
Estoy vacunado/a contra ... m/f
es·*toy* va·koo·*na*·do/a *kon*·tra ...

hepatitis A/B/C	hepatitis A/B/C	e·pa·*tee*·tees a/be/se
tetanus	tétanos	*te*·ta·nos
typhoid	tifoidea	tee·foy·*de*·a
yellow fever	fiebre amarilla	*fye*·bre a·ma·*ree*·ya

I need new contact lenses.
Necesito pupilentes nuevos.
ne·se·*see*·to poo·pee·*len*·tes *nwe*·vos

I need new glasses.
Necesito lentes nuevos.
ne·se·*see*·to *len*·tes *nwe*·vos

I've run out of my medication.
Se me acabó mi medicamento.
se me a·ka·*bo* mee mod·oo

This is my usual medicine.
Esta es mi medicina habitual.
es·te es mee me·dee·*see*·na a·bee·*twal*

Can I have a receipt for my insurance?	¿Me da un recibo para mi seguro médico? me da oon re·*see*·bo *pa*·ra mee se·*goo*·ro *me*·dee·ko

SYMPTOMS & CONDITIONS

I'm sick.	Estoy enfermo/a. m/f es·*toy* en·*fer*·mo/a
My friend is sick.	Mi amigo está enfermo. m mee a·*mee*·go es·*ta* en·*fer*·mo Mi amiga está enferma. f mee a·*mee*·ga es·*ta* en·*fer*·ma
It hurts here.	Me duele aquí. me *dwe*·le a·*kee*
I've been injured.	Me lastimé. me las·tee·*me*
I've been vomiting.	He estado vomitando. e es·*ta*·do vo·mee·*tan*·do
I'm dehydrated.	Estoy deshidratado/a. m/f es·*toy* des·ee·dra·*ta*·do/a
I'm all hot and cold.	Tengo escalofríos. *ten*·go es·ka·lo·*free*·os
I can't sleep.	No puedo dormir. no *pwe*·do dor·*meer*

LISTEN FOR

¿Usted bebe?	oos·*ted* *be*·be Do you drink?
¿Usted fuma?	oos·*ted* *foo*·ma Do you smoke?
¿Usted consume drogas?	oos·*ted* kon·*soo*·me *dro*·gas Do you take drugs?

LISTEN FOR

¿Dónde le duele?	*don*·de le *dwe*·le Where does it hurt?
¿Está tomando algún medicamento?	es·*ta* to·*man*·do al·*goon* me·dee·ka·*men*·to Are you on any medication?
¿Desde cuándo se siente así?	*des*·de *kwan*·do se *syen*·te a·*see* How long have you felt like this?
¿Ha tenido ésto antes?	a te·*nee*·do *es*·to *an*·tes Have you had this before?

I feel ... — Me siento ... *me syen*·to ...

anxious	ansioso/a m/f	an·*syo*·so/a
dizzy	mareado/a m/f	ma·re·a·do/a
nauseous	con náuseas	kon *now*·se·as
shivery	destemplado/a m/f	des·tem·*pla*·do/a
weak	débil	*de*·beel

I've (recently) had ...	(Hace poco) Tuve ... (a·se *po*·ko) *too*·ve ...
I'm on medication for ...	Tomo medicamento para ... *to* mo me·dee·ka·*men*·to *pa*·ra ...
I'm asthmatic.	Soy asmático/a. m/f soy as·*ma*·tee·ko/a
I'm diabetic.	Soy diabético/a. m/f soy dya·*be*·tee·ko/a

I'm epileptic.	Soy epiléptico/a. m/f soy e·pee·*lep*·tee·ko/a

For more symptoms and conditions, see the **dictionary** (p205).

WOMEN'S HEALTH

(I think) I'm pregnant.	(Creo que) Estoy embarazada. (*kre*·o ke) es·*toy* em·ba·ra·*sa*·da
I haven't had my period for (three) days/weeks.	Hace (tres) días/ semanas que no tengo mi período. *a*·se (tres) *dee*·as/ se·*ma*·nas ke no *ten*·go mee pe·*ree*·o·do
I'm on the pill.	Tomo pastillas anticonceptivas. *to*·mo pas·*tee*·yas an·tee·kon·sep·*tee*·vas

LISTEN FOR

¿Está menstruando?	es·*ta* men·*strwan*·do Are you menstruating?
¿Cuándo tuvo su último período?	*kwan*·do *too*·vo soo *ool*·tee·mo pe·*ree*·o·do When did you last have your period?
¿Usa anticonceptivos?	*oo*·sa an·tee·kon·sep·*tee*·vos Are you using contraception?
¿Está embarazada?	es·*ta* em·ba·ra·*sa*·da Are you pregnant?
Está embarazada.	es·*ta* em·ba·ra·*sa*·da You're pregnant.

I need contraception.	Necesito anticonceptivos. ne·se·*see*·to an·tee·kon·sep·*tee*·vos
I need the morning-after pill.	Necesito la pastilla del día siguiente. ne·se·*see*·to la pas·*tee*·ya del *dee*·a see·*gyen*·te
I need a pregnancy test.	Necesito una prueba del embarazo. ne·se·*see*·to *oo*·na *prwe*·ba de em·ba·*ra*·so
I've noticed a lump here.	He notado un bulto aquí. e no·*ta*·do oon *bool*·to a·*kee*

ALLERGIES

I have a skin allergy.	Tengo alergia en la piel. *ten*·go a·*ler*·gya en la pyel
I'm allergic to ...	Soy alérgico/a a ... m/f soy a·*ler*·hee·ko/a a ...

anti-histamines	los anti-histamínicos	los an·tee·ees·ta·*mee*·nee·kos
anti-inflammatories	los anti-inflamatorios	los an·tee·een·fla·ma·*to*·ryos
inhalers	los inhaladores	los ee·na·la·*do*·res
penicillin	la penicilina	la pe·nee·see·*lee*·na

For food-related allergies, see **vegetarian & special meals** (p186).

PARTS OF THE BODY

My (stomach) hurts.	Me duele (el estómago). me *dwe*·le (el es·*to*·ma·go)
I can't move my (ankle).	No puedo mover (el tobillo). no *pwe*·do mo·*ver* (el to·*bee*·yo)
I have a cramp in my (foot).	Tengo un calambre en (el pie). *ten*·go oon ka·*lam*·bre en (el pye)
My ... is swollen.	Mi ... está hinchado/a. m/f mee ... es·*ta* een·*cha*·do/a

For more parts of the body, see the **dictionary** (p205).

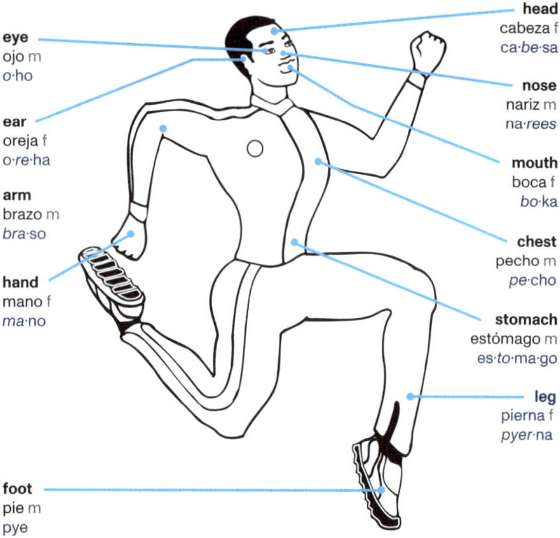

LISTEN FOR

¿Ha tomado ésto antes?	a to·*ma*·do es·to *an*·tes Have you taken this before?
Debe terminar el tratamiento.	*de*·be ter·mee·*nar* el tra·ta·*myen*·to You must complete the course.
Dos veces al día (con la comida).	dos *ve*·ses al *dee*·a (kon la ko·*mee*·da) Twice a day (with food).

CHEMIST/PHARMACY

I need something for (fever).	Necesito algo para (la fiebre). ne·se·*see*·to *al*·go *pa*·ra (la *fye*·bre)
Do I need a prescription for (antihistamines)?	¿Necesito receta para (antihistamínicos)? ne·se·*see*·to re·*se*·ta *pa*·ra (an·tee·ees·ta·*mee*·nee·kos)
How many times a day?	¿Cuántas veces al día? *kwan*·tas *ve*·ses al *dee*·a
Will it make me drowsy?	¿Me dará sueño? me da·*ra* *swe*·nyo

For more chemist/pharmacy items, see the **dictionary** (p205).

DENTIST

I have a toothache.	Tengo dolor de muelas. *ten*·go do·*lor* de *mwe*·las
I have a cavity.	Tengo una caries. *ten*·go *oo*·na *ka*·ryes

LISTEN FOR

Abra grande.	a·bra *gran*·de	Open wide.
Muerda ésto.	*mwer*·da *es*·to	Bite down on this.
No se mueva.	no se *mwe*·va	Don't move.
Esto no le dolerá.	*es*·to no le do·le·*ra*	This won't hurt.
Enjuáguese.	en·*hwa*·ge·se	Rinse.

I have a broken tooth.	Tengo un diente roto. *ten*·go oon *dyen*·te *ro*·to
I've lost a filling.	Se me cayó una amalgama. se me ka·*yo* *oo*·na a·mal·*ga*·ma
My dentures are broken.	Se me rompió la dentadura postiza. se me rom·*pyo* la den·ta·*doo*·ra pos·*tee*·sa
I need a filling.	Necesito una amalgama. ne·se·*see*·to *oo*·na a·mal·*ga*·ma
I need a crown.	Necesito una corona. ne·se·*see*·to *oo*·na ko·*ro*·na
My gums hurt.	Me duelen las encías. me *dwe*·len las en·*see*·as
I don't want it extracted.	No quiero que me lo saque. no *kye*·ro ke me lo *sa*·ke
I need an anaesthetic.	Necesito una anestesia. ne·se·*see*·to *oo*·na a·nes·*te*·sya

FOOD

Eating Out

KEY PHRASES

Can you recommend a restaurant?	¿Me puede recomendar un restaurante?	me *pwe*·de re·ko·men·*dar* oon res·tow·*ran*·te
A table for (two), please.	Una mesa para (dos), por favor.	*oo*·na *me*·sa *pa*·ra (dos) por fa·*vor*
I'd like the menu, please.	Quisiera la carta, por favor.	kee·*sye*·ra la *kar*·ta por fa·*vor*
I'd like a beer, please.	Quisiera una cerveza, por favor.	kee·*sye*·ra·*oo*·na ser·*ve*·sa por fa·*vor*
Please bring us the bill.	Por favor, nos trae la cuenta.	por fa·*vor* nos *tra*·e la *kwen*·ta

BASICS

breakfast	desayuno m de·sa·*yoo*·no
lunch	comida f ko·*mee*·da
dinner	cena f se·na
eat	comer ko·*mer*
drink	beber be·*ber*
I'm starving!	¡Me muero de hambre! me *mwe*·ro de *am*·bre
Enjoy the meal!	¡Buen provecho! bwen pro·*ve*·cho

FINDING A PLACE TO EAT

Can you recommend a ...?	¿Me puede recomendar ...?	me *pwe*·de re·ko·men·*dar* ...

bar	un bar	oon bar
cafe	un café	oon ka·*fe*
coffee bar	una cafetería	*oo*·na ka·fe·te·*ree*·a
eatery	un comedor	oon ko·me·*dor*
restaurant	un restaurante	oon res·tow·*ran*·te
stall (market/ street)	un puesto	oon *pwes*·to

Where would you go for a celebration?	¿Dónde recomienda ir para festejar? *don*·de re·ko·*myen*·da eer *pa*·ra fes·te·*har*
Where would you go for a cheap meal?	¿Dónde se come barato? *don*·de se ko·*me* ba·*ra*·to
Where would you go for local specialities?	¿Adónde se va para comida típica? a·*don*·de se va *pa*·ra ko·*mee*·da *tee*·pee·ka
I'd like to reserve a table for (five) people.	Quisiera reservar una mesa para (cinco). kee·*sye*·ra re·ser·*var oo*·na *me*·sa *pa*·ra (*seen*·ko)
I'd like to reserve a table for (eight) o'clock.	Quisiera reservar una mesa para las (ocho). kee·*sye*·ra re·ser·*var oo*·na *me*·sa *pa*·ra las (*o*·cho)

CULTURE TIP: TACOS

Fresh tacos are cheap, tasty and you can find them absolutely everywhere in Mexico. Don't leave without trying these three favourites:

tacos m pl **al pastor** *ta*·kos al pas·*tor*
tacos with thinly-sliced pork, pineapple, onions and coriander/cilantro

tacos m pl **de carne asada** *ta*·kos de *kar*·ne a·*sa*·da
tacos with marinated minced steak, fresh onions and coriander/cilantro

tacos m pl **de carnitas** *ta*·kos de kar·*nee*·tas
tacos with finely-diced pork, onions and coriander/cilantro

Are you still serving food?	¿Siguen sirviendo comida? *see*·gen seer·*vyen*·do ko·*mee*·da
How long is the wait?	¿Cuánto hay que esperar? *kwan*·to ai ke es·pe·*rar*

AT THE RESTAURANT

In any *comedor* ko·me·*dor*, or run-of-the-mill restaurant, Mexicans greet all the other diners when they walk past them (coming in or going out) by saying *¡Provecho!* pro·*ve*·cho (short for *¡Buen provecho!* bwen pro·*ve*·cho, or 'Enjoy the meal!'). You also say it if you start talking to someone and they're in the middle of eating, even just a snack.

I'd like a table for (two), please.	Quisiera una mesa para (dos), por favor. kee·*sye*·ra *oo*·na *me*·sa *pa*·ra (dos) por fa·*vor*

For two, please.	Para dos, por favor.	*pa*·ra dos por fa·*vor*

I'd like the (non)smoking section, please.	Quisiera el área de (no) fumar, por favor. kee·*sye*·ra el *a*·re·a de (no) foo·*mar* por fa·*vor*
We're just having drinks.	Sólo queremos tomar algo. *so*·lo ke·*re*·mos to·*mar al*·go

Just drinks. Sólo bebidas. *so*·lo be·*bee*·das

I'd like the drinks list, please.	Quisiera la carta de bebidas, por favor. kee·*sye*·ra la *kar*·ta de be·*bee*·das por fa·*vor*
I'd like the menu, please.	Quisiera la carta, por favor. kee·*sye*·ra la *kar*·ta por fa·*vor*

Menu, please. La carta, por favor. la *kar*·ta por fa·*vor*

Do you have a menu (in English)?	¿Tienen una carta (en inglés)? *tye*·nen *oo*·na *kar*·ta (en een·*gles*)

LISTEN FOR

No tenemos mesas.	no te·*ne*·mos *me*·sas We have no tables.
Ya no hay cupo.	ya no ai *koo*·po We're fully booked.
Ya cerramos.	ya se·*ra*·mos We're closed.
¿Dónde le gustaría sentarse?	*don*·de le goos·ta·*ree*·a sen·*tar*·se Where would you like to sit?

Do you have children's meals?	¿Tienen menú infantil? *tye*·nen me·*noo* een·fan·*teel*
What would you recommend?	¿Qué recomienda? ke re·ko·*myen*·da
What's in that dish?	¿Qué lleva ese platillo? ke *ye*·va e·se pla·*tee*·yo
Does it take long to prepare?	¿Se tarda mucho en prepararlo? se *tar*·da *moo*·cho en pre·pa·*rar*·lo

For dishes and ingredients, see the **menu decoder** (p189).

REQUESTS

Please bring us (a napkin).	Por favor, nos trae (una servilleta). por fa·*vor* nos *tra*·e (*oo*·na ser·vee·*ye*·ta)

LISTEN FOR

¿Quiere tomar algo?	*kye*·re to·*mar al*·go Would you like a drink?
¿Qué desea ordenar?	ke de·*se*·a or·de·*nar* What can I get for you?
¿Cómo lo quiere preparado?	*ko*·mo lo *kye*·re pre·pa·*ra*·do How would you like that cooked?
¿Le gusta ...?	le *goos*·ta ... Do you like ...?
Le recomiendo ...	le re·ko·*myen*·do ... I suggest the ...
Aquí tiene.	a·*kee tye*·ne Here you go!

Eating Out

CAN I SEE THE MENU, PLEASE?

¿Puedo ver la carta, por favor?

pwe·do ver la *kar*·ta por fa·*vor*

WHAT WOULD YOU RECOMMEND FOR ...?

¿Qué recomienda para ...?

ke re·ko·*myen*·da *pa*·ra ...

THE MAIN MEAL
el plato fuerte
el *pla*·to *fwer*·te

DESSERT
postre
pos·tre

DRINKS
beber
be·*ber*

CAN YOU BRING ME SOME ..., PLEASE?

Por favor me trae ...

por fa·*vor* me *tra*·e ...

I'D LIKE THE BILL, PLEASE.

Quisiera la cuenta, por favor.

kee·*sye*·ra la *kwen*·ta por fa·*vor*

Is there any (chili sauce)?	¿Hay (salsa picante)? ai (*sal*·sa pee·*kan*·te)
I'd like it ...	Lo quiero ... lo *kye*·ro ...
I don't want it ...	No lo quiero ... no lo *kye*·ro ...

boiled	hervido/a m/f	er·*vee*·do/a
broiled/grilled	asado/a m/f	a·*sa*·do/a
deep-fried	sumergido/a en aceite m/f	soo·mer·*hee*·do/a en a·*say*·te
fried	frito/a m/f	*free*·to/a
medium	término medio	*ter*·mee·no *me*·dyo
rare	roja	*ro*·ha
reheated	recalentado/a m/f	re·ka·len·*ta*·do/a
steamed	al vapor	al va·*por*
well done	bien cocido/a m/f	byen ko·*see*·do/a
with (the dressing on the side)	con (el aderezo aparte)	kon (el a·de·*re*·so a·*par*·te)
without (chili)	sin (chile)	seen (*chee*·le)

COMPLIMENTS & COMPLAINTS

That was delicious!	¡Estuvo delicioso! es·*too*·vo de·lee·*syo*·so
I love this dish.	Me encanta este platillo. me en·*kan*·ta es·te pla·*tee*·yo
I love the local cuisine.	Me encanta la comida típica. me en·*kan*·ta la ko·*mee*·da *tee*·pee·ka

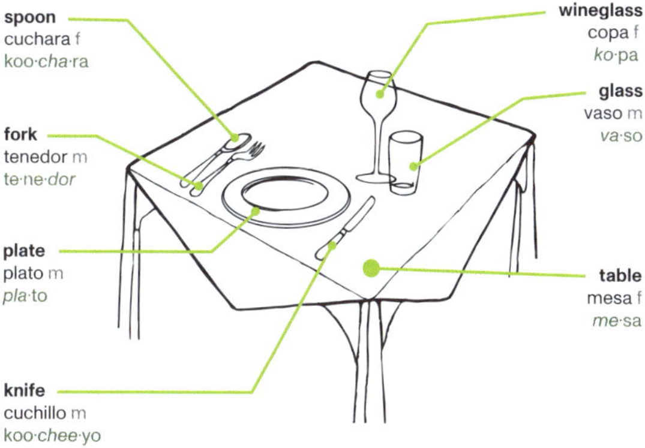

I'm full.	Estoy satisfecho/a. m/f es·*toy* sa·tees·*fe*·cho/a
My compliments to the chef.	Mis felicitaciones al chef. mees fe·lee·see·ta·*syo*·nes al chef
This is ...	Esto está ... es·to es·*ta* ...

burnt	quemado	ke·*ma*·do
cold	frío	*free*·o
hot	caliente	kal·*yen*·te
(too) spicy	(demasiado) picante	(de·ma·*sya*·do) pee·*kan*·te
superb	exquisito	es·kee·*see*·to

LOOK FOR

Botanas	bo·*ta*·nas	Appetisers
Entradas	en·*tra*·das	Starters
Antojitos	an·to·*hee*·tos	Snacks/Meals
Comida Corrida	ko·*mee*·da ko·*ree*·da	Set Meals
Platillo Principal	pla·*tee*·yo preen·see·*pal*	Main Course
Guarniciones	gwar·nee·*syo*·nes	Side Dishes
Sopas	*so*·pas	Soups
Ensaladas	en·sa·*la*·das	Salads
Postre	*pos*·tre	Dessert
Aperitivos	a·pe·ree·*tee*·vos	Aperitifs
Bebidas	be·bee·*das*	Drinks
Aguas Frescas	a·gwas *fres*·kas	Fruit Drinks
Refrescos	re·*fres*·kos	Soft Drinks
Licores	lee·*ko*·res	Spirits
Cervezas	ser·*ve*·sas	Beers
Vinos Blancos	*vee*·nos *blan*·kos	White Wines
Vinos Dulces	*vee*·nos *dool*·ses	Dessert Wines
Vinos Espumosos	*vee*·nos es·poo·*mo*·sos	Sparkling Wines
Vinos Tintos	*vee*·nos *teen*·tos	Red Wines
Digestivos	dee·hes·*tee*·vos	Digestifs

PAYING THE BILL

Please bring us the bill.

Por favor, nos trae la cuenta.
por fa·*vor* nos *tra*·e la *kwen*·ta

Bill, please.	La cuenta, por favor.	la *kwen*·ta por fa·*vor*

Is service included in the bill?	¿La cuenta incluye el servicio? la *kwen*·ta een·*kloo*·ye el ser·*vee*·syo
There's a mistake in the bill.	Hay un error en la cuenta. ai oon e·*ror* en la *kwen*·ta

For more on paying bills, see **money & banking** (p90).

NONALCOHOLIC DRINKS

coffee	café m ka·*fe*
juice	jugo m *hoo*·go
lemonade	limonada f lee·mo·*na*·da
milk	leche f *le*·che
milkshake	malteada f mal·te·*a*·da licuado m lee·*kwa*·do
orangeade	naranjada f na·ran·*ha*·da
rice water	horchata f or·*cha*·ta
soft drink (general)	refresco m re·*fres*·ko
soft drink (north Mexico)	soda f *so*·da
tea	té m te
with (milk)	con (leche) kon (*le*·che)
without (sugar)	sin (azúcar) seen (a·*soo*·kar)

CULTURE TIP: TEX-MEX CUISINE

Some foods that you may have thought were Mexican – such as fajitas, burritos and nachos – are actually all from Texas. Some say these dishes are a pale imitation of Mexican food, while others claim Tex-Mex cuisine belongs in a class of its own. Homesick Texans should order *tacos dorados* *ta*·kos do·*ra*·dos (deep-fried tacos) if they need a bit of crunch.

... water	agua ... a·gwa ...

boiled	hervida	er·*vee*·da
fruit mixed with	de fruta	de *froo*·ta
hibiscus-flower	de jamaica	de ha·*may*·ka
lime	de limón	de lee·*mon*
mineral	mineral	mee·ne·*ral*
sparkling	con gas	kon gas
still	sin gas	seen gas
tamarind	de tamarindo	de ta·ma·*reen*·do

ALCOHOLIC DRINKS

a shot of (gin)	un caballito de (ginebra) oon ka·ba·*yee*·to de (hee·*ne*·bra)
champagne	champán m cham·*pan*
cocktail	coctel m kok·*tel*
rum	ron m ron

a bottle/glass of ... wine	una botella/copa de vino ... *oo*·na bo·*te*·ya/*ko*·pa de *vee*·no ...

dessert	dulce	*dool*·se
red	tinto	*teen*·to
rose	rosado	ro·*sa*·do
sparkling	espumoso	es·poo·*mo*·so
white	blanco	*blan*·ko

a ... of beer	... de cerveza ... de ser·*ve*·sa

glass	un tarro	oon *ta*·ro
jug	una jarra	*oo*·na *ha*·ra
large bottle (940ml)	una caguama	*oo*·na ka·*gwa*·ma
small bottle (325ml)	una botella	*oo*·na bo·*te*·ya

IN THE BAR

Excuse me!	¡Con permiso! kon per·*mee*·so
I'm next.	Sigo yo. *see*·go yo
I'll buy you a drink.	Te invito una copa. te een·*vee*·to *oo*·na *ko*·pa
Q **What would you like?**	¿Qué quieres tomar? ke *kye*·res to·*mar*
A **I'll have (a shot of tequila).**	Quiero (un caballito de tequila). *kye*·ro (oon ka·ba·*yee*·to de te·*kee*·la)

CULTURE TIP: MEXICAN SPIRITS

mezcal m — mes·*kal*
liquor distilled from agave

posh/pox m — posh
sugar-cane liquor flavoured with herbs

pulque m — *pool*·ke
alcohol from fermented agave sap

rompope m — rom·*po*·pe
eggnog with sugar-cane alcohol and cinnamon

tepache m — te·*pa*·che
alcohol from fermented pineapple rinds

tequila f — te·*kee*·la
popular spirit distilled from the *maguey* plant

I'd like a beer, please.	Quisiera una cerveza, por favor. kee·*sye*·ra *oo*·na ser·*ve*·sa por fa·*vor*
Same again, please.	Otro igual, por favor. *o*·tro ee·*gwal* por fa·*vor*
No ice, please.	Sin hielo, por favor. seen *ye*·lo por fa·*vor*
It's my round.	Yo invito esta ronda. yo een·*vee*·to *es*·ta *ron*·da
You can get the next one.	Tu invitas la que sigue. too een·*vee*·tas la ke *see*·ge
Do you serve meals here?	¿Sirven comidas aquí? *seer*·ven ko·*mee*·das a·*kee*

DRINKING UP

Cheers!	¡Salud! *sa·lood*
Thanks, but I don't feel like it.	Gracias, pero no se me antoja. *gra·syas pe·ro no se me an·to·ha*
I don't drink alcohol.	No bebo. *no be·bo*
This is hitting the spot.	Es justo lo que necesitaba. *es hoo·sto lo ke ne·se·see·ta·ba*
I think I've had one too many.	Creo que ya tomé de más. *kre·o ke ya to·meh de mas*
I'm feeling drunk.	Se me está subiendo mucho. *se me es·ta soo·byen·do moo·cho*
I feel ill.	Me siento mal. *me syen·to mal*

LOOK FOR

In Mexico, toilets are widely known as *baños* ba·nyos, while public toilets may also advertise themselves as *sanitarios* sa·nee·ta·ryos or *servicios* ser·vee·syos.

Caballeros	*ka·ba·yo·ros*	Gentlemen
Damas	*da·mas*	Ladies
Hombres	*om·bres*	Men
Mujeres	*moo·he·res*	Women
Señores	*sen·yo·res*	Sirs
Señoras	*sen·yo·ras*	Madams

Self-Catering

KEY PHRASES

What's the local speciality?	¿Cuál es la especialidad de la zona?	kwal es la es·pe·sya·lee·*dad* de la *so*·na
Where can I find the ... section?	¿Dónde está la sección de ...?	*don*·de es·*ta* la sek·*syon* de ...
I'd like some ...	Quisiera algunos/as ... **m/f**	kee·*sye*·ra al·*goo*·nos/as ...

BUYING FOOD

How much is (a kilo of cheese)?	¿Cuánto vale (un kilo de queso)? *kwan*·to *va*·le (oon *kee*·lo de *ke*·so)
Do you sell locally produced food?	¿Vende productos locales? *ven*·de pro·*dook*·tos lo·*ka*·les
What's the local speciality?	¿Cuál es la especialidad de la región? kwal es la es·pe·sya·lee·*dad* de la re·*hyon*
Do you sell organic produce?	¿Vende productos orgánicos? *ven*·de pro·*dook*·tos or·*ga*·nee·kos
Can I taste it?	¿Puedo probarlo? *pwe*·do pro·*bar*·lo

I'd like ...	Quisiera ... *kee·sye·ra ...*

(100) grams	(cien) gramos	(syen) *gra*·mos
a kilo	un kilo	oon *kee*·lo
(two) kilos	(dos) kilos	(dos) *kee*·los
a bottle	una botella	*oo*·na bo·*te*·ya
a dozen	una docena	*oo*·na do·*sen*·a
a jar	una jarra	*oo*·na *ha*·ra
a packet	un paquete	oon pa·*ke*·te
a piece	una pieza	*oo*·na *pye*·sa
(three) pieces	(tres) piezas	(tres) *pye*·sas
a slice	una rebanada	*oo*·na re·ba·*na*·da
(six) slices	(seis) rebanadas	(says) re·ba·*na*·das
a tin	una lata	*oo*·na *la*·ta
that one	ése/ésa m/f	*e*·se/*e*·sa
this one	ésto	*es*·to
a bit more	un poco más	oon *po*·ko mas
less	menos	*me*·nos

That's enough, thanks.	Así está bien, gracias. *a·see es·ta byen gra·syas*
Do you have anything cheaper?	¿Tiene algo más barato? *tye·ne al·go mas ba·ra·to*

LISTEN FOR

Se me terminó.	se me ter·mee·*no*	There's none left.
¿Algo más?	*al*·go mas	Anything else?

Do you have any other kinds?	¿Tiene otros tipos? *tye*·ne *o*·tros *tee*·pos
Where can I find the ... section?	¿Dónde está la sección de ...? *don*·de es·*ta* la sek·*syon* de ...

dairy	lácteos	*lak*·te·os
fish and seafood	pescados y mariscos	*pes*·ka·dos ee ma·*rees*·kos
frozen goods	productos congelados	pro·*dook*·tos kon·he·*la*·dos
fruit and vegetable	frutas y verduras	*froo*·tas ee ver·*doo*·ras
meat	carnes	*kar*·nes
poultry	aves	*a*·ves

COOKING

Could I please borrow (a)?	¿Me presta ... por favor? me pres·*ta* ... por fa·*vor*

chopping board	una tabla para picar	*oo*·na *ta*·bla *pa*·ra pee·*kar*
corkscrew	un sacacorchos	oon sa·ka·*kor*·chos
saucepan	una olla	*oo*·na *o*·ya

☑ CULTURE TIP: MARKET MUNCHIES

The glory of fresh food in a Mexican market can really work up your appetite. For a cheap local meal in a rowdy atmosphere, grab a seat at a *comedor* ko·me·*dor* (lit: eatery) usually found in the centre of the market.

¿Puedo probarlo?

pwe·do pro·*bar*·lo

Can I taste it?

Where's (a frying pan)?	¿Dónde hay (un sartén)? *don*·de ai (oon sar·*ten*)
cooked	cocido/a m/f ko·see·do/a
dried	seco/a m/f se·ko/a
fresh	fresco/a m/f *fres*·ko/a
frozen	congelado/a m/f kon·he·*la*·do/a
raw	crudo/a m/f *kroo*·do/a

For more cooking implements, see the **dictionary** (p205).

Vegetarian & Special Meals

KEY PHRASES

Do you have vegetarian food?	¿Tienen comida vegetariana?	*tye*·nen ko·*mee*·da ve·he·ta·*rya*·na
Could you prepare a meal without ...?	¿Me puede preparar una comida sin ...?	me *pwe*·de pre·pa·*rar oo*·na ko·*mee*·da seen ...
I'm allergic to ...	Soy alérgico/a a ... m/f	soy a·*ler*·hee·ko/a a ...

SPECIAL DIETS & ALLERGIES

Is there a (vegetarian) restaurant near here?	¿Hay un restaurante (vegetariano) por aquí? ai oon res·tow·*ran*·te (ve·he·ta·*rya*·no) por a·*kee*
Do you have vegetarian food?	¿Tienen opciones vegetarianas? *tye*·nen op·syon·es ve·he·ta·*rya*·nas
Do you have halal/kosher food?	¿Tienen opciones halal/kosher? *tye*·nen op·syon·es ha·*lal*/*ko*·sher
I'm (vegan).	Soy (vegano/a). m/f soy (veh·*ga*·no/a)

I'm on a special diet.	Tengo una dieta especial. *ten*·go *oo*·na *dye*·ta es·pe·*syal*
I don't eat (meat).	No como (carne). no *ko*·mo (*kar*·ne)
I'm allergic to ...	Soy alérgico/a ... m/f soy a·*ler*·hee·ko/a ...

dairy produce	a los productos lácteos	a los pro·*dook*·tos *lak*·te·os
eggs	a los huevos	a los *we*·vos
gelatin	a la gelatina	a la he·la·*tee*·na
gluten	al gluten	al *gloo*·ten
nuts	a las nueces	a las *nwe*·ses
peanuts	a los cacahuates	a los ka·ka·*wa*·tes
seafood	a los mariscos	a los ma·*rees*·kos
shellfish	a los crustáceos	a los kroos·*ta*·syos
wheat products	a los productos de trigo	a los pro·*dook*·tos de *tree*·go

ORDERING FOOD

Is it cooked in/with (oil)?	¿Está cocinado en/con (aceite)? es·*ta* ko·see·*na*·do en/con (a·*say*·te)

LISTEN FOR

¿Puede comer ...?	*pwe*·de ko·*mer* ... Can you eat ...?
Le preguntaré al cocinero.	le pre·goon·ta·*re* al ko·see·*ne*·ro I'll check with the cook.
Todo tiene (carne).	*to*·do *tye*·ne (*kar*·ne) It all has (meat) in it.

Is this ...? ¿Esto es ...? *es·to es ...*

decaffeinated	descafeinado	des·ka·fay·*na*·do
free of animal produce	sin productos animales	seen pro·*dook*·tos a·nee·*ma*·les
free range	de corral	de ko·*ral*
genetically modified	transgénico	trans·*he*·nee·ko
gluten-free	sin gluten	seen *gloo*·ten
low-fat	bajo en grasas	*ba*·ho en *gra*·sas
low in sugar	bajo en azúcar	*ba*·ho en a·*soo*·kar
organic	orgánico	or·*gan*·ee·ko
salt-free	sin sal	seen sal

Could you prepare a meal without ...? ¿Me puede preparar una comida sin ...? me *pwe*·de pre·pa·*rar* *oo*·na ko·*mee*·da seen ...

butter	mantequilla	man·te·*kee*·ya
chicken stock	caldo de gallina	*kal*·do de ga·*yee*·na
eggs	huevos	*we*·vos
fish	pescado	pes·*ka*·do
lard	manteca	man·*te*·ka
(red) meat	carne (roja)	*kar*·ne (*ro*·ha)
meat/fish stock	consomé de carne/pescado	kon·so·*me* de *kar*·ne/pes·*ka*·do
pork	cerdo	*ser*·do
poultry	aves	*a*·ves

MENU Decoder

LÉXICO CULINARIO

This miniguide to Mexican cuisine lists dishes and ingredients in Spanish alphabetical order (see **alphabet**, p12). Spanish nouns have their gender indicated by ⓜ or ⓕ. If it's a plural noun, you'll also see pl.

A

abulón ⓜ a·boo·*lon* abalone
aceite ⓜ a·*say*·te oil
— de girasol de hee·ra·*sol* sunflower oil
— de oliva de o·*lee*·va olive oil
— vegetal ve·he·*tal* vegetable oil
aceituna ⓕ a·say·*too*·na olive
— negra *ne*·gra black olive
— verde *ver*·de green olive
acitrón ⓜ a·see·*tron* cactus prepared as a sweet but also used in savoury dishes
acocil ⓜ a·ko·*seel* small red prawn
achiote ⓜ a·*chyo*·te red, musky-flavoured spice used as a colouring agent in **mole** & other foods (also called **annatto**)
adobo ⓜ a·*do*·bo paste of garlic, vinegar, herbs & chilies – can be used as a sauce, marinade or pickling agent
agave ⓜ a·*ga*·ve American aloe, also known as 'century plant' – source of alcoholic beverages such as **pulque**, **mezcal** & **tequila**
— azul a·*sool* blue agave – used to produce **tequila** & **mezcal**
agua ⓕ *a*·gwa water
— caliente ka·*lyen*·te hot water
— con gas kon gas soda water • carbonated water
— de jamaica de ha·*mai*·ka drink made by steeping dried hibiscus flowers in warm water – served chilled
— de la llave de la *ya*·ve tap water
— de manantial de ma·nan·*tyal* spring water
— embotellada em·bo·te·*ya*·da bottled water
— fresca *fres*·ka fruit-flavoured water
— fría *free*·a cold water
— mineral mee·ne·*ral* mineral water
— purificada poo·ree·fee·*ka*·da purified water
— quina *kee*·na tonic water
— sin gas seen gas still mineral water
— tónica to·*nee*·ka tonic water
aguacate ⓜ a·gwa·*ka*·te avocado
aguamiel ⓜ a·gwa·*myel* agave juice
aguardiente ⓜ a·gwar·*dyen*·te sugar cane alcohol
ajo ⓜ *a*·ho garlic
ajonjolí ⓜ a·hon·ho·*lee* sesame seeds
albahaca ⓕ al·*ba*·ka sweet basil

albóndigas ⓕ pl al·*bon*·dee·gas meatballs
alcachofa ⓕ al·ka·*cho*·fa artichoke
alcaparras ⓕ pl al·ka·*pa*·ras capers
alegrías ⓕ pl a·le·*gree*·as sweet cake made of amaranth seeds & molasses
alfajor ⓜ **de coco** al·fa·*hor* de *ko*·ko pastry filled with jam & sprinkled with grated coconut
algodón ⓜ **de azúcar** al·go·*don* de a·*soo*·kar candy floss • cotton candy
alimentos ⓜ pl a·lee·*men*·tos food
almeja ⓕ al·*me*·ha clam • scallop
almendra ⓕ al·*men*·dra almond
almuerzo ⓜ al·*mwer*·so brunch, also translated as 'lunch' – a late-morning meal typically consisting of a quick plate of **tacos**, eggs or a sandwich
alubia ⓕ a·*loo*·bya haricot bean
amaranto ⓜ a·ma·*ran*·to amaranth (a native plant similar to spinach)
anchoa ⓕ an·*cho*·a anchovy
anguila ⓕ an·*gee*·la eel
anís ⓜ a·*nees* anise • aniseed (used in desserts, liqueurs & breads)
annatto a·*na*·to see **achiote**
antojitos ⓜ pl an·to·*hee*·tos 'little whimsies' – small portions of classic Mexican dishes, such as **quesadillas**, **sopes** & **tostadas**, served as snack food for street eating or as appetisers
añejo/a ⓜ/ⓕ a·*nye*·ho/a 'aged' – describes cheeses, meat & **tequila**
apio ⓜ *a*·pyo celery
arándano ⓜ a·*ran*·da·no bilberry
— agrio *a*·gryo cranberry
arenque ⓜ a·*ren*·ke herring • kipper
arroz ⓜ a·*ros* rice
— a la Mexicana a la me·hee·*ka*·na 'Mexican rice' – may be coloured red with tomatoes & cooked with diced carrots & peas
— a la poblana a la po·*bla*·na pilaf with **chile poblano**, corn & melted cheese
— con leche kon *le*·che rice pudding
— de grano corto de *gra*·no *kor*·to short-grain rice
— glutinoso gloo·tee·*no*·so glutinous rice
— integral een·te·*gral* brown rice
— salvaje sal·*va*·he wild rice
— verde *ver*·de green rice, made with **chile poblano**
asadero ⓜ a·sa·*de*·ro white cheese used in **quesadillas**
atole ⓜ a·*to*·le thin porridge or gruel of maize flour or cornflour, usually served hot for breakfast
— de chocolate de cho·ko·*la*·te chocolate **atole**
— de fresa de *fre*·sa strawberry **atole**
— de nuez de *nwes* pecan **atole**
— de vainilla de vai·*nee*·ya vanilla **atole**
atún ⓜ a·*toon* tuna
avellana ⓕ a·ve·*ya*·na hazelnut
avena ⓕ a·*ve*·na rolled oats – a breakfast staple usually served with milk
azafrán ⓜ a·sa·*fran* saffron
azúcar ⓜ a·*soo*·kar sugar
— blanca *blan*·ka white sugar
— morena mo·*re*·na brown sugar

B

bacalao ⓜ ba·ka·*la*·o cod – usually dried
balché ⓜ bal·*che* Maya alcoholic drink made from the fermented bark of the balché tree
banderillas ⓕ pl ban·de·*ree*·yas long flaky pastries
barbacoa ⓕ bar·ba·*ko*·a Mexican-style barbecue – a lamb, goat or chicken is steamed with vegetables, then baked in the ground
bebida ⓕ be·*bee*·da drink
— alcohólica al·*ko*·lee·ka alcoholic drink
berenjena ⓕ be·ren·*he*·na aubergine • eggplant
betabel ⓜ be·ta·*bel* beet • beetroot

birria Ⓕ *bee*·rya soupy stew made with meat (usually goat) in a tomato-based broth
bistec Ⓜ bees·*tek* steak (beef)
blanquillos Ⓜ pl blan·kee·yos eggs (also **huevos**)
bolillo Ⓜ bo·*lee*·yo large, French-style bread roll, served with meals
borrego Ⓜ bo·*re*·go lamb (see also **cordero**)
botana Ⓕ bo·*ta*·na appetiser
botella Ⓕ bo·*te*·ya bottle
brocheta Ⓕ bro·*che*·ta skewer • kebab
brócoli Ⓜ *bro*·ko·lee broccoli
buey Ⓜ bway ox
buñuelo Ⓜ boo·*nywe*·lo tortilla-sized fritter sprinkled with sugar & cinnamon

C

cabra Ⓕ *ka*·bra goat
cabrito Ⓜ ka·*bree*·to milk-fed kid rubbed with butter or oil & seasoned with salt, pepper & lime, then roasted whole on a spit
cacahuates Ⓜ pl ka·ka·*wa*·tes peanuts
— japoneses ha·po·*ne*·ses Japanese-style peanuts, covered with a crunchy coating
cacao Ⓜ ka·*ka*·o cocoa
café Ⓜ ka·*fe* café • coffee
— con leche kon *le*·che coffee with milk
— de olla de *o*·ya coffee flavoured with cinnamon & sweetened with **piloncillo**
— expresso ek·*spre*·so espresso
cajeta Ⓕ ka·*he*·ta goat's milk caramel
calabacita Ⓕ ka·la·ba·*see*·ta zucchini • courgette • vegetable marrow
calabaza Ⓕ ka·la·*ba*·sa pumpkin • squash
calamar Ⓜ ka·la·*mar* squid
calaveras Ⓕ pl ka·la·*ve*·ras confectionery skulls primarily intended as decorative offerings for the Day of the Dead
— de azúcar de a·*soo*·kar skulls made from sugar
— de chocolate de cho·ko·*la*·te skulls made from chocolate
caldo Ⓜ *kal*·do broth
— tlalpeño tlal·*pe*·nyo vegetable soup
— xóchitl *so*·cheetl fiery hot soup with serrano peppers on top
camarón Ⓜ ka·ma·*ron* prawn • shrimp
— para pelar *pa*·ra pe·*lar* whole unpeeled shrimp boiled in a very weak broth, milled & then served with lime
camote Ⓜ ka·*mo*·te sweet potato
canela Ⓕ ka·*ne*·la cinnamon
cangrejo Ⓜ kan·*gre*·ho crab (also **jaiba**)
— moro *mo*·ro stone crab
caña Ⓕ **de azúcar** *ka*·nya de a·*soo*·kar sugar cane
capeado Ⓜ ka·pe·*a*·do fried, egg-battered seafood or vegetables
capirotada Ⓕ ka·pee·ro·*ta*·da Mexican-style bread pudding
capulines Ⓜ pl ka·poo·*lee*·nes black cherries
cardo Ⓜ *kar*·do cardoon (vegetable similar to an artichoke)
carne Ⓕ *kar*·ne meat
— asada a·*sa*·da thinly cut, grilled tenderloin or steak, served with sliced onion & grilled sweet pepper strips, rice, beans & **guacamole**
— a la Tampiqueña a la tam·pee·*ke*·nya plate piled with a small piece of meat, **chile poblano**, a **taco** or **enchilada**, beans, **guacamole** & shredded lettuce
— de cerdo de *ser*·do pork
— de res de res beef
— de vaca de *va*·ka beef
— molida mo·*lee*·da ground meat
— para asar *pa*·ra a·*sar* for grilling
— para taquear *pa*·ra ta·ke·*ar* meat for use in **tacos**
carnero Ⓜ kar·*ne*·ro mutton

carnitas Ⓕ pl kar·*nee*·tas slow-simmered chunks of seasoned pork served on **tortillas** with salsa, chopped onion & fresh coriander
cáscara Ⓕ *kas*·ka·ra rind • shell • husk
castaña Ⓕ kas·*ta*·nya chestnut
cátsup Ⓜ *kat*·soop tomato sauce • ketchup
caza Ⓕ *ca*·sa game (animals)
cebada Ⓕ se·*ba*·da barley
cebolla Ⓕ se·*bo*·ya onion
— **blanca** *blan*·ka white onion
— **de Cambray** de kam·*bray* spring onion
— **morada** mo·*ra*·da red onion • Spanish onion
cena Ⓕ *se*·na supper • dinner
cerdo Ⓜ *ser*·do pig • pork
cereal Ⓜ se·re·*al* cereal
cerveza Ⓕ ser·*ve*·sa beer
— **amarga** a·*mar*·ga bitter
— **clara** *kla*·ra blonde beer • light beer
— **de barril** de ba·*reel* draught beer
— **oscura** os·*koo*·ra stout
ceviche Ⓜ se·*vee*·che cocktail with fish, prawn, oysters or crab, mixed with onion, coriander & tomato
chabacano Ⓜ cha·ba·*ka*·no apricot
chalote Ⓜ cha·*lo*·te shallot onion
chalupas Ⓕ pl cha·*loo*·pas small **tortillas** made with cornflour, chili, beans & cheese
chamorro Ⓜ cha·*mo*·ro leg of pork marinated in **adobo** then oven-roasted at a very low heat
champiñones Ⓜ pl cham·pee·*nyo*·nes mushrooms
champurrado Ⓜ cham·poo·*ra*·do similar to **atole** but made with chocolate, water & cornflour
chapulín Ⓜ cha·poo·*leen* grasshopper
charal Ⓜ cha·*ral* sardine-like fish
chaya Ⓕ *cha*·ya type of spinach
chayote Ⓜ cha·*yo*·te popular type of squash, stuffed & baked or used raw in salad
chícharo Ⓜ *chee*·cha·ro pea
— **seco** *se*·ko green split pea
— **verde** *ver*·de snap pea
chicharra Ⓕ chee·*cha*·ra cricket
chicharrones Ⓜ pl chee·cha·*ro*·nes deep-fried pork rinds, usually sold by street vendors with a topping • flour-based fried snack
chilaquiles Ⓜ pl chee·la·*kee*·les crisp **tortillas** topped with chicken, onion, cream, fresh cheese & salsa; sometimes made with scrambled eggs & **chorizo**
chile Ⓜ *chee*·le chili – a huge variety of fresh & dried chilies is available at markets, sometimes pickled
— **ancho** *an*·cho 'broad chili' – has wrinkled, reddish-brown skin & is the most common form of dried **chile poblano**
— **cayena** ka·*ye*·na cayenne
— **chipotle** chee·*pot*·le smoke-dried version of **chile jalapeño**
— **dulce en adobo** *dool*·se en a·*do*·bo sweet, non-spicy pickled chili
— **en nogada** en no·*ga*·da a green **chile poblano** stuffed with a stew of beef & fruits, topped with **nogada** & decorated with pomegranate seeds
— **guajillo** gwa·*hee*·yo very hot, dried chili, almost black in colour
— **habanero** a·ba·*ne*·ro extremely hot type of chili
— **jalapeño** ha·la·*pe*·nyo Jalapeno pepper, often eaten in pickled form
— **mulato** moo·*la*·to dried **chile poblano** – its almost-black colour means it can be substituted for **chilhuacle negro** in the dish **mole negro**
— **pasilla** pa·*see*·ya dark, dried & very spicy **chile** used in **mole** and marinades

— poblano po·*bla*·no medium-green to purple-black chili, sometimes dried to produce **chile ancho** & **chile mulato** – this mildly hot, arrow-shaped chili is also used for making stuffed peppers
— relleno re·*ye*·no green **chile poblano** stuffed with cheese, covered in egg batter & fried
— serrano se·*ra*·no fiery green chili used in **moles** & **salsa**
chilhuacle ⓜ **negro** cheel·*wa*·kle *ne*·gro very dark, spicy strain of **chilhuacle**, a chili about the shape & size of a small bell pepper
chilpachole ⓜ **de jaiba** cheel·pa·*cho*·le de *hai*·ba a spicy soup made with crab
chirimoya ⓕ chee·ree·*mo*·ya custard apple • cherimoya
chocolate ⓜ **oaxaqueño** cho·ko·*la*·te wa·ha·*ke*·nyo chocolate from Oaxaca mixed with hot milk
chongos ⓜ pl **zamoranos** *chon*·gos sa·mo·*ra*·nos popular dessert of curdled milk, sugar, cinnamon & egg yolks
choriqueso ⓜ cho·ree·*ke*·so **chorizo** & melted cheese
chorizo ⓜ cho·*ree*·so spicy pork sausage, fried with eggs as breakfast, or cooked with potatoes as a filling for **tacos**
chuletas ⓕ choo·*le*·tas chops
— de cerdo de *ser*·do pork chops
— de res de res small beef steaks
churro ⓜ *choo*·ro long doughnut covered with sugar
cidra ⓕ *see*·dra cider
cilantro ⓜ see·*lan*·tro coriander • cilantro
ciruela ⓕ seer·*rwe*·la plum
— pasa *pa*·sa prune
clayuda ⓕ kla·*yoo*·da large, crisp **tortilla** with toppings (also **tlayuda**)
cocada ⓕ ko·*ka*·da traditional candy made with coconut, eggs, milk, almonds & sugar
coco ⓜ *ko*·ko coconut
coctél ⓜ kok·*tel* cocktail
— de camarón de ka·ma·*ron* prawn cocktail
cochinita ⓕ **pibil** ko·chee·*nee*·ta pee·*beel* pork cooked with **achiote**, red onions & orange juice
codorniz ⓕ ko·dor·*nees* quail
col ⓕ kol cabbage
cola ⓕ *ko*·la tail
coles ⓕ pl **de Bruselas** *ko*·les de broo·*se*·las Brussels sprouts
coliflor ⓕ ko·lee·*flor* cauliflower
comida ⓕ ko·*mee*·da food • lunch (the biggest meal of the day, taken between 1pm and 4pm)
comino ⓜ ko·*mee*·no cumin
conchas ⓕ pl **de vainilla** kon·chas de vay·*nee*·ya mini loaves topped with vanilla icing
conchas ⓕ pl **de chocolate** kon·chas de cho·ko·*la*·te mini loaves topped with chocolate icing
conejillo ⓜ **de indias** ko·ne·*hee*·yo de *een*·dyas guinea pig
conejo ⓜ ko·*ne*·ho rabbit
consomé *kal*·do meat broth • stock
— de camarón de ka·ma·*ron* prawn soup
— de pollo de *po*·yo chicken broth • soup with chicken, vegetables & sometimes rice & chickpeas
— de res de res beef & vegetable soup
corazón ⓜ ko·ra·*son* heart
cordero ⓜ kor·*de*·ro lamb • mutton
corundas ⓕ pl ko·*roon*·das little **tamales**
costillas ⓕ pl kos·*tee*·yas ribs
crema ⓕ *kre*·ma cream
— ácida *a*·see·da sour cream
— batida ba·*tee*·da whipping cream
— chantilly chan·tee·*yee* chantilly
— espesa es·*pe*·sa clotted cream
crepas ⓕ pl *kre*·pas crepes
croqueta ⓕ kro·*ke*·ta croquette

Cuba Ⓕ **libre** *koo*·ba *lee*·bre rum & cola (also simply called 'Cuba')
cubierta Ⓕ koo·*byer*·ta topping
cubiertos Ⓜ pl koo·*byer*·tos cutlery
cuerno Ⓜ *kwer*·no croissant
cuitlacoche Ⓜ kwee·tla·*ko*·che black corn fungus (also **huitlacoche**)
culebra Ⓕ koo·*le*·bra snake
cúrcuma Ⓕ *koor*·koo·ma turmeric
curry Ⓜ *koo*·ree curry
— en polvo en *pol*·vo curry powder
cus cus Ⓜ koos koos cous cous

D

dátiles Ⓜ pl *da*·tee·les dates
desayuno Ⓜ de·sa·*yoo*·no breakfast – Mexicans usually eat eggs or meat for breakfast, including one or more staples such as **tortillas**, beans, chilies & **atole**
diente Ⓜ **de ajo** *dyen*·te de *a*·ho garlic clove
dona Ⓕ *do*·na doughnut
dulce Ⓜ *dool*·se sweet • candy
durazno Ⓜ doo·*ras*·no peach

E

elote Ⓜ e·*lo*·te maize • corn
— tierno *tyer*·no sweet corn
empanada Ⓕ em·pa·*na*·da pastry turnover with a savoury meat & vegetable filling, baked or fried, or filled with fruit & served as a dessert
encebollado en·se·bo·*ya*·do served with onion
encurtidos Ⓜ pl en·koor·*tee*·dos table condiment consisting of a bowl of chilies marinated in vinegar, combined with onions, carrots & other vegetables
enchiladas Ⓕ pl en·chee·*la*·das meat or cheese wrapped in **tortillas** & smothered in red or green salsa, cream & melted cheese
— adobadas a·do·*ba*·das beef or chicken **enchiladas** in **adobo** sauce
— queretanas ke·re·*ta*·nas fresh **enchiladas** topped with shredded lettuce & other raw vegetables
— rojas *ro*·has meat or cheese **enchiladas** with a red **chile ancho sauce**, the most popular **enchiladas** on menus
— suizas *swee*·sas mild & creamy Swiss-style **enchiladas** filled with chicken or cheese, served with creamy green tomato sauce
— verdes *ver*·des served with a delicate green **tomatillo** sauce
endivia Ⓕ en·*dee*·vya endive
enebro Ⓜ e·*ne*·bro juniper
eneldo Ⓜ e·*nel*·do dill
enfrijolado/a Ⓜ/Ⓕ en·free·ho·*la*·do/a anything cooked in a bean sauce, most commonly corn **tortillas** in a smooth black bean sauce & topped with thinly sliced onions, cream & crumbed cheese
enmolado/a Ⓜ/Ⓕ en·mo·*la*·do/a anything cooked in a **mole** sauce
ensalada Ⓕ en·sa·*la*·da salad
— César *se*·sar Caesar salad, named after its inventor César Cardini, an Italian immigrant to Mexico
— de verduras de ver·*doo*·ras salad of cooked vegetables, a mix of fresh vegetables, or a combination of the two
— mixta *meek*·sta mix of lettuce, red tomatoes, cucumber, peas, avocado & fresh onion rings
entrada Ⓕ en·*tra*·da starter
entremés Ⓜ en·tre·*mes* appetiser
epazote Ⓜ e·pa·*so*·te wormseed, a pungent herb similar to coriander, used in sauces, beans & **quesadillas**
escabeche Ⓜ es·ka·*be*·che a brine used as a pickling agent or as a fish marinade

escamoles ⓜ pl es·ka·*mo*·les ant eggs, a delicacy that looks like rice – usually sauteed in butter & wine, served as an accompaniment to meat or with **tortillas**, avocado & salad
espárragos ⓜ pl es·*pa*·ra·gos asparagus
especias ⓕ pl es·*pe*·syas spices
espinaca ⓕ es·pee·*na*·ka spinach
esquites ⓜ pl es·*kee*·tes fresh corn grains boiled with butter, **epazote** & onions, served with fresh lime juice, chili powder & grated cheese
estofado ⓜ es·to·*fa*·do stew • Oaxacan **mole** served over chicken or pork, prepared with tomatoes, almonds, bread, raisins, cloves & ground **chile guajillo**
estragón ⓜ es·tra·*gon* tarragon
esturión ⓜ es·too·*ryon* sturgeon

F

faisán ⓜ fay·*san* pheasant
filete ⓜ fee·*le*·te fillet
filete ⓜ **a la Mexicana** fee·*le*·te a la me·hee·*ka*·na grilled white fish with a tomato-based sauce
flan ⓜ flan a caramel egg custard flavoured with vanilla & covered in a syrupy topping
— **napolitano** na·po·lee·*ta*·no whiter & thicker than the custard-style flan, sometimes flavoured with liqueur
flautas ⓕ pl *flow*·tas tube-shaped tacos topped with chicken meat, deep-fried & served with cream, cheese & green or red sauce
flor ⓕ **de calabaza** flor de ka·la·*ba*·sa large squash flowers used in soups & other dishes
frambuesa ⓕ fram·*bwe*·sa raspberry
fresa ⓕ *fre*·sa strawberry
fideos ⓜ pl fee·*de*·os noodles
frijoles ⓜ pl free·*ho*·les beans, of which nearly 100 varieties are included in the Mexican cuisine
— **borrachos** bo·*ra*·chos 'drunken beans', made as **frijoles charros** but flavoured with flat beer
— **charros** *cha*·ros 'cowboy beans' – pork rind, fried tomatoes, onion & coriander, served as a soup
— **molidos** mo·*lee*·dos ground beans
— **negros** *ne*·gros 'black beans' – served mashed & refried, pureed as a soup or whole, usually seasoned with **epazote**
— **refritos** re·*free*·tos mashed beans fried in lard or vegetable oil
frutas ⓕ pl *froo*·tas fruits
— **cristalizadas** krees·ta·lee·*sa*·das different fruits cooked with sugar & water until crunchy
— **secas** *se*·kas dried fruit

G

galleta ⓕ ga·*ye*·ta biscuit • cookie • cracker
galletas ⓕ pl **saladas** ga·*ye*·tas sa·*la*·das crackers
gallina ⓕ ga·*yee*·na hen
ganso ⓜ *gan*·so goose
garbanzo ⓜ gar·*ban*·so chickpea
gelatina ⓕ he·la·*tee*·na gelatin
germen ⓜ **de trigo** *her*·men de *tree*·go wheat germ
germinado ⓜ **de soya** her·mee·*na*·do de *so*·ya bean sprout
ginebra ⓕ hee·*ne*·bra gin
gorditas ⓕ pl gor·*dee*·tas thick corn **tortillas** fried then filled with beef, chicken or pork, then topped with cheese & lettuce
granada ⓕ gra·*na*·da grenadine • pomegranate
granola ⓕ gra·*no*·la muesli
grosella ⓕ gro·se·ya currant

guacamole ⓜ gwa·ka·*mo*·le mashed avocado mixed with onion & chili
guaraches ⓜ pl gwa·*ra*·ches **tortilla** shells piled high with **chorizo**, meat, potato, coriander & chili salsa
guarnición ⓕ gwar·nee·*syon* garnish
guisado ⓜ gee·*sa*·do stew
guiso ⓜ *gee*·so stew
gusano ⓜ goo·*sa*·no worm
gusanos ⓜ pl **de maguey** goo·*sa*·nos de ma·*gay* worms that live in **maguey** – usually at the bottom of the bottle as a sign of true **mezcal**
— con salsa borracha kon *sal*·sa bo·*ra*·cha a dish of **maguey** worms fried in oil & accompanied by a sauce of roasted **chile pasilla**, garlic, onion, cheese & **pulque**

H

haba ⓕ *a*·ba broad bean
habanero ⓜ a·ba·*ne*·ro extremely spicy type of chili
hamburguesa ⓕ am·boor·*ge*·sa hamburger
helado ⓜ e·*la*·do ice cream
hielo ⓜ *ye*·lo ice
hígado ⓜ *ee*·ga·do liver
— encebollado en·se·bo·*ya*·do liver with onions
higo ⓜ *ee*·go fig
hinojo ⓜ ee·*no*·ho fennel
hojas ⓕ pl *o*·has leaves (banana, avocado, corn or **maguey**) used for flavouring, to wrap food for steaming or to line or cover earthenware pots
— de laurel de low·*rel* bay leaves
— de plátano de *pla*·ta·no banana leaves
— santas *san*·tas large anise-flavoured leaves
hojuelas ⓕ pl **de maíz** o·*hwe*·las de ma·*ees* corn flakes
huachinango ⓜ wa·chee·*nan*·go red snapper
— a la Veracruzana a la ve·ra·kroo·*sa*·na speciality of the port city of Veracruz where fresh red snapper is grilled in a lightly spiced sauce of tomato, onion & green olives
huarache ⓜ wa·*ra*·che flat & oval **tortilla** with beans and/or meat, topped with cream, cheese & various sauces (common street food)
huatape ⓜ **tamaulipeco** wa·*ta*·pe ta·mow·lee·*pe*·ko green prawn soup thickened with corn dough
huauzontle ⓜ wow·*son*·tle green vegetable whose buds are dipped in flour & fried
huevos ⓜ pl *hwe*·vos eggs
— entomatados en·to·ma·*ta*·dos eggs in a tomato sauce
— estrellados es·tre·*ya*·dos fried (sunny side up) eggs
— fritos *free*·tos fried eggs
— revueltos re·*vwel*·tos scrambled eggs
— rancheros ran·*che*·ros eggs on **tortillas**, topped with chili sauce
— tibios *tee*·byos soft-boiled eggs
huitlacoche ⓜ weet·la·*ko*·che black fungus that grows on young corn during the rainy season, used in crepes, **quesadillas** & soups

I

iguana ⓕ ee·*gwa*·na iguana – some species are protected and should not be eaten

J

jabalí ⓜ ha·ba·*lee* boar
jaiba ⓕ *hai*·ba crab
— de río de *ree*·o crayfish
jalapeño ⓜ ha·la·*pe*·nyo hot green chil from Jalapa
jamón ⓜ ha·*mon* ham

jengibre ⓜ hen·*hee*·bre ginger
jerez ⓜ he·*res* sherry
jícama ⓕ *hee*·ka·ma crunchy, sweet turnip • potato-like tuber often sold by street vendors, sliced & garnished with red chili powder, salt & fresh lime juice
jitomates ⓜ pl hee·to·*ma*·tes red tomatoes, specifically plum or roma
— cereza se·*re*·sa cherry tomatoes
— deshidratados des·ee·dra·*ta*·dos sun-dried tomatoes
jugo ⓜ *hoo*·go juice
— de fruta de *froo*·ta fruit juice
— de naranja de na·*ran*·ha orange juice
— fresco *fres*·ko freshly squeezed juice

L

langosta ⓕ lan·*gos*·ta lobster
laurel ⓜ low·*rel* bay leaf
lavanda ⓕ la·*van*·da lavender
leche ⓕ *le*·che milk
— de soya de *so*·ya soy milk
— descremada des·kre·*ma*·da skimmed milk
— entera en·*te*·ra full cream milk
lechuga ⓕ le·*choo*·ga lettuce
lengua ⓕ *len*·gwa tongue
lenguado ⓜ len·*gwa*·do sole (fish)
lentejas ⓕ pl len·*te*·has brown lentils
— rojas *ro*·has red lentils
— verdes *ver*·des green lentils
levadura ⓕ le·va·*doo*·ra yeast
licor ⓜ lee·*kor* liqueur
licores ⓜ pl lee·*ko*·res spirits
lichi ⓜ *lee*·chee lychee
liebre ⓕ *lye*·bre hare
lima ⓕ *lee*·ma fragrant citrus fruit native to the Yucatán Peninsula
limón ⓜ lee·*mon* lime
— agrio *a*·gryo bitter lime
— sin semilla seen se·*mee*·ya seedless lime
limonada ⓕ lee·mo·*na*·da lemonade
lomo ⓜ *lo*·mo loin • rump • shoulder
longaniza ⓕ lon·ga·*nee*·sa dried speciality pork sausage
lonche ⓜ *lon*·che sandwich made with a long bun – in Guadalajara most of the bread is filled with meat, cheese, avocado & mayonnaise or cream
lucio ⓜ *loo*·syo pike (fish)

M

macadamia ⓕ ma·ka·*da*·mya macadamia
machaca ⓕ ma·*cha*·ka sheets of dried beef or beef jerky
machacado ⓜ ma·cha·*ka*·do dried meat
maguey ⓜ ma·*gay* any of the agave plants, used to make alcoholic drinks such as **pulque** and **tequila**
maíz ⓜ ma·*ees* corn • maize
— molido mo·*lee*·do de-husked dried maize kernels with the germ removed that is ground into cornmeal
malta ⓕ *mal*·ta malt
malteada ⓕ mal·te·*a*·da milkshake
mamey ⓜ ma·*may* rough brown fruit with bitter yellow inner skin & orangey flesh, used to make smoothies, gelatin, ice cream & mousses
mandarina ⓕ man·da·*ree*·na mandarin
mantequilla ⓕ man·te·*kee*·ya butter
manzana ⓕ man·*sa*·na apple
maracuyá ⓕ ma·ra·koo·*ya* passion fruit
margarina ⓕ mar·ga·*ree*·na margarine
Margarita ⓕ mar·ga·*ree*·ta cocktail made with **tequila**, lime juice, orange liqueur & crushed ice, served in a chilled glass with salt on the rim

mariscos ⓜ pl ma·*rees*·kos seafood
masa ⓕ *ma*·sa ground, cooked corn mixed with slaked lime and made into a dough or batter used for **tortillas**
— de harina de maíz de a·*ree*·na de ma·*ees* cornflour
— de harina de trigo de a·*ree*·na de *tree*·go wheat flour
maseca ⓕ ma·*se*·ka type of cornflour used in **tortillas** & **tamales**
mayonesa ⓕ ma·yo·*ne*·sa mayonnaise
mazapán ⓜ ma·sa·*pan* marzipan
medio *me*·dyo half • medium cooked
médula ⓕ *me*·doo·la bone marrow, also called **tuétano**
mejillón ⓜ me·hee·*yon* mussel
mejorana ⓕ me·ho·*ra*·na marjoram
melón ⓜ me·*lon* melon • cantaloupe
membrillo ⓜ mem·*bree*·yo quince
menta ⓕ *men*·ta peppermint • mint
menudo ⓜ me·*noo*·do tripe stew – a hangover remedy (an acquired taste)
merienda ⓕ me·*ryen*·da the equivalent of English afternoon tea
merluza ⓕ mer·*loo*·sa hake
mermelada ⓕ mer·me·*la*·da fruit jam • jelly • marmalade
mezcal ⓜ mes·*kal* distilled liquor made from **agave**
miel ⓕ myel honey
migajas ⓕ pl mee·*ga*·has crumbs
mijo ⓜ *mee*·ho millet
milanesa ⓕ mee·la·*ne*·sa pork, beef or chicken schnitzel – inferior cuts of beef are pounded to a thin slab, then fried in an egg & bread batter, served with fresh limes & accompanied by rice, beans & salad
mixiotes ⓜ pl mee·*shyo*·tes lamb, chicken or rabbit meat wrapped in a thin layer of **maguey** leaves & steamed in a rich broth, then served with a mild green sauce, sliced avocado & **tortillas**
modongo ⓜ **jarocho** mon·*don*·go ha·*ro*·cho rich, stew-like dish with ham, tripe, pork, chickpeas, coriander & **tortillas**
mojarra ⓕ **a la veracruzana** mo·*ha*·ra a la ve·ra·kroo·*sa*·na spicy baked perch in a tomato, onion & green olive salsa
mole ⓜ *mo*·le the quintessential Mexican sauce, made using a variety of chilies, herbs, spices & chocolate
— almendrado al·men·*dra*·do a **mole** made mainly with almonds
— coloradito ko·lo·ra·*dee*·to Oaxacan **mole** made with chilies, sesame seeds, almonds, raisins, bananas & spices, ladled over chicken
— de olla de *o*·ya type of **mole** prepared with pork, lamb or smoked meat, cactus fruit & **epazote**
— de xico de *hee*·ko a slightly sweet **mole**
— naolinco na·o·*leen*·ko a spicy **mole**
— negro *ne*·gro a dark **mole**
— poblano po·*bla*·no type of **mole** made from deseeded & pureed chilies, onion, coriander, anise, cinnamon, garlic, toasted peanuts, almonds & sweetened chocolate
mollejas ⓕ pl mo·*ye*·has giblets
molletes ⓜ pl mo·*ye*·tes savoury, filled bread roll spread with refried beans & melted cheese & topped with fresh **salsa**
mondongo ⓜ mon·*don*·go a kind of stew with several regional variations
mora ⓕ *mo*·ra mulberry
moronga ⓕ mo·*ron*·ga black pudding • blood sausage
mostaza ⓕ mos·*ta*·sa mustard

N

nabo ⓜ *na*·bo turnip
naranja ⓕ na·*ran*·ha orange
— agria *a*·grya bitter orange used in marinades & sauces
— china ⓕ *chee*·na kumquat

nieves ⓕ pl *nye*·ves sherbets made-with fruits or other ingredients such as **tequila**, avocado, prawn, rosehips or sweet corn

nixtamal ⓜ neek·sta·*mal* mixture of corn & lime used in tortilla dough (see **masa**)

nogada ⓕ no·*ga*·da walnut or walnut sauce

nogal no·*gal* walnut tree

nopal ⓜ no·*pal* prickly pear cactus – the cactus pads (leaves) are cut into strips & boiled as a vegetable or added to scrambled eggs

nudillo ⓜ noo·*dee*·yo knuckle

nueva cocina ⓕ **mexicana** *nwe*·va ko·*see*·na me·hee·*ka*·na 'new Mexican cuisine' – a movement among some chefs to combine traditional ingredients with contemporary preparations & presentations

nuez ⓕ nwes nut • pecan • walnut

— cruda *kroo*·da raw nut

— de Castilla de kas·*tee*·ya walnut

— del Brasil del bra·*seel* brazil nut

— de la India de la *een*·dya cashew

— moscada mos·*ka*·da nutmeg

— pacana pa·*ka*·na pecan

— tostada tos·*ta*·da roasted nut

O

obleas ⓕ pl o·*ble*·as coloured wafers filled with raw brown sugar syrup & decorated with toasted pumpkin seeds

octli ⓜ *ok*·tlee alcoholic drink made from a combination of juices from different agave plants

olivo ⓜ o·*lee*·vo olive tree

oporto ⓜ o·*por*·to port

ostión ⓜ os·*tyon* oyster

ostra ⓕ *os*·tra oyster

oveja ⓕ o·*ve*·ha sheep

P

palanquetas ⓕ pl pa·lan·*ke*·tas traditional sweets made with peanuts or pumpkin seeds formed into rectangular or round shapes using caramelised sugar

paleta ⓕ pa·*le*·ta ice lolly • popsicle

— de agua de *a*·gwa ice lolly made with water & fruit juice

— de leche de *le*·che ice lolly made with milk & fruits or other ingredient such as vanilla, chocolate or nuts

palomitas ⓕ pl pa·lo·*mee*·tas pop corn

pan ⓜ pan bread

— árabe *a*·ra·be pita bread

— de levadura fermentada de le·va·*doo*·ra fer·men·*ta*·da sourdough

— de muerto de *mwer*·to heavy bread used as an offering on the Day of the Dead

— de yema de *ye*·ma yellow, rich & heavy bread made with egg yolks

— dulce *dool*·se sweet bread

— duro *doo*·ro stale bread

— integral een·te·*gral* brown bread

— tostado tos·*ta*·do toasted bread

panuchos ⓜ pl pa·*noo*·chos bean-stuffed **tortillas**, fried crisp then topped with a tower of shredded turkey or chicken, tomato, lettuce & onions

papas ⓜ pl *pa*·pas potatoes

— a la francesa a la fran·*se*·sa chips • French fries

papadzules ⓜ pl pa·pad·*soo*·les fresh corn **tortillas** wrapped around a filling of chopped hard-boiled eggs then covered with sauce made from pumpkin seed & **epazote**

papitas ⓕ pl **del monte** pa·*pee*·tas del *mon*·te wild potatoes
paprika ⓕ pap·*ree*·ka paprika
parillada ⓕ pa·ree·*ya*·da flame-grilled meat platter
pasa ⓕ **(de uva)** *pa*·sa (de *oo*·va) raisin
pastel ⓜ pas·*tel* pastry • cake
— de tres leches de tres *le*·ches cake made with evaporated milk, condensed milk & evaporated cream
pastelería ⓕ pas·te·le·*ree*·a cake shop
pastelito ⓜ pas·te·*lee*·to pastry
patas ⓕ pl *pa*·tas hooves
pato ⓜ *pa*·to duck
pavo ⓜ *pa*·vo turkey
pechuga ⓕ pe·*choo*·ga breast
— de pollo de *po*·yo chicken breast
pepinillo ⓜ pe·pee·*nee*·yo gherkin • pickle
pepino ⓜ pe·*pee*·no cucumber
pepitoria ⓕ pe·pee·*to*·rya traditional sweets made with coloured **obleas**
pera ⓕ *pe*·ra pear
perejil ⓜ pe·re·*heel* parsley
pescadería ⓕ pes·ka·de·*ree*·a fishmonger
pescado ⓜ pes·*ka*·do fish
pibil ⓜ pee·*beel* sauce made from **achiote**, bitter orange juice, garlic, salt & pepper, used as a marinade for chicken or pork
picadillo ⓜ pee·ka·*dee*·yo minced meat cooked with potatoes, carrots & onion, simmered in a light tomato sauce
pierna ⓕ *pyer*·na leg
piloncillo ⓜ pee·lon·*see*·yo raw brown sugar
pimentón ⓜ pee·men·*ton* cayenne • red pepper • paprika
pimienta ⓕ pee·*myen*·ta black pepper
— de cayena de ka·*ye*·na cayenne pepper
— entera en·*te*·ra ground pepper
— inglesa een·*gle*·sa allspice
— negra *ne*·gra black pepper
— recién molida re·*syen* mo·*lee*·da freshly ground black pepper
— verde *ver*·de green pepper
pimiento ⓜ pee·*myen*·to pepper (bell)
pinole ⓜ pee·*no*·le flour made with a mixture of toasted corn & amaranth seeds
piña ⓕ *pee*·nya pineapple
piñatas ⓕ pl pee·*nya*·tas balloons or animal-shaped dolls made with clay or papier mache, filled with sweets, fruits, peanuts & toys
piñón ⓜ pee·*nyon* pine nut
pipián verde ⓜ pee·*pyan ver*·de a type of **mole** made with ground spices & pumpkin or squash seeds, green tomatoes, peanuts – served over pork or chicken
pistaches ⓜ pl pees·*ta*·ches pistachios
plátano ⓜ *pla*·ta·no banana • plantain
— dominico do·mee·*nee*·ko small & very sweet banana
— macho *ma*·cho large fried banana, served with sour cream & sugar
poc chuc ⓜ pok chook thin slice of pork, cooked on a grill & served on a sizzling plate with a bitter orange sauce & chopped onions
pollo ⓜ *po*·yo chicken
— a la pibil a la pee·*beel* chicken marinated in **pibil** sauce
— frito *free*·to fried chicken
— rostizado ros·tee·*sa*·do roast chicken
ponche ⓜ **de frutas** pon·che de *froo*·tas fruit punch prepared during Christmas made with guava, **tejocotes**, sugar cane, cinnamon, raisins, cloves & raw sugar
— con piquete kon pee·*ke*·te fruit punch with a shot of **tequila** or rum
poro ⓜ *po*·ro leek
postre ⓜ *pos*·tre dessert

pozole ⓜ po·so·le soup made of hominy corn, chicken or pork, lettuce & slices of radish, traditionally eaten at Christmas
— **blanco** *blan*·ko hominy corn soup prepared with stock but without chilies
— **rojo** *ro*·ho hominy corn soup made with chili
— **verde** *ver*·de hominy corn soup made with green chilies & toasted pumpkin seeds
puchero ⓜ poo·*che*·ro stew made of chicken & vegetables
puerro ⓜ *pwe*·ro leek
pulpo ⓜ *pool*·po octopus
— **en su tinta** en soo *teen*·ta octopus prepared in a rich squid-ink sauce
pulque ⓜ *pool*·ke white, thick, sweet alcoholic drink made from the fermented sap of agave plants, especially the **maguey**

Q

queretanas ⓕ pl ke·re·*ta*·nas Queretaro-style **enchiladas** topped with shredded lettuce & other raw vegetables
quesadillas ⓕ pl ke·sa·dee·yas flour or corn **tortillas** with a savoury cheese filling • corn dough filled with different toppings such as mushrooms, mashed potatoes, **huitlacoche** & **rajas**
quesillo ⓜ ke·see·yo stringy goat's milk cheese from Oaxaca
queso ⓜ *ke*·so cheese
— **añejo** a·nye·ho hard, aged cheese with a sharp flavour similar to Parmesan
— **Chihuahua** chee·*wa*·wa creamy yellow cheese often used in **quesadillas**
— **crema** *kre*·ma cream cheese
— **de cabra** de *ka*·bra goat's cheese
— **fresco** fres·ko cheese made from cow's milk
— **fundido** foon·*dee*·do cheese fondue
— **manchego** man·*che*·go although this cheese is originally from La Mancha in Spain, it's popular in Mexico & used in many recipes
— **Oaxaca** wa·*ha*·ka Oaxacan cheese, made from goat's milk (see **quesillo)**
— **parmesano** par·me·sa·no Parmesan cheese

R

rábano ⓜ *ra*·ba·no radish
— **picante** pee·*kan*·te horseradish
rabo ⓜ *ra*·bo tail
rajas ⓕ pl *ra*·has slices of chili
— **con crema** kon *kre*·*ma* a dish made with **chile poblano** & sour cream
— **en escabeche** en es·ka·*be*·che pickled chilies
rana ⓕ *ra*·na frog
ranchera ⓕ ran·*che*·ra sauce made with chilies, tomatoes, onions, coriander – used for eggs or **enchiladas**
raspados ⓜ pl ras·*pa*·dos 'scrapings' – flavoured ice with fruit juice, sold by pushcart vendors as a refreshing treat
rebanada ⓕ re·ba·*na*·da a slice
regaliz ⓜ re·ga·*lees* liquorice
refresco ⓜ re·*fres*·ko soft drink
relleno ⓜ re·*ye*·no stuffing
— **negro** *ne*·gro green pepper, **chiles anchos** & **achiote**, served over shredded turkey & a hard-boiled egg
relleno/a ⓜ/ⓕ re·*ye*·no/a stuffed
reposado ⓜ re·po·sa·do an alcoholic drink such as **tequila** that has been aged two to 12 months
requesón ⓜ re·ke·*son* cottage cheese
res ⓕ res beef
riñón ⓜ ree·*nyon* kidney

robalo ⓜ ro·*ba*·lo sea bass
romero ⓜ ro·*me*·ro rosemary
ron ⓜ ron rum
rosca ⓕ **de reyes** *ros*·ka de *re*·yes eaten on Epiphany, this large, wreath-shaped pastry has a small china doll representing Christ, baked into it – whoever gets the piece with the doll in it throws a party on Candlemas Day (2 February)

S

sal ⓕ sal salt
salbutes ⓜ pl sal·*boo*·tes fried crisp **tortillas** topped with a tower of shredded turkey or chicken, tomato, lettuce & onions
salchicha ⓕ sal·*chee*·cha frankfurter
— de coctél de kok·*tel* small cocktail sausage
— de Viena de *vye*·na sausages used for hot dogs
salmón ⓜ sal·*mon* salmon
salsa ⓕ *sal*·sa a spicy, tomato-based sauce
— a la veracruzana a la ve·ra·kroo·*sa*·na sauce of tomato, onion & green olives
— bandera ban·*de*·ra 'flag sauce' – named for the red of the tomato, the white of the onion & the green of the chili
— borracha bo·*ra*·cha 'drunken sauce' – made from roasted **chile pasilla**, garlic, onion, cheese & **pulque**
— de tomatillos sauce with green chilies, onion & coriander
— picante pee·*kan*·te hot sauce
— roja *ro*·ha red sauce made with plum tomatoes, onions, garlic & salt
— tártara *tar*·ta·ra tartare sauce
— verde *ver*·de green sauce made with **tomatillos**, green chilies, onion & coriander

sandía ⓕ san·*dee*·a watermelon – a symbol of Mexico (the red, white & green correspond to the colours of the Mexican flag)
sangría ⓕ san·*gree*·a refreshing cold drink of Spanish origin made with red wine, brandy, orange liqueur, fresh citrus juices & sliced fresh fruit
sangrita ⓕ san·*gree*·ta bright red, thickish mixture of crushed tomatoes (or tomato juice), orange juice, grenadine, chili & salt – served chilled with a shot of **tequila**
sardina ⓕ sar·*dee*·na sardine
semilla ⓕ se·*mee*·ya seed
— de ajonjolí de a·hon·ho·*lee* sesame seed
— de amapola de a·ma·*po*·la poppy seed
— de apio de a·pyo celery seed
— de hinojo de ee·*no*·ho fennel seed
semita ⓕ se·*mee*·ta round & flat sweet bread
semillas ⓕ pl **de alcaravea** se·*mee*·yas de al·ka·ra·*ve*·a caraway seed
sémola ⓕ *se*·mo·la semolina
sesos ⓜ pl *se*·sos brains
sidra ⓕ *see*·dra cider
sopa ⓕ *so*·pa soup • chowder
— de coco de *ko*·ko coconut soup
— de lima de *lee*·ma soup made from a fragrant citrus fruit native to the Yucatán Peninsula
— de nopales de no·*pa*·les soup with cactus leaves
— de tortilla de tor·*tee*·ya chicken broth-based soup featuring strips of leftover corn **tortillas**
— seca *se*·ka 'dry soup' – a rice, pasta or tortilla-based dish
sope ⓜ *so*·pe thick cornflour **tortilla** stuffed with refried beans, served with chicken or other meat with lettuce & cream on the top

T

tablillas ⓕ pl **de chocolate** ta·*blee*·yas de cho·ko·*la*·te blocks of chocolate (for heating with water and drinking)
tacos ⓜ pl *ta*·kos folded corn **tortillas** filled with meat, beans & other ingredients
— al pastor al pas·*tor* **tacos** with meat cut from a roasting spit, served with fresh pineapple, onions, coriander & salsa
— árabe a·ra·be **tacos** made with slightly thicker wheat bread (pita bread)
— de carne asada de kar·ne a·sa·da **tacos** with grilled beef
— de carnitas de kar·nee·tas **tacos** with finely chopped pork
— de pollo de *po*·yo chicken **tacos**
— dorados do·*ra*·dos deep fried **tacos**
tallo ⓜ *ta*·yo shank
tamales ⓜ pl ta·*ma*·les corn dough stuffed with meat, **mole**, green or red salsa, fruit or nothing at all, usually wrapped in banana leaves or in corn husks & steamed
tamarindo ⓜ ta·ma·*reen*·do tamarind, a fruit used for making **aguas**, **nieves** & desserts
taquería ⓕ ta·ke·*ree*·a place that specialises in serving **tacos**
taquito ⓜ ta·*kee*·to a small **tortilla** wrapped around meat or chicken
té ⓜ te tea
— de hierbabuena de yer·ba·*bwe*·na peppermint tea
— de limón de lee·*mon* lemongrass tea
— de manzanilla de man·sa·*nee*·ya chamomile tea
— de menta de *men*·ta mint tea
— descafeinado des·ka·fay·*na*·do decaffeinated tea
— negro *ne*·gro black tea
tejate ⓜ te·*ha*·te Oaxacan recipe for chocolate that includes **mamey** seeds, cacao flowers & corn dough
tejocote ⓜ te·ho·*ko*·te hawthorn
telera ⓕ te·*le*·ra French-style bread roll used to make **tortas**
tepache ⓜ te·*pa*·che alcoholic drink made from fermented pineapple
tequila ⓕ te·*kee*·la classic Mexican spirit distilled from the **maguey** plant
ternera ⓕ ter·*ne*·ra veal
tescalate ⓜ tes·ka·*la*·te type of chocolate popular in Chiapas, made by grinding the cacao beans with toasted corn & **achiote**
tlayuda ⓕ tla·*yoo*·da large, crisp **tortilla** topped with Oaxacan cheese, tomatoes & beans, also called **clayuda**
tocino ⓜ to·*see*·no bacon
— de lomo de *lo*·mo back bacon
tomate ⓜ **verde** to·*ma*·te *ver*·de see **tomatillo**
tomates ⓜ pl **deshidratados** to·*ma*·tes des·ee·dra·*ta*·dos sun-dried tomatoes
tomatillo ⓜ to·ma·*tee*·yo small green native tomato wrapped in a brownish papery husk – used for salsas (also known as **tomate verde**)
tomillo ⓜ to·*mee*·yo thyme
to'owloche ⓜ tow·*lo*·che 'wrapped in corn leaves' – Mayan **tamal** made by home chefs & served to people in the street on festival days
toro ⓜ *to*·ro bull
toronja ⓕ to·*ron*·ha grapefruit
torta ⓕ *tor*·ta sandwich made with crusty bread
tortillas ⓕ tor·*tee*·yas ubiquitous round flatbread made with corn or wheat flour, a staple in the Mexican diet for thousands of years – used in making **tacos**, **chalupas**, **huaraches**, **sopes** & **tostadas**
— de maíz de ma·*ees* corn **tortillas**

— de trigo de *tree*·go wheat **tortillas**
— yucatecas yoo·ka·*te*·kas see **papadzules**
tortillería ⓕ tor·tee·ye·*ree*·a bakery in which Mexicans buy their **tortillas** by the kilo
tostadas ⓕ pl tos·*ta*·das fried corn **tortillas**
totopos ⓜ pl to·*to*·pos deep-fried wedges of stale corn **tortillas**
trigo ⓜ *tree*·go wheat
— integral een·te·*gral* whole-grain wheat
— sarraceno ⓜ sa·ra·*se*·no buckwheat
tripa ⓕ *tree*·pa tripe
trucha ⓕ *troo*·cha trout
tuna ⓕ *too*·na prickly pear • cactus fruit
tuétano ⓜ *twe*·ta·no marrow
turrón ⓜ too·*ron* nougat

U

uchepos ⓜ pl oo·*che*·pos corn dough, wrapped in corn husks, steamed & served with fresh cream
uva ⓕ **pasa** *oo*·va *pa*·sa raisin
uvas ⓕ pl *oo*·vas grapes

V

vainilla ⓕ vay·*nee*·ya vanilla
venado ⓜ ve·*na*·do venison • deer
verdulería ⓕ ver·doo·le·*ree*·a greengrocer
verduras ⓕ pl ver·*doo*·ras mixed greens
vinagre ⓜ vee·*na*·gre vinegar
— balsámico bal·*sa*·mee·ko balsamic vinegar
vino ⓜ *vee*·no wine
— afrutado a·froo·*ta*·do fruity wine
— blanco *blan*·ko white wine
— de la casa de la *ka*·sa house wine
— dulce *dool*·se sweet wine
— espumoso es·poo·*mo*·so sparkling wine
— ligeramente dulce lee·he·ra·*men*·te *dool*·se lightly sweet wine
— muy seco mooy *se*·ko very dry wine
— nacional na·syo·*nal* Mexican wine
— seco *se*·ko dry wine
— semi-seco *se*·mee *se*·ko semi-dry wine
— tinto *teen*·to red wine
vuelve a la vida ⓜ *vwel*·ve a la *vee*·da 'return to life' – seafood cocktail in a tomato salsa that serves as a popular hangover cure

W

whiskey ⓜ *wees*·kee whiskey
— canadiense ka·na·*dyen*·se rye whiskey
— de centeno de sen·*te*·no bourbon whiskey

X

xcatik ⓜ shka·*teek* kind of chili found in Yucatán state
xtabentún ⓜ shta·ben·*toon* Maya liqueur made from native flowers of the same name & anise seeds

Z

zanahoria ⓕ sa·na·*o*·rya carrot
zapote ⓜ sa·*po*·te a fruit used for making desserts which comes in two varieties: **negro** (black) or **blanco** (white)
zarzamora ⓕ sar·sa·*mo*·ra blackberry • dewberry

DICTIONARY

English to Mexican Spanish

INGLÉS – ESPAÑOL MEXICANO

Nouns in the dictionary have their gender indicated by ⓜ or ⓕ. If it's a plural noun, you'll also see pl. Where a word that could be either a noun or a verb has no gender indicated, it's a verb.

A

(to be) able poder po·der
aboard a bordo a bor·do
abortion aborto ⓜ a·bor·to
about sobre so·bre
above arriba a·ree·ba
abroad en el extranjero en el ek·stran·he·ro
accept aceptar a·sep·tar
accident accidente ⓜ ak·see·den·te
accommodation alojamiento ⓜ a·lo·ha·myen·to
across a través a tra·ves
activist activista ⓜ&ⓕ ak·tee·vees·ta
acupuncture acupuntura ⓕ a·koo·poon·too·ra
adaptor adaptador ⓜ a·dap·ta·dor
address dirección ⓕ dee·rek·syon
administration administración ⓕ ad·mee·nees·tra·syon
admission price precio ⓜ de entrada pre·syo de en·tra·da
admit (acknowledge) reconocer re·ko·no·ser
admit (allow to enter) dejar entrar de·har en·trar
admit (accept) admitir ad·mee·teer
adult adulto/a ⓜ/ⓕ a·dool·to/a
advertisement anuncio ⓜ a·noon·syo
advice consejo ⓜ kon·se·ho
advise aconsejar a·kon·se·har
aerobics aeróbics ⓜ a·e·ro·beeks
Africa África a·free·ka
after después de des·pwes de
aftershave loción ⓕ para después del afeitado lo·syon pa·ra des·pwes del a·fay·ta·do
again otra vez o·tra ves
age edad ⓕ e·dad
aggressive agresivo/a ⓜ/ⓕ a·gre·see·vo/a
agree estar de acuerdo es·tar de a·kwer·do
agriculture agricultura ⓕ a·gree·kool·too·ra
AIDS SIDA ⓜ see·da
air aire ⓜ ai·re
airmail correo ⓜaéreo ko·re·o a·e·re·o

(by) airmail (por) vía ⓕ aérea (por) *vee*·a a·e·re·a
air-conditioning aire ⓜ acondicionado *ai*·re a·kon·dee·syo·*na*·do
airline aerolínea ⓕ a·e·ro·*lee*·ne·a
airport aeropuerto ⓜ a·e·ro·*pwer*·to
airport tax tarifa de uso ⓕ de aeropuerto (TUA) ta·*ree*·fa de·oo·so de a·e·ro·*pwer*·to (*too*·a)
alarm clock despertador ⓜ des·per·ta·*dor*
alcohol alcohol ⓜ al·*kol*
all todo *to*·do
allergy alergia ⓕ a·*ler*·hya
allow permitir per·mee·*teer*
almond almendra ⓕ al·*men*·dra
almost casi *ka*·see
alone solo/a ⓜ/ⓕ *so*·lo/a
already ya ya
also también tam·*byen*
altar altar ⓜ al·*tar*
altitude altura ⓕ al·*too*·ra
always siempre *syem*·pre
amateur amateur ⓜ&ⓕ a·ma·*ter*
ambassador embajador/embajadora ⓜ/ⓕ em·ba·ha·*dor*/em·ba·ha·*do*·ra
among entre *en*·tre
anarchist anarquista ⓜ&ⓕ a·nar·*kees*·ta
ancient antiguo/a ⓜ/ⓕ an·*tee*·gwo/a
and y ee
angry enojado/a ⓜ/ⓕ e·no·*ha*·do/a
animal animal ⓜ a·nee·*mal*
ankle tobillo ⓜ to·*bee*·yo
answer respuesta ⓕ res·*pwes*·ta
answering machine contestadora ⓕ kon·tes·ta·*do*·ra
ant hormiga ⓕ or·*mee*·ga
anthology antología ⓕ an·to·lo·*hee*·a
antibiotics antibióticos ⓜ pl an·tee·*byo*·tee·kos
antimalarial tablets pastillas ⓕ pl antipalúdicas pas·*tee*·yas an·tee·pa·*loo*·dee·kas
antinuclear antinuclear an·tee·noo·kle·*ar*
antique antigüedad ⓕ an·tee·gwe·*dad*
antiseptic antiséptico ⓜ an·tee·*sep*·tee·ko
any (singular) alguno/a ⓜ/ⓕ al·*goo*·no/a
any (plural) algunos/as ⓜ/ⓕ al·*goo*·nos/as
appendix apéndice ⓜ a·*pen*·dee·se
apple manzana ⓕ man·*sa*·na
appointment cita ⓕ *see*·ta
apricot chabacano ⓜ cha·ba·*ka*·no
archaeological arqueológico/a ⓜ/ⓕ ar·ke·o·*lo*·hee·ko/a
archaeologist arqueólogo/a ⓜ/ⓕ ar·ke·o·*lo*·go/a
architect arquitecto/a ⓜ/ⓕ ar·kee·*tek*·to/a
architecture arquitectura ⓕ ar·kee·tek·*too*·ra
argue discutir dees·koo·*teer*
arm brazo ⓜ *bra*·so
army ejército ⓜ e·*her*·see·to
arrest arrestar/detener a·res·*tar*/de·te·*ner*
arrivals llegadas ⓕ pl ye·*ga*·das
arrive llegar ye·*gar*
art arte ⓜ *ar*·te
art gallery galería ⓕ de arte ga·le·*ree*·a de *ar*·te
artichoke alcachofa ⓕ al·ka·*cho*·fa
artist artista ⓜ&ⓕ ar·*tees*·ta
ashtray cenicero ⓜ se·nee·*se*·ro
Asia Asia ⓕ *a*·sya
ask (a question) preguntar pre·goon·*tar*
ask (for something) pedir pe·*deer*
aspirin aspirina ⓕ as·pee·*ree*·na
assault agresión ⓕ a·gre·*syon*
asthma asma ⓜ *as*·ma
at the back (behind) detrás de de·*tras* de
athletics atletismo ⓜ at·le·*tees*·mo
atmosphere atmósfera ⓕ at·*mos*·fe·ra
aubergine berenjena ⓕ be·ren·*he*·na

aunt tía ⓕ *tee*·a
Australia Australia ⓕ ow·*stra*·lya
Australian Rules football fútbol ⓜ australiano *foot*·bol ows·tra·*lya*·no
automatic teller machine cajero ⓜ automático ka·*he*·ro ow·to·*ma*·tee·ko
autumn otoño ⓜ o·*to*·nyo
avenue avenida ⓕ a·ve·*nee*·da
avocado aguacate ⓜ a·gwa·*ka*·te
Aztec azteca ⓜ&ⓕ as·*te*·ka

B

B&W (film) blanco y negro *blan*·ko ee *ne*·gro
baby bebé ⓜ be·*be*
baby food alimento ⓜ para bebé a·lee·*men*·to *pa*·ra be·*be*
baby powder talco ⓜ para bebé *tal*·ko *pa*·ra be·*be*
babysitter niñera ⓕ nee·*nye*·ra
back (of body) espalda ⓕ es·*pal*·da
back (of chair) respaldo ⓜ res·*pal*·do
backpack mochila ⓕ mo·*chee*·la
bacon tocino ⓜ to·*see*·no
bad malo/a ⓜ/ⓕ *ma*·lo/a
bag bolsa ⓕ *bol*·sa
baggage equipaje ⓜ e·kee·*pa*·he
baggage allowance límite ⓜ de equipaje *lee*·mee·te de e·kee·*pa*·he
baggage claim entrega ⓕ de equipaje en·*tre*·ga de e·kee·*pa*·he
bakery panadería ⓕ pa·na·de·*ree*·a
balance (account) saldo ⓜ *sal*·do
balcony balcón ⓜ bal·*kon*
ball pelota ⓕ pe·*lo*·ta
ballet ballet ⓜ ba·*le*
banana plátano ⓜ *pla*·ta·no
band grupo ⓜ *groo*·po
bandage vendaje ⓜ ven·*da*·he
Band-Aids curitas ⓕ pl koo·*ree*·tas
bank banco ⓜ *ban*·ko
bank account cuenta ⓕ bancaria *kwen*·ta ban·*ka*·rya
banknotes billetes ⓜ pl bee·*ye*·tes
baptism bautizo ⓜ bow·*tee*·so
bar bar ⓜ bar
bar (with live music) bar ⓜ con música en vivo bar kon *moo*·see·ka en *vee*·vo
barber barbero ⓜ bar·*beh*·ro
baseball béisbol ⓜ *bays*·bol
basket canasta ⓕ ka·*nas*·ta
basketball básquetbol/básquet ⓜ *bahs*·ket·bol/*bahs*·ket
bathtub tina ⓕ *tee*·na
bathing suit traje ⓜ de baño *tra*·he de *ba*·nyo
bathroom baño ⓜ *ba*·nyo
battery (car) batería ⓕ ba·te·*ree*·a
battery (small) pila ⓕ *pee*·la
be (ongoing) ser ser
be (temporary) estar es·*tar*
beach playa ⓕ *pla*·ya
beans frijoles ⓜ pl free·*ho*·les
beautiful hermoso/a ⓜ/ⓕ er·*mo*·so/a
beauty salon salón ⓜ de belleza sa·*lon* de be·*ye*·sa
because porque *por*·ke
bed cama ⓕ *ka*·ma
bedding ropa ⓕ de cama *ro*·pa de *ka*·ma
bedroom habitación ⓕ a·bee·ta·*syon*
bee abeja ⓕ a·*be*·ha
beef carne ⓕ de res *kar*·ne de res
beer cerveza ⓕ ser·*ve*·sa
beetroot betabel ⓜ be·ta·*bel*
before antes *an*·tes
beggar limosnero/a ⓜ/ⓕ lee·mos·*ne*·ro/a
begin comenzar ko·men·*sar*
behind detrás de de·*tras* de
below abajo a·*ba*·ho
best mejor me·*hor*
bet apuesta ⓕ a·*pwes*·ta
better mejor me·*hor*
between entre *en*·tre
Bible Biblia ⓕ *bee*·blya
bicycle bicicleta ⓕ bee·see·*kle*·ta
big grande *gran*·de
bike bici ⓕ *bee*·see

B ENGLISH – MEXICAN SPANISH

bike chain cadena ⓕ de bici ka·*de*·na de *bee*·see
bike path ciclovía ⓕ see·klo·*vee*·a
bill (account) cuenta ⓕ *kwen*·ta
biodegradable biodegradable bee·o·de·gra·*da*·ble
biography biografía ⓕ bee·o·gra·*fee*·a
bird pájaro ⓜ *pa*·ha·ro
birth certificate acta ⓕ de nacimiento *ak*·ta de na·see·*myen*·to
birthday cumpleaños ⓜ koom·ple·*a*·nyos
birthday cake pastel ⓜ de cumpleaños pas·*tel* de koom·ple·*a*·nyos
biscuit galleta ⓕ ga·*ye*·ta
bite (dog) mordedura ⓕ mor·de·*doo*·ra
bite (food) bocado ⓜ bo·*ka*·do
bite (insect) picadura ⓕ pee·ka·*doo*·ra
black negro/a ⓜ/ⓕ *ne*·gro/a
blanket cobija ⓕ ko·*bee*·ha
bleed sangrar san·*grar*
blind ciego/a ⓜ/ⓕ *sye*·go/a
blister ampolla ⓕ am·*po*·ya
blocked bloqueado/a ⓜ/ⓕ blo·ke·*a*·do/a
blood sangre ⓕ *san*·gre
blood group grupo ⓜ sanguíneo *groo*·po san·*gee*·ne·o
blood pressure presión ⓕ arterial pre·*syon* ar·te·*ryal*
blood test análisis ⓜ de sangre a·*na*·lee·sees de *san*·gre
blue azul a·*sool*
board (ship, etc) embarcar em·bar·*kar*
boarding house pensión ⓕ pen·*syon*
boarding pass pase ⓜ de abordar *pa*·se de a·bor·*dar*
boat barco ⓜ *bar*·ko
body cuerpo ⓜ *kwer*·po
bomb bomba ⓕ *bom*·ba
bone hueso ⓜ *we*·so
book libro ⓜ *lee*·bro
book (reserve) reservar re·ser·*var*
booked out lleno/a ⓜ/ⓕ *ye*·no/a
bookshop librería ⓕ lee·bre·*ree*·a
boots botas ⓕ pl *bo*·tas
border frontera ⓕ fron·*te*·ra
boring aburrido/a ⓜ/ⓕ a·boo·*ree*·do/a
borrow pedir prestado pe·*deer* pres·*ta*·do
botanic garden jardín ⓜ botánico k\ har·*deen* bo·*ta*·nee·ko
both ambos/as ⓜ/ⓕ pl *am*·bos/as
bottle botella ⓕ bo·*te*·ya
bottle opener destapador ⓜ des·ta·pa·*dor*
bottle shop tienda ⓕ de abarrotes *tyen*·da de a·ba·*ro*·tes
bowl tazón ⓜ ta·*son*
box caja ⓕ *ka*·ha
boxer shorts boxers ⓜ pl *bok*·sers
boxing boxeo ⓜ bok·*se*·o
boy niño ⓜ *nee*·nyo
boyfriend novio ⓜ *no*·vyo
bra brassiere ⓜ bra·*syer*
braille braille ⓜ *brai*·le
brakes frenos ⓜ pl *fre*·nos
branch office sucursal ⓕ soo·koor·*sal*
brandy brandy ⓜ *bran*·dee
brave valiente va·*lyen*·te
bread pan ⓜ pan
bread roll bolillo ⓜ bo·*lee*·yo
brown bread pan ⓜ integral pan een·te·*gral*
rye bread pan ⓜ de centeno pan de sen·*te*·no
sourdough bread pan ⓜ de levadura fermentada pan de le·va·*doo*·ra fer·men·*ta*·da
white bread pan ⓜ blanco pan *blan*·ko
break romper rom·*per*
break down descomponerse des·kom·po·*ner*·se
breakfast desayuno ⓜ de·sa·*yoo*·no
breast (poultry) pechuga ⓕ pe·*choo*·ga
breasts senos ⓜ pl *se*·nos
breasts (colloquial) chichis ⓕ pl *chee*·chees

breathe respirar *res·pee·rar*
bribe soborno ⓜ / mordida ⓕ *so·bor·no/mor·dee·da*
bribe sobornar/dar mordida *so·bor·nar/dar mor·dee·da*
bridge puente ⓜ *pwen·te*
briefcase portafolios ⓜ *por·ta·fo·lyos*
brilliant brillante *bree·yan·te*
bring traer *tra·er*
brochure folleto ⓜ *fo·ye·to*
broken roto/a ⓜ/ⓕ *ro·to/a*
bronchitis bronquitis ⓜ *bron·kee·tees*
brother hermano ⓜ *er·ma·no*
brown café *ka·fe*
bruise moretón ⓜ *mo·re·ton*
bucket cubeta ⓕ *koo·be·ta*
Buddhist budista ⓜ&ⓕ *boo·dees·ta*
budget presupuesto ⓜ *pre·soo·pwes·to*
buffet buffet ⓜ *boo·fe*
bug bicho ⓜ *bee·cho*
build construir *kon·stroo·eer*
building edificio ⓜ *e·dee·fee·syo*
bull toro ⓜ *to·ro*
bullfight corrida ⓕ (de toros) *ko·ree·da (de to·ros)*
bullring plaza ⓕ de toros *pla·sa de to·ros*
bum (body) nalga ⓕ *nal·ga*
burn quemadura ⓕ *ke·ma·doo·ra*
burn (something) quemar *ke·mar*
bus (city) autobús ⓜ *ow·to·boos*
bus (intercity) camión ⓜ *ka·myon*
bus station estación ⓕ de autobuses *es·ta·syon de ow·to·boo·ses*
bus stop parada ⓕ de autobuses *pa·ra·da de ow·to·boo·ses*
business negocios ⓜ pl *ne·go·syos*
business class clase ⓕ ejecutiva *kla·se e·he·koo·tee·va*
business person comerciante ⓜ&ⓕ *ko·mer·syan·te*
busker artista callejero/a ⓜ/ⓕ *ar·tees·ta ka·ye·he·ro/a*
busy ocupado/a ⓜ/ⓕ *o·koo·pa·do/a*
but pero *pe·ro*
butcher's shop carnicería ⓕ *kar·nee·se·ree·a*
butter mantequilla ⓕ *man·te·kee·ya*
butterfly mariposa ⓕ *ma·ree·po·sa*
buttons botones ⓜ pl *bo·to·nes*
buy comprar *kom·prar*

C

cabbage col ⓕ *kol*
cable cable ⓜ *ka·ble*
cable car teleférico ⓜ *te·le·fe·ree·ko*
cactus cactus ⓜ *kak·toos*
cactus worms gusanos ⓜ pl de maguey *goo·sa·nos de ma·gay*
cafe café ⓜ *ka·fe*
cake pastel ⓜ *pas·tel*
cake shop pastelería ⓕ *pas·te·le·ree·a*
calculator calculadora ⓕ *kal·koo·la·do·ra*
calendar calendario ⓜ *ka·len·da·ryo*
calf becerro ⓜ *be·se·ro*
camera cámara ⓕ *ka·ma·ra*
camera shop tienda ⓕ de fotografía *tyen·da de fo·to·gra·fee·a*
camp acampar *a·kam·par*
camping store tienda ⓕ de camping *tyen·da de kam·peen*
campsite área ⓕ para acampar *a·re·a pa·ra a·kam·par*
can (tin) lata ⓕ *la·ta*
can (be able) poder *po·der*
can opener abrelatas ⓜ *a·bre·la·tas*
Canada Canadá *ka·na·da*
cancel cancelar *kan·se·lar*
cancer cáncer ⓜ *kan·ser*
candle vela ⓕ *ve·la*
candy dulces ⓜ pl *dool·ses*
cantaloupe melón ⓜ cantaloupe *me·lon kan·ta·loop*
capsicum pimiento ⓜ *pee·myen·to*
car coche ⓜ *ko·che*
car hire renta ⓕ de coches *ren·ta de ko·ches*
car owner's title factura ⓕ del coche *fak·too·ra del ko·che*

car park estacionamiento ⓜ es·ta·syo·na·*myen*·to
car registration matrícula ⓕ ma·*tree*·koo·la
caravan caravana ⓕ ka·ra·*va*·na
cards (game) cartas ⓕ pl *kar*·tas
cards (paper) tarjetas ⓕ pl tar·*heh*·tas
care (about something) preocuparse por pre·o·koo·*par*·se por
care (for someone) cuidar de kwee·*dar* de
caring bondadoso/a ⓜ/ⓕ bon·da·*do*·so/a
carpenter carpintero ⓜ kar·peen·*te*·ro
carrot zanahoria ⓕ sa·na·*o*·rya
carry llevar ye·*var*
carton cartón ⓜ kar·*ton*
cash efectivo ⓜ e·fek·*tee*·vo
cash (a cheque) cambiar (un cheque) kam·*byar* (oon *che*·ke)
cash register caja ⓕ *ka*·ha
cashew nut nuez ⓕ de la India nwes de la *een*·dya
cashier cajero/a ⓜ/ⓕ ka·*he*·ro/a
casino casino ⓜ ka·*see*·no
cassette cassette ⓜ ka·*set*
castle castillo ⓜ kas·*tee*·yo
casual work trabajo ⓜ eventual tra·*ba*·ho e·ven·*twal*
cat gato/a ⓜ/ⓕ *ga*·to/a
cathedral catedral ⓕ ka·te·*dral*
Catholic católico/a ⓜ/ⓕ ka·*to*·lee·ko/a
cauliflower coliflor ⓕ ko·lee·*flor*
caves cuevas ⓕ pl *kwe*·vas
celebrate (an event) celebrar se·le·*brar*
celebration celebración ⓕ se·le·bra·*syon*
cell phone celular ⓜ se·loo·*lar*
cemetery cementerio ⓜ se·men·*te*·ryo
cent centavo ⓜ sen·*ta*·vo
centimetre centímetro ⓜ sen·*tee*·me·tro
Central America Centroamérica ⓕ sen·tro·a·*me*·ree·ka
central heating calefacción ⓕ central ka·le·fak·*syon* sen·*tral*
centre centro ⓜ *sen*·tro
ceramic cerámica ⓕ se·*ra*·mee·ka
cereal cereal ⓜ se·re·*al*
certificate certificado ⓜ ser·tee·fee·*ka*·do
chair silla ⓕ *see*·ya
champagne champán ⓜ cham·*pan*
chance oportunidad ⓕ o·por·too·nee·*dad*
change (money) cambio ⓜ *kam*·byo
change cambiar kam·*byar*
changing rooms probadores ⓜ pl pro·ba·*do*·res
charming encantador/encantadora ⓜ/ⓕ en·kan·ta·*dor*/en·kan·ta·*do*·ra
chat up ligar lee·*gar*
cheap barato/a ⓜ/ⓕ ba·*ra*·to/a
cheat tramposo/a ⓜ/ⓕ tram·*po*·so/a
check revisar re·vee·*sar*
check (bank) cheque ⓜ *che*·ke
check (bill) cuenta ⓕ *kwen*·ta
check-in (flight) documentación ⓕ do·koo·men·ta·*syon*
check-in (hotel) registro ⓜ re·*hees*·tro
checkpoint control ⓜ kon·*trol*
cheese queso ⓜ *ke*·so
chef chef ⓜ&ⓕ chef
chemist (person) farmacéutico/a ⓜ/ⓕ far·ma·*sew*·tee·ko/a
chemist (shop) farmacia ⓕ far·*ma*·sya
cheque cheque ⓜ *che*·ke
chess ajedrez ⓜ a·he·*dres*
chest pecho ⓜ *pe*·cho
chewing gum chicle ⓜ *chee*·kle
chicken pollo ⓜ *po*·yo
chicken breast pechuga ⓕ de pollo pe·*choo*·ga de *po*·yo
chickpeas garbanzos ⓜ pl gar·*ban*·sos
child niño/a ⓜ/ⓕ *nee*·nyo/a

child's car seat asiento ⓜ de seguridad para bebés a·*syen*·to de se·goo·ree·*dad* pa·ra be·*bes*
childminding service servicio de niñera ⓜ ser·*vee*·cyo de nee·*nye*·ra
children niños ⓜ&ⓕ pl *nee*·nyos
chili chile ⓜ *chee*·le
chili sauce salsa ⓕ picante *sal*·sa pee·*kan*·te
chocolate chocolate ⓜ cho·ko·*la*·te
choose elegir e·le·*heer*
Christian cristiano/a ⓜ/ⓕ krees·*tya*·no/a
Christmas Day Navidad ⓕ na·vee·*dad*
Christmas Eve Nochebuena ⓕ no·che·*bwe*·na
church iglesia ⓕ ee·*gle*·sya
cider sidra ⓕ *see*·dra
cigar puro ⓜ *poo*·ro
cigarette cigarro ⓜ see·*ga*·ro
cigarette lighter encendedor ⓜ en·sen·de·*dor*
cigarette machine máquina ⓕ de tabaco *ma*·kee·na de ta·*ba*·ko
cigarette papers papel ⓜ de fumar pa·*pel* de foo·*mar*
cinema cine ⓜ *see*·ne
cinnamon canela ⓕ ka·*ne*·la
circus circo ⓜ *seer*·ko
citizenship ciudadanía ⓕ syoo·da·da·*nee*·a
city ciudad ⓕ syoo·*dad*
city centre centro ⓜ de la ciudad *sen*·tro de la syoo·*dad*
city walls murallas ⓕ pl moo·*ra*·yas
civil rights derechos ⓜ pl civiles de·*re*·chos see·*vee*·les
classical clásico/a ⓜ/ⓕ *kla*·see·ko/a
clean limpio/a ⓜ/ⓕ *leem*·pyo/a
cleaning trabajo ⓜ de limpieza tra·*ba*·ho de leem·*pye*·sa
client cliente/a ⓜ/ⓕ klee·*en*·te/a
cliff acantilado ⓜ a·kan·tee·*la*·do
climb escalar es·ka·*lar*
cloak capa ⓜ *ka*·pa
cloakroom guardarropa ⓜ gwar·da·*ro*·pa
clock reloj ⓜ re·*loh*
close (nearby) cerca *ser*·ka
close (shut) cerrar se·*rar*
closed cerrado/a ⓜ/ⓕ se·*ra*·do/a
clothes line tendedero ⓜ ten·de·*de*·ro
clothing ropa ⓕ *ro*·pa
clothing store tienda ⓕ de ropa *tyen*·da de *ro*·pa
cloud nube ⓕ *noo*·be
cloudy nublado noo·*bla*·do
clove (of garlic) diente (de ajo) *dyen*·te (de *a*·ho)
cloves clavos ⓜ pl de olor *kla*·vos de o·*lor*
clutch embrague ⓜ em·*bra*·ge
coach entrenador/entrenadora ⓜ/ⓕ en·tre·na·*dor*/en·tre·na·*do*·ra
coast costa ⓕ *kos*·ta
cocaine cocaína ⓕ ko·ka·*ee*·na
cockroach cucaracha ⓕ koo·ka·*ra*·cha
cocoa cacao ⓜ ka·*kow*
coconut coco ⓜ *ko*·ko
codeine codeína ⓕ ko·de·*ee*·na
coffee café ⓜ ka·*fe*
coins monedas ⓕ pl mo·*ne*·das
cold frío/a ⓜ/ⓕ *free*·o/a
cold (illness) resfriado ⓜ res·free·*a*·do
colleague colega ⓜ&ⓕ ko·*le*·ga
collect call llamada ⓕ por cobrar ya·*ma*·da por ko·*brar*
college universidad ⓕ oo·nee·ver·see·*dad*
colour color ⓜ ko·*lor*
colour film película ⓕ en color pe·*lee*·koo·la en ko·*lor*
comb peine ⓜ *pay*·ne
comb peinar pay·*nar*
come venir ve·*neer*
come (arrive) llegar ye·*gar*
comedy comedia ⓕ ko·*me*·dya
comfortable cómodo/a ⓜ/ⓕ *ko*·mo·do/a
communion comunión ⓕ ko·moo·*nyon*

communist comunista ⓜ&ⓕ ko·moo·*nees*·ta
companion compañero/a ⓜ/ⓕ kom·pa·*nye*·ro/a
company compañía ⓕ kom·pa·*nyee*·a
compass brújula ⓕ *broo*·hoo·la
complain quejarse ke·*har*·se
computer computadora ⓕ kom·poo·ta·*do*·ra
computer game juego ⓜ de computadora *hwe*·go de kom·poo·ta·*do*·ra
concert concierto ⓜ kon·*syer*·to
conditioner acondicionador ⓜ a·kon·dee·syo·na·*dor*
condoms condones ⓜ pl kon·*do*·nes
confession confesión ⓕ kon·fe·*syon*
confirm confirmar kon·feer·*mar*
connection conexión ⓕ ko·nek·*syon*
conservative conservador/conservadora ⓜ/ⓕ kon·ser·va·*dor*/kon·ser·va·*do*·ra
constipation estreñimiento ⓜ es·tre·nyee·*myen*·to
consulate consulado ⓜ kon·soo·*la*·do
contact lenses pupilentes ⓜ pl poo·pee·*len*·tes
contraceptives anticonceptivos ⓜ pl an·tee·kon·sep·*tee*·vos
contract contrato ⓜ kon·*tra*·to
convenience store tienda ⓕ de abarrotes *tyen*·da de a·ba·*ro*·tes
convenience liquor store depósito ⓜ de·*po*·see·to
convent convento ⓜ kon·*ven*·to
cook cocinero/a ⓜ/ⓕ ko·see·*ne*·ro/a
cook cocinar ko·see·*nar*
cookie galleta ⓕ ga·*ye*·ta
corn maíz ⓜ ma·*ees*
corn flakes hojuelas ⓕ pl de maíz o·*hwe*·las de ma·*ees*
corner esquina ⓕ es·*kee*·na
corrupt corrupto/a ⓜ/ⓕ ko·*roop*·to/a
cost costo ⓜ *kos*·to
cost costar kos·*tar*
cottage cheese queso ⓜ cottage *ke*·so *ko*·ta·he
cotton algodón ⓜ al·go·*don*
cotton balls bolas ⓕ pl de algodón *bo*·las de al·go·*don*
cough tos ⓕ tos
cough medicine jarabe ⓜ para la tos ha·*ra*·be *pa*·ra la tos
count contar kon·*tar*
counter (in shop) mostrador ⓜ mos·tra·*dor*
country país ⓜ pa·*ees*
countryside campo ⓜ *kam*·po
coupon cupón ⓜ koo·*pon*
courgette calabacita ⓕ ka·la·ba·*see*·ta
court (tennis) cancha ⓕ de tenis *kan*·cha de *te*·nees
cous cous cus cus ⓜ koos koos
cover charge cover ⓜ *ko*·ver
cow vaca ⓕ *va*·ka
crab cangrejo ⓜ kan·*gre*·ho
crackers galletas ⓕ pl saladas ga·*ye*·tas sa·*la*·das
craft artesanía ⓕ pl ar·te·sa·*nee*·a
crash choque ⓜ *cho*·ke
crazy loco/a ⓜ/ⓕ *lo*·ko/a
cream crema ⓕ *kre*·ma
cream cheese queso ⓜ crema *ke*·so *kre*·ma
creche guardería ⓕ gwar·de·*ree*·a
credit card tarjeta ⓕ de crédito tar·*he*·ta de *kre*·dee·to
cricket (sport) críquet ⓜ *kree*·ket
crop cosecha ⓕ ko·*se*·cha
crowded lleno/a ⓜ/ⓕ *ye*·no/a
cucumber pepino ⓜ pe·*pee*·no
cuddle abrazo ⓜ a·*bra*·so
cuddle abrazar a·bra·*sar*
cup taza ⓕ *ta*·sa
cupboard alacena ⓕ a·la·*se*·na
currency exchange cambio ⓜ (de moneda) *kam*·byo (de mo·*ne*·da)
current (electricity) corriente ⓕ ko·*ryen*·te
current affairs informativo ⓜ een·for·ma·*tee*·vo
curry curry ⓜ *koo*·ree

curry powder curry ⓜ en polvo koo·ree en pol·vo
custard flan ⓜ flan
customs aduana ⓕ a·dwa·na
cut cortar kor·tar
cutlery cubiertos ⓜ pl koo·byer·tos
CV currículum ⓜ koo·ree·koo·loom
cycle andar en bicicleta an·dar en bee·see·kle·ta
cycling ciclismo ⓜ see·klees·mo
cyclist ciclista ⓜ&ⓕ see·klees·ta
cystitis cistitis ⓕ sees·tee·tees

D

dad papá ⓜ pa·pa
daily diariamente dya·rya·men·te
dance bailar bai·lar
dancing/dance baile ⓜ bai·le
dangerous peligroso/a ⓜ/ⓕ pe·lee·gro·so/a
dark oscuro/a ⓜ/ⓕ os·koo·ro/a
data projector cañon ⓜ proyector ka·nyon pro·yek·tor
date (appointment) cita ⓕ see·ta
date (day) fecha ⓕ fe·cha
date (a person) salir con sa·leer kon
date of birth fecha ⓕ de nacimiento fe·cha de na·see·myen·to
daughter hija ⓕ ee·ha
dawn amanecer ⓜ a·ma·ne·ser
day día ⓜ dee·a
day after tomorrow pasado mañana pa·sa·do ma·nya·na
day before yesterday antier an·tyer
dead muerto/a ⓜ/ⓕ mwer·to/a
deaf sordo/a ⓜ/ⓕ sor·do/a
deal (cards) repartir re·par·teer
decide decidir de·see·deer
deep profundo/a ⓜ/ⓕ pro·foon·do/a
deforestation deforestación ⓕ de·fo·res·ta·syon
degree título ⓜ tee·too·lo
delay demora ⓕ de·mo·ra
delirious delirante de·lee·ran·te
deliver entregar en·tre·gar
democracy democracia ⓕ de·mo·kra·sya
demonstration (protest) manifestación ⓕ ma·nee·fes·ta·syon
dental floss hilo ⓜ dental ee·lo den·tal
dentist dentista ⓜ den·tees·ta
deny negar ne·gar
deodorant desodorante ⓜ de·so·do·ran·te
depart salir de sa·leer de
department store tienda ⓕ departamental tyen·da de·par·ta·men·tal
departure salida ⓕ sa·lee·da
deposit (bank) depósito ⓜ de·po·see·to
descendant descendiente ⓜ de·sen·dyen·te
desert desierto ⓜ de·syer·to
design diseño ⓜ dee·se·nyo
destination destino ⓜ des·tee·no
destroy destruir des·troo·eer
detail detalle ⓜ de·ta·ye
diabetes diabetes ⓕ dee·a·be·tes
dial tone tono de marcar ⓜ toh·no de mar·kar
diaper pañal ⓜ pa·nyal
diaphragm diafragma ⓜ dee·a·frag·ma
diarrhoea diarrea ⓕ dee·a·re·a
diary agenda ⓕ a·hen·da
dice dados ⓜ pl da·dos
dictionary diccionario ⓜ deek·syo·na·ryo
die morir mo·reer
diet dieta ⓕ dye·ta
different diferente dee·fe·ren·te
difficult difícil dee·fee·seel
dining car vagón ⓜ restaurante va·gon res·tow·ran·te
dinner cena ⓕ se·na
direct directo/a ⓜ/ⓕ dee·rek·to/a
direct-dial marcación ⓕ directa mar·ka·syon dee·rek·ta
director director/directora ⓜ/ⓕ dee·rek·tor/dee·rek·to·ra

dirty sucio/a ⓜ/ⓕ *soo·syo/a*
disabled discapacitado/a ⓜ/ⓕ *dees·ka·pa·see·ta·do/a*
disco discoteca ⓕ *dees·ko·te·ka*
discount descuento ⓜ *des·kwen·to*
discover descubrir *des·koo·breer*
discrimination discriminación ⓕ *dees·kree·mee·na·syon*
disease enfermedad ⓕ *en·fer·me·dad*
disk disco ⓜ *dees·ko*
disposable desechable *de·se·cha·ble*
diving buceo ⓜ *boo·se·o*
diving equipment equipo ⓜ de buceo *e·kee·po de boo·se·o*
divorced divorciado/a ⓜ/ⓕ *dee·vor·sya·do/a*
dizzy mareado/a ⓜ/ⓕ *ma·re·a·do/a*
do hacer *a·ser*
doctor doctor/doctora ⓜ/ⓕ *dok·tor/dok·to·ra*
documentary documental ⓜ *do·koo·men·tal*
dog perro/a ⓜ/ⓕ *pe·ro/a*
dole paro ⓜ *pa·ro*
doll muñeca ⓕ *moo·nye·ka*
dollar dólar ⓜ *do·lar*
domestic flight vuelo ⓜ nacional *vwe·lo na·syo·nal*
donkey burro ⓜ *boo·ro*
door puerta ⓕ *pwer·ta*
dope mota ⓕ *mo·ta*
double doble *do·ble*
double bed cama ⓕ matrimonial *ka·ma ma·tree·mo·nyal*
double room habitación ⓕ doble *a·bee·ta·syon do·ble*
down hacia abajo *a·sya a·ba·ho*
downhill cuesta abajo *kwes·ta a·ba·ho*
dozen docena ⓕ *do·se·na*
drama drama ⓜ *dra·ma*
draw dibujar *dee·boo·har*
dream soñar *so·nyar*
dress vestido ⓜ *ves·tee·do*
dried fruit fruta ⓕ seca *froo·ta se·ka*
drink bebida ⓕ *be·bee·da*
drink tomar *to·mar*
drive conducir *kon·doo·seer*
driving licence licencia ⓕ de manejo *lee·sen·sya de ma·ne·ho*
drug (medicinal) medicina ⓕ *me·dee·see·na*
drug addiction drogadicción ⓕ *dro·ga·deek·syon*
drug dealer traficante ⓜ&ⓕ de drogas *tra·fee·kan·te de dro·gas*
drugs (illegal) drogas ⓕ pl *dro·gas*
drums batería ⓕ *ba·te·ree·a*
drumstick muslo ⓜ de pollo *moos·lo de po·yo*
drunk borracho/a ⓜ/ⓕ *bo·ra·cho/a*
dry seco/a ⓜ/ⓕ *se·ko/a*
dry secar *se·kar*
duck pato ⓜ *pa·to*
dummy (pacifier) chupón ⓜ *choo·pon*
during durante *doo·ran·te*

E

each cada *ka·da*
ear oreja ⓕ *o·re·ha*
early temprano *tem·pra·no*
earn ganar *ga·nar*
earplugs tapones ⓜ pl para los oídos *ta·po·nes pa·ra los o·ee·dos*
earrings aretes ⓜ pl *a·re·tes*
Earth Tierra ⓕ *tye·ra*
earthquake terremoto ⓜ *te·re·mo·to*
east este *es·te*
Easter Pascua ⓕ *pas·kwa*
easy fácil *fa·seel*
eat comer *ko·mer*
economy class clase ⓕ turísta *kla·se too·rees·ta*
eczema eczema ⓕ *ek·se·ma*
editor editor/editora ⓜ/ⓕ *e·dee·tor/e·dee·to·ra*
education educación ⓕ *e·doo·ka·syon*
eggplant berenjena ⓕ *be·ren·he·na*
egg huevo ⓜ *we·vo*
elections elecciones ⓕ pl *e·lek·syo·nes*

electrical store tienda ⓕ de electrónica tyen·da de el·ek·tron·ica
electricity electricidad ⓕ e·lek·tree·see·dad
elevator elevador ⓜ e·le·va·dor
embarrassed apenado/a ⓜ/ⓕ a·pe·na·do/a
embassy embajada ⓕ em·ba·ha·da
emergency emergencia ⓕ e·mer·hen·sya
emotional emocional e·mo·syo·nal
employee empleado/a ⓜ/ⓕ em·ple·a·do/a
employer jefe/jefa ⓜ/ⓕ he·fe/he·fa
empty vacío/a ⓜ/ⓕ va·see·o/a
end fin ⓜ feen
end terminar ter·mee·nar
endangered species especies ⓕ pl en peligro de extinción es·pe·syes en pe·lee·gro de ek·steen·syon
engine motor ⓜ mo·tor
engineer ingeniero/a ⓜ/ⓕ een·he·nye·ro/a
engineering ingeniería ⓕ een·he·nye·ree·a
England Inglaterra ⓕ een·gla·te·ra
English (language) inglés ⓜ een·gles
enjoy (oneself) divertirse dee·ver·teer·se
enough suficiente soo·fee·syen·te
enter entrar en·trar
entertainment guide guía ⓕ del ocio gee·a del o·syo
envelope sobre ⓜ so·bre
environment medio ⓜ ambiente me·dyo am·byen·te
epilepsy epilepsia ⓕ e·pee·lep·sya
equal opportunity igualdad ⓕ de oportunidades ee·gwal·dad de o·por·too·nee·da·des
equality igualdad ⓕ ee·gwal·dad
equipment equipo ⓜ e·kee·po
escalator escaleras ⓕ pl eléctricas es·ka·le·ras e·lek·tree·kas
Euro euro ⓜ e·oo·ro
Europe Europa ⓕ e·oo·ro·pa
euthanasia eutanasia ⓕ e·oo·ta·na·sya
evening noche ⓕ no·che
everything todo to·do
example ejemplo ⓜ e·hem·plo
excellent excelente ek·se·len·te
excess baggage exceso ⓜ de equipage ek·se·so de e·kee·pa·he
exchange cambio ⓜ kam·byo
exchange (money) cambiar kam·byar
exchange rate tipo ⓜ de cambio tee·po de kam·byo
excluded excluído/a ⓜ/ⓕ ek·skloo·ee·do/a
exhaust agotar a·go·tar
exhaust (car) escape ⓜ es·ka·pe
exhibit exponer ek·spo·ner
exhibition exposición ⓕ ek·spo·see·syon
exit salida ⓕ sa·lee·da
expensive caro/a ⓜ/ⓕ ka·ro/a
experience experiencia ⓕ ek·spe·ryen·sya
express expreso ⓜ ek·spre·so
express mail correo ⓜ expresso ko·re·o ek·spre·so
extension (visa) prórroga ⓕ pro·ro·ga
eye ojo ⓜ o·ho
eyebrows cejas ⓕ pl se·has
eye drops gotas ⓕ pl para los ojos go·tas pa·ra los o·hos

F

fabric tela ⓕ te·la
face cara ⓕ ka·ra
face cloth toallita ⓕ facial to·a·yee·ta fa·syal
factory fábrica ⓕ fa·bree·ka
factory worker obrero/a ⓜ/ⓕ o·bre·ro/a
fall caída ⓕ ka·ee·da
fall (season) otoño ⓜ o·to·nyo
family familia ⓕ fa·mee·lya
family name apellido ⓜ a·pe·yee·do
famous famoso/a ⓜ/ⓕ fa·mo·so/a

fan (supporter) aficionado ⓜ a·fee·syo·*na*·do
fan (machine) ventilador ⓜ ven·tee·la·*dor*
far lejos *le*·hos
farewell despedida ⓕ des·pe·*dee*·da
farm granja ⓕ *gran*·ha
farmer granjero/a ⓜ/ⓕ gran·*he*·ro/a
fart pedo ⓜ *pe*·do
fast rápido/a ⓜ/ⓕ *ra*·pee·do/a
fat (person) gordo/a ⓜ/ⓕ *gor*·do/a
fat (grease) grasa ⓕ *gra*·sa
father padre ⓜ *pa*·dre
father-in-law suegro ⓜ *swe*·gro
faucet llave ⓕ (del agua) *ya*·ve (del a·gwa)
fault falta ⓕ *fal*·ta
faulty defectuoso/a ⓜ/ⓕ de·fek·*two*·so/a
feed alimentar a·lee·men·*tar*
feel sentir sen·*teer*
feelings sentimientos ⓜ pl sen·tee·*myen*·tos
fence cerca ⓕ *ser*·ka
fencing (sport) esgrima ⓕ es·*gree*·ma
festival festival ⓜ fes·tee·*val*
fever fiebre ⓕ *fye*·bre
few pocos/as ⓜ/ⓕ pl *po*·kos/as
fiancé(e) prometido/a ⓜ/ⓕ pro·me·*tee*·do/a
fiction ficción ⓕ feek·*syon*
field campo ⓜ *kam*·po
fig higo ⓜ *ee*·go
fight pelea ⓕ pe·*le*·a
fight luchar loo·*char*
fill llenar ye·*nar*
film película ⓕ pe·*lee*·koo·la
film speed sensibilidad ⓕ de la película sen·see·bee·lee·*dad* de la pe·*lee*·koo·la
filtered con ⓕ filtro kon *feel*·tro
find encontrar en·kon·*trar*
fine (payment) multa ⓕ *mool*·ta
finger dedo ⓜ *de*·do
finish terminar ter·mee·*nar*
fire (general) fuego ⓜ *fwe*·go
fire (building) incendio ⓜ een·*sen*·dyo
fireplace chimenea ⓕ chee·me·*ne*·a
firewood leña ⓕ *le*·nya
first primero/a ⓜ/ⓕ pree·*me*·ro/a
first class primera clase ⓕ pree·*me*·ra *kla*·se
first name nombre ⓜ *nom*·bre
first-aid kit botiquín de primeros auxilios ⓜ bo·tee·*keen* de pree·*me*·ros awk·*see*·lyos
fish pez ⓜ pes
fish (as food) pescado ⓜ pes·*ka*·do
fish shop pescadería ⓕ pes·ka·de·*ree*·a
fishing pesca ⓕ *pes*·ka
fizzy con gas kon gas
flag bandera ⓕ ban·*de*·ra
flannel franela ⓕ fra·*ne*·la
flashlight linterna ⓕ leen·*ter*·na
flat plano/a ⓜ/ⓕ *pla*·no/a
flat (apartment) apartamento ⓜ a·par·ta·*men*·to
flea pulga ⓕ *pool*·ga
flippers aletas ⓕ pl a·*le*·tas
flooding inundación ⓕ ee·noon·da·*syon*
floor (ground) suelo ⓜ *swe*·lo
floor (storey) piso ⓜ *pee*·so
florist florista ⓜ&ⓕ flo·*rees*·ta
flour harina ⓕ a·*ree*·na
flower flor ⓕ flor
flower seller vendedor/vendedora de flores ⓜ/ⓕ ven·de·*dor*/ven·de·*do*·ra de *flo*·res
flu gripe ⓕ *gree*·pe
fly volar vo·*lar*
foggy neblinoso/a ⓜ/ⓕ ne·blee·*no*·so/a
folk (music) folklórico/a ⓜ/ⓕ fol·*klo*·ree·ko/a
follow seguir se·*geer*
food comida ⓕ ko·*mee*·da
food supplies víveres ⓜ pl *vee*·ve·res
fool imbécil ⓜ&ⓕ eem·*be*·seel
foot pie ⓜ pye
football (soccer) fútbol ⓜ *foot*·bol

footpath banqueta ⓕ ban·*ke*·ta
for para *pa*·ra
foreign extranjero/a ⓜ/ⓕ ek·stran·*he*·ro/a
foreign exchange office casa ⓕ de cambio *ka*·sa de *kam*·byo
forest bosque ⓜ *bos*·ke
forever para siempre *pa*·ra *syem*·pre
forget olvidar ol·vee·*dar*
forgive perdonar per·do·*nar*
fork tenedor ⓜ te·ne·*dor*
fortnight quincena ⓕ keen·*se*·na
foul asqueroso/a ⓜ/ⓕ as·ke·*ro*·so/a
foyer vestíbulo ⓜ ves·*tee*·boo·lo
fragile frágil *fra*·heel
France Francia ⓕ *fran*·sya
free (not bound) libre *lee*·bre
free (of charge) gratis *gra*·tees
freeze congelar kon·he·*lar*
friend amigo/a ⓜ/ⓕ a·*mee*·go/a
frost escarcha ⓕ es·*kar*·cha
frozen foods productos ⓜ pl congelados pro·*dook*·tos kon·he·*la*·dos
fruit fruta ⓕ *froo*·ta
fruit picking recolección ⓕ de fruta re·ko·lek·*syon* de *froo*·ta
fry freír fre·*eer*
frying pan sartén ⓜ sar·*ten*
fuel combustible ⓜ kom·boos·*tee*·ble
full (place/thing) lleno/a ⓜ/ⓕ *ye*·no/a
full-time tiempo ⓜ completo *tyem*·po kom·*ple*·to
fun diversión ⓕ dee·ver·*syon*
funeral funeral ⓜ foo·ne·*ral*
funny divertido/a ⓜ/ⓕ dee·ver·*tee*·do/a
furniture muebles ⓜ pl *mwe*·bles
future futuro ⓜ foo·*too*·ro

G

garlic ajo ⓜ *a*·ho
gas (for cooking) gas ⓜ gas
gas (petrol) gasolina ⓕ ga·so·*lee*·na
gay gay gay
gelatin gelatina ⓕ he·la·*tee*·na
general general he·ne·*ral*
Germany Alemania ⓕ a·le·*ma*·nya
gift regalo ⓜ re·*ga*·lo
gin ginebra ⓕ hee·*ne*·bra
ginger jengibre ⓜ hen·*hee*·bre
girl chica ⓕ *chee*·ka
girl (child) niña ⓕ *nee*·nya
girlfriend novia ⓕ *no*·vya
give dar dar
give (a gift) regalar re·ga·*lar*
glandular fever mononucleosis ⓜ mo·no·nyoo·klee·*oh*·sees
glass (drinking) vaso ⓜ *va*·so
glass (material) vidrio ⓜ *vee*·dryo
glass (of wine) copa ⓕ (de vino) *ko*·pa (de *vee*·no)
glasses lentes ⓜ pl *len*·tes
gloves guantes ⓜ pl *gwan*·tes
go ir eer
go out with salir con sa·*leer* kon
go shopping ir de compras eer de *kom*·pras
goal gol ⓜ gol
goalkeeper portero/a ⓜ/ⓕ por·*te*·ro/a
goat cabra ⓕ *ka*·bra
god dios ⓜ dyos
goddess diosa ⓕ *dyo*·sa
goggles goggles ⓜ pl *go*·gles
golf golf ⓜ golf
golf ball pelota ⓕ de golf pe·*lo*·ta de golf
golf course campo ⓜ de golf *kam*·po de golf
good bueno/a ⓜ/ⓕ *bwe*·no/a
goodbye adiós a·*dyos*
gorgeous guapo/a ⓜ/ⓕ *gwa*·po/a
government gobierno ⓜ go·*byer*·no
gram gramo ⓜ *gra*·mo
grandchild nieto/a ⓜ/ⓕ *nye*·to/a
grandfather abuelo ⓜ a·*bwe*·lo
grandmother abuela ⓕ a·*bwe*·la
grapefruit toronja ⓕ to·*ron*·ha
grapes uvas ⓕ pl *oo*·vas
grass pasto ⓜ *pas*·to
grasshoppers chapulines ⓜ pl cha·poo·*lee*·nes

grave tumba ⓕ *toom*·ba
gray gris grees
grease grasa ⓕ *gra*·sa
great padrísimo/a ⓜ/ⓕ pa·*dree*·see·mo/a
green verde *ver*·de
greengrocery 'supermercado ⓜ soo·per·mer·*ka*·do
grey gris grees
grocery tienda ⓕ de abarrotes *tyen*·da de a·ba·*ro*·tes
groundnut cacahuate ⓜ ka·ka·*wa*·te
grow crecer kre·*ser*
g-string tanga ⓕ *tan*·ga
guess adivinar a·dee·vee·*nar*
guide (audio) audioguía ⓕ ow·dyo·*gee*·a
guide (person) guía ⓜ&ⓕ *gee*·a
guide dog perro ⓜ guía *pe*·ro *gee*·a
guidebook guía ⓕ turística *gee*·a too·*rees*·tee·ka
guided tour recorrido ⓜ guiado re·ko·*ree*·do gee·a·do
guilty culpable kool·*pa*·ble
guitar guitarra ⓕ gee·*ta*·ra
gum chicle ⓕ *chee*·kle
gymnastics gimnasia ⓕ heem·*na*·sya
gynaecologist ginecólogo/a ⓜ/ⓕ hee·ne·*ko*·lo·go/a

H

hair peloⓜ *pe*·lo
hairbrush cepillo ⓜ se·*pee*·yo
haircut corte ⓜ de pelo *kor*·te de *pe*·lo
hairdresser peluquero/a ⓜ/ⓕ pe·loo·*ke*·ro/a
halal halal ha·*lal*
half medio/a ⓜ/ⓕ *me*·dyo/a
half a litre medio litro ⓜ *me*·dyo *lee*·tro
hallucinate alucinar a·loo·see·*nar*
ham jamón ⓜ ha·*mon*
hammer martillo ⓜ mar·*tee*·yo
hammock hamaca ⓕ a·*ma*·ka
hand mano ⓕ *ma*·no
handbag bolsa ⓕ *bol*·sa
handicrafts artesanías ⓕ pl ar·te·sa·*nee*·as
handkerchief pañuelo ⓜ pa·*nywe*·lo
handlebar manubrio ⓜ ma·*noo*·bryo
handmade hecho/a ⓜ/ⓕ a mano e·cho/a a *ma*·no
handsome guapo/a ⓜ/ⓕ *gwa*·po/a
happy feliz fe·*lees*
harassment acoso ⓜ a·*ko*·so
harbour puerto ⓜ *pwer*·to
hard duro/a ⓜ/ⓕ *doo*·ro/a
hardware store ferretería ⓕ fe·re·te·*ree*·a
hash hachís ⓜ ha·*shees*
hat sombrero ⓜ som·*bre*·ro
have tener te·*ner*
have a cold tener gripa te·*ner gree*·pa
have fun divertirse dee·ver·*teer*·se
hay fever alergia ⓕ al polen a·*ler*·hya al *po*·len
he él el
head cabeza ⓕ ka·*be*·sa
headache dolor ⓜ de cabeza do·*lor* de ka·*be*·sa
headlights faros ⓜ pl *fa*·ros
health salud ⓕ sa·*lood*
hear oír o·*eer*
hearing aid audífono ⓜ ow·*dee*·fo·no
heart corazón ⓜ ko·ra·*son*
heart condition cardiopatía ⓕ kar·dyo·pa·*tee*·a
heat calor ⓜ ka·*lor*
heater calentador ⓜ ka·len·ta·*dor*
heating calefacción ⓕ ka·le·fak·*syon*
heavy pesado/a ⓜ/ⓕ pe·*sa*·do/a
helmet casco ⓜ *kas*·ko
help ayudar a·yoo·*dar*
hepatitis hepatitis ⓕ e·pa·*tee*·tees
her su soo
herbalist yerbero/a ⓜ/ⓕ yer·*be*·ro/a
herbs hierbas ⓕ pl *yer*·bas
here aquí a·*kee*
heroin heroína ⓕ e·ro·*ee*·na
herring arenque ⓜ a·*ren*·ke
high alto/a ⓜ/ⓕ *al*·to/a

high school preparatoria ⓕ pre·pa·ra·to·rya
hike hacer senderismo a·ser sen·de·rees·mo
hiking senderismo ⓜ sen·de·rees·mo
hiking boots botas ⓕ pl de montaña bo·tas de mon·ta·nya
hiking routes senderos ⓜ pl sen·de·ros
hill colina ⓕ ko·lee·na
Hindu hindú ⓜ&ⓕ een·doo
hire rentar ren·tar
his su soo
historical histórico/a ⓜ/ⓕ ees·to·ree·ko/a
hitchhike pedir aventón pe·deer a·ven·ton
HIV positive seropositivo/a ⓜ/ⓕ se·ro·po·see·tee·vo/a
hockey hockey ⓜ ho·kee
holiday día ⓜ festivo dee·a fes·tee·vo
holidays vacaciones ⓕ pl va·ka·syo·nes
Holy Week Semana ⓕ Santa se·ma·na san·ta
home casa ⓕ ka·sa
homeless sin hogar seen o·gar
homemaker ama ⓕ de casa a·ma de ka·sa
homosexual homosexual ⓜ&ⓕ o·mo·sek·swal
honey miel ⓕ myel
honeymoon luna ⓕ de miel loo·na de myel
horoscope horóscopo ⓜ o·ros·ko·po
horse caballo ⓜ ka·ba·yo
horse riding equitación ⓕ e·kee·ta·syon
hospital hospital ⓜ os·pee·tal
hospitality hotelería ⓕ o·te·le·ree·a
hot caliente ka·lyen·te
hot water agua ⓜ caliente a·gwa ka·lyen·te
hotel hotel ⓜ o·tel
house casa ⓕ ka·sa
housework quehacer ⓜ ke·a·ser
how cómo ko·mo
how much cuánto kwan·to
hug abrazo ⓜ a·bra·so
huge enorme e·nor·me
human rights derechos ⓜ pl humanos de·re·chos oo·ma·nos
humanities humanidades ⓕ pl oo·ma·nee·da·des
hungover crudo/a ⓜ/ⓕ kroo·do/a
(be) hungry tener hambre te·ner am·bre
hunting caza ⓕ ka·sa
(be in a) hurry tener prisa te·ner pree·sa
hurt lastimar las·tee·mar
husband esposo ⓜ es·po·so

I

I yo yo
ice hielo ⓜ ye·lo
ice axe piolet ⓜ pyo·let
ice cream helado ⓜ e·la·do
ice-cream parlour heladería ⓕ e·la·de·ree·a
ice hockey hockey ⓜ sobre hielo ho·kee so·bre ye·lo
identification identificación ⓕ ee·den·tee·fee·ka·syon
idiot idiota ⓜ&ⓕ ee·dyo·ta
if si see
ill enfermo/a ⓜ/ⓕ en·fer·mo/a
immigration inmigración ⓕ een·mee·gra·syon
important importante eem·por·tan·te
in a hurry de prisa pree·sa
in front of enfrente de en·fren·te de
included incluído/a ⓜ/ⓕ een·kloo·ee·do/a
income tax impuesto ⓜ sobre la renta (ISR) eem·pwes·to so·bre la ren·ta (ee·ese·ere)
India India ⓕ een·dya
indicator indicador ⓜ een·dee·ka·dor
indigestion indigestión ⓕ een·dee·hes·tyon
industry industria ⓕ een·doos·trya

infection infección ⓕ een·fek·*syon*
inflammation inflamación ⓕ een·fla·ma·*syon*
influenza gripe ⓕ *gree*·pe
ingredient ingrediente ⓜ een·gre·*dyen*·te
inject inyectar een·yek·*tar*
injection inyección ⓕ een·yek·*syon*
injury herida ⓕ e·*ree*·da
innocent inocente ee·no·*sen*·te
inside adentro a·*den*·tro
instructor instructor/instructora ⓜ/ⓕ een·strook·*tor*/eens·trook·*to*·ra
insurance seguro ⓜ se·*goo*·ro
interesting interesante een·te·re·*san*·te
intermission intermedio ⓜ een·ter·*me*·dyo
international internacional een·ter·na·syo·*nal*
internet internet ⓕ een·ter·*net*
— cafe cibercafé ⓜ see·ber·ka·*fe*
interpreter intérprete ⓜ&ⓕ een·*ter*·pre·te
intersection intersección ⓕ een·ter·sek·*syon*
interview entrevista ⓕ en·tre·*vees*·ta
invite invitar een·vee·*tar*
Ireland Irlanda ⓕ eer·*lan*·da
iron (for clothes) plancha ⓕ *plan*·cha
island isla ⓕ *ees*·la
IT informática ⓕ een·for·*ma*·tee·ka
itch comezón ⓜ ko·me·*son*
itemised detallado/a ⓜ/ⓕ de·ta·*ya*·do/a
itinerary itinerario ⓜ ee·tee·ne·*ra*·ryo
IUD DIU ⓜ dee·ee·*oo*

J

jacket chamarra ⓕ cha·*ma*·ra
jail cárcel ⓕ *kar*·sel
jam mermelada ⓕ mer·me·*la*·da
Japan Japón ⓜ ha·*pon*
jar jarra ⓕ *ha*·ra
jaw mandíbula ⓕ man·*dee*·boo·la
jealous celoso/a ⓜ/ⓕ se·*lo*·so/a
jeans pantalones de mezclilla ⓜ pl pan·ta·*lo*·nes de mes·klee·ya
jeep jeep ⓜ yeep
Jehovah's Witness testigo ⓜ de Jehová tes·*tee*·go de he·o·*va*
jet lag jet lag ⓜ yet lag
jewellery joyería ⓕ ho·ye·*ree*·a
Jewish judío/a ⓜ/ⓕ hoo·*dee*·o/a
job trabajo ⓜ tra·*ba*·ho
jockey jockey ⓜ *yo*·kee
jogging correr ko·*rer*
joke broma ⓕ *bro*·ma
joke bromear bro·me·*ar*
journalist periodista ⓜ&ⓕ pe·ryo·*dees*·ta
judge juez ⓜ&ⓕ hwes
juice jugo ⓜ *hoo*·go
jump saltar sal·*tar*
jumper (sweater) sweater ⓜ *swe*·ter
jumper leads cables ⓜ pl pasacorrientes *ka*·bles pa·sa·ko·*ryen*·tes

K

ketchup cátsup ⓜ *kat*·soop
key llave ⓕ *ya*·ve
keyboard teclado ⓜ te·*kla*·do
kick patear pa·te·*ar*
kick (a goal) meter (un gol) me·*ter* (oon gol)
kill matar ma·*tar*
kilogram kilo ⓜ *kee*·lo
kilometre kilómetro ⓜ kee·*lo*·me·tro
kind amable a·*ma*·ble
kindergarten jardín ⓜ de niños har·*deen* de *nee*·nyos
king rey ⓜ ray
kiss beso ⓜ *be*·so
kiss besar be·*sar*
kitchen cocina ⓕ ko·*see*·na
kitten gatito/a ⓜ/ⓕ ga·*tee*·to/a
kiwifruit kiwi ⓜ *kee*·wee
knapsack mochila ⓕ mo·*chee*·la
knee rodilla ⓕ ro·*dee*·ya

knife cuchillo ⓜ *koo·chee·yo*
know (someone) conocer *ko·no·ser*
know (something) saber *sa·ber*
kosher kosher *ko·sher*

L

labourer obrero/a ⓜ/ⓕ *o·bre·ro/a*
lace encaje ⓜ *en·ka·he*
lager cerveza ⓕ clara *ser·ve·sa kla·ra*
lake lago ⓜ *la·go*
lamb borrego ⓜ *bo·re·go*
land tierra ⓕ *tye·ra*
landlady propietaria ⓕ *pro·pye·ta·rya*
landlord propietario ⓜ *pro·pye·ta·ryo*
languages idiomas ⓜ pl *ee·dyo·mas*
laptop laptop ⓜ *lap·top*
lard manteca ⓕ *man·te·ka*
large grande *gran·de*
laser pointer señalador ⓜ láser *se·nya·la·dor la·ser*
late tarde *tar·de*
laugh reír *re·eer*
laundrette lavandería ⓕ *la·van·de·ree·a*
laundry lavandería ⓕ *la·van·de·ree·a*
law ley ⓕ *lay*
law (field of study) derecho ⓜ *de·re·cho*
lawyer abogado/a ⓜ/ⓕ *a·bo·ga·do/a*
leader líder ⓜ&ⓕ *lee·der*
leaf hoja ⓕ *o·ha*
learn aprender *a·pren·der*
leather cuero ⓜ *kwe·ro*
lecturer profesor/profesora ⓜ/ⓕ *pro·fe·sor/pro·fe·so·ra*
ledge saliente ⓜ *sa·lyen·te*
leek poro ⓜ *po·ro*
left izquierda ⓕ *ees·kyer·da*
left luggage consigna ⓕ *kon·seeg·na*
left-wing de izquierda *de ees·kyer·da*
leg pierna ⓕ *pyer·na*
legal legal *le·gal*
legislation legislación ⓕ *le·hees·la·syon*
lemon limón amarillo ⓜ *lee·mon a·ma·ree·yo*
lemonade limonada ⓕ *lee·mo·na·da*
lens lente ⓜ *len·te*
Lent Cuaresma ⓕ *kwa·res·ma*
lentils lentejas ⓕ pl *len·te·has*
lesbian lesbiana ⓕ *les·bee·a·na*
less menos *me·nos*
letter carta ⓕ *kar·ta*
lettuce lechuga ⓕ *le·choo·ga*
LGBTIQ+ LGBTI+ *eh·leh·heh·beh·teh·ee·mas*
liar mentiroso/a ⓜ/ⓕ *men·tee·ro·so/a*
library biblioteca ⓕ *bee·blyo·te·ka*
lice piojos ⓜ pl *pyo·hos*
licence plate number número ⓜ de placa *noo·me·ro de pla·ka*
lie (not stand) recostarse *re·kos·tar·se*
life vida ⓕ *vee·da*
life jacket chaleco ⓜ salvavidas *cha·le·ko sal·va·vee·das*
lift elevador ⓜ *e·le·va·dor*
light (of weight) ligero/a ⓜ/ⓕ *lee·he·ro/a*
light luz ⓕ *loos*
light bulb foco ⓜ *fo·ko*
light meter fotómetro ⓜ *fo·to·me·tro*
lighter encendedor ⓜ *en·sen·de·dor*
lights luces ⓕ pl *loo·ses*
like gustar *goos·tar*
lime limón ⓕ *lee·mon*
line línea ⓕ *lee·ne·a*
lip balm bálsamo ⓜ labial *bal·sa·mo la·byal*
lips labios ⓜ pl *la·byos*
lipstick lápiz ⓜ labial *la·pees la·byal*
liquor store licorería ⓕ *lee·ko·re·rya*
listen escuchar *es·koo·char*
live vivir *vee·veer*
liver hígado ⓜ *ee·ga·do*
lizard lagartija ⓕ *la·gar·tee·ha*
local local *lo·kal*
lock cerradura ⓕ *se·ra·doo·ra*
lock cerrar *se·rar*

locked cerrado/a con llave ⓜ/ⓕ *se·ra·do/a kon ya·ve*
lollies dulces ⓜ pl *dool·ses*
long largo/a ⓜ/ⓕ *lar·go/a*
long-distance larga distancia ⓕ *lar·ga dees·tan·sya*
look mirar *mee·rar*
look after cuidar *kwee·dar*
look for buscar *boos·kar*
lookout mirador ⓜ *mee·ra·dor*
loose suelto/a ⓜ/ⓕ *swel·to/a*
loose change cambio ⓜ *kam·byo*
lose perder *per·der*
lost perdido/a ⓜ/ⓕ *per·dee·do/a*
lost property office oficina ⓕ de objetos perdidos *o·fee·see·na de ob·he·tos per·dee·dos*
loud ruidoso/a ⓜ/ⓕ *rwee·do·so/a*
love amar *a·mar*
lover amante ⓜ&ⓕ *a·man·te*
low bajo/a ⓜ/ⓕ *ba·ho/a*
lubricant lubricante ⓜ *loo·bree·kan·te*
luck suerte ⓕ *swer·te*
lucky afortunado/a ⓜ/ⓕ *a·for·too·na·do/a*
luggage equipaje ⓜ *e·kee·pa·he*
luggage lockers casilleros ⓜ pl *ka·see·ye·ros*
luggage tag etiqueta ⓕ de equipaje *e·tee·ke·ta de e·kee·pa·he*
lump bulto ⓜ *bool·to*
lunch almuerzo ⓜ *al·mwer·so*
lungs pulmones ⓜ pl *pool·mo·nes*
luxury lujo ⓜ *loo·ho*

M

machine máquina ⓕ *ma·kee·na*
made of (cotton) hecho/a ⓜ/ⓕ de (algodón) *e·cho/a de (al·go·don)*
magazine revista ⓕ *re·vees·ta*
magician mago/a ⓜ/ⓕ *ma·go/a*
mail correo ⓜ *ko·re·o*
mailbox buzón ⓜ *boo·son*
main principal *preen·see·pal*
make hacer *a·ser*
make fun of burlarse de *boor·lar·se de*
make-up maquillaje ⓜ *ma·kee·ya·he*
mammogram mamograma ⓜ *ma·mo·gra·ma*
man hombre ⓜ *om·bre*
manager director/directora ⓜ/ⓕ *dee·rek·tor/dee·rek·to·ra*
mandarin mandarina ⓕ *man·da·ree·na*
mango mango ⓜ *man·go*
manual worker obrero/a ⓜ/ⓕ *o·bre·ro/a*
many muchos/as ⓜ/ⓕ pl *moo·chos/as*
map mapa ⓜ *ma·pa*
margarine margarina ⓕ *mar·ga·ree·na*
marijuana marihuana ⓕ *ma·ree·wa·na*
marital status estado ⓜ civil *es·ta·do see·veel*
market mercado ⓜ *mer·ka·do*
marmalade mermelada ⓕ *mer·me·la·da*
marriage matrimonio ⓜ *ma·tree·mo·nyo*
married casado/a ⓜ/ⓕ *ka·sa·do/a*
marry casarse *ka·sar·se*
martial arts artes ⓜ pl marciales *ar·tes mar·sya·les*
mass misa ⓕ *mee·sa*
massage masaje ⓜ *ma·sa·he*
masseur/masseuse masajista ⓜ&ⓕ *ma·sa·hees·ta*
mat petate ⓜ *pe·ta·te*
match (game) partido ⓜ *par·tee·do*
matches cerillos ⓜ pl *se·ree·yos*
mattress colchón ⓜ *kol·chon*
maybe tal vez *tal ves*
mayonnaise mayonesa ⓕ *ma·yo·ne·sa*
mayor alcalde ⓜ&ⓕ *al·kal·de*
measles sarampión ⓜ *sa·ram·pyon*
meat carne ⓕ *kar·ne*
mechanic mecánico/a ⓜ/ⓕ *me·ka·nee·ko/a*

media medios (m) pl de comunicación me·dyos de ko·moo·nee·ka·syon
medicine medicina (f) me·dee·see·na
meet encontrar en·kon·trar
melon melón (m) me·lon
member miembro (m) myem·bro
menstruation menstruación (f) men·strwa·syon
menu carta (f) kar·ta
message mensaje (m) men·sa·he
metal metal (m) me·tal
metre metro (m) me·tro
metro station estación (f) del metro es·ta·syon del me·tro
microwave horno (m) de microondas or·no de mee·kro·on·das
midnight medianoche (f) me·dya·no·che
migraine migraña (f) mee·gra·nya
military militar mee·lee·tar
military service servicio (m) militar ser·vee·syo mee·lee·tar
milk leche (f) le·che
millimetre milímetro (m) mee·lee·me·tro
million millón (m) mee·yon
minced meat carne (f) molida kar·ne mo·lee·da
mind cuidar kwee·dar
mineral water agua (m) mineral a·gwa mee·ne·ral
mints pastillas (f) pl de menta pas·tee·yas de men·ta
minute minuto (m) mee·noo·to
mirror espejo (m) es·pe·ho
miscarriage aborto (m) natural a·bor·to na·too·ral
miss (feel absence of) extrañar ek·stra·nyar
mistake error (m) e·ror
mix mezclar mes·klar
mobile phone celular (m) se·loo·lar
modem módem (m) mo·dem
moisturiser crema (f) hidratante kre·ma ee·dra·tan·te
monastery monasterio (m) mo·nas·te·ryo
money dinero (m) dee·ne·ro
month mes (m) mes
monument monumento (m) mo·noo·men·to
moon luna (f) loo·na
morning mañana (f) ma·nya·na
morning sickness náuseas (f) pl del embarazo now·se·as del em·ba·ra·so
mosque mezquita (f) mes·kee·ta
mosquito mosquito (m) mos·kee·to
mosquito coil repelente (m) de mosquitos re·pe·len·te de mos·kee·tos
mosquito net mosquitero (m) mos·kee·te·ro
mother madre (f) ma·dre
mother-in-law suegra (f) swe·gra
motorboat lancha (f) a motor lan·cha a mo·tor
motorcycle motocicleta (f) mo·to·see·kle·ta
motorway carretera (f) ka·re·te·ra
mountain montaña (f) mon·ta·nya
mountain bike bicicleta (f) de montaña bee·see·kle·ta de mon·ta·nya
mountain path sendero de montaña (m) sen·de·ro de mon·ta·nya
mountain range cordillera (f) kor·dee·ye·ra
mountaineering alpinismo (m) al·pee·nees·mo
mouse ratón (m) ra·ton
mouse (computer) mouse (m) mows
mouth boca (f) bo·ka
movie película (f) pe·lee·koo·la
mud lodo (m) lo·do
muesli granola (f) gra·no·la
mum mamá (f) ma·ma
muscle músculo (m) moos·koo·lo
museum museo (m) moo·se·o
mushroom champiñón (m) cham·pee·nyon
music música (f) moo·see·ka

musician músico/a ⓜ/ⓕ *moo·see·ko/a*
Muslim musulmán/musulmana ⓜ/ⓕ *moo·sool·man/moo·sool·ma·na*
mussels mejillones ⓜ pl *me·hee·yo·nes*
mustard mostaza ⓕ *mos·ta·sa*
mute mudo/a ⓜ/ⓕ *moo·do/a*
my mi/mis sg/pl *mee/mees*

N

nail clippers cortauñas ⓜ *kor·ta·oo·nyas*
name nombre ⓜ *nom·bre*
napkin servilleta ⓕ *ser·vee·ye·ta*
nappy pañal ⓜ *pa·nyal*
nappy rash rosadura ⓕ *ro·sa·doo·ra*
national park parque ⓜ nacional *par·ke na·syo·nal*
nationality nacionalidad ⓕ *na·syo·na·lee·dad*
nature naturaleza ⓕ *na·too·ra·le·sa*
naturopathy naturopatía ⓕ *na·too·ro·pa·tee·a*
nausea náusea ⓕ *now·se·a*
near cerca *ser·ka*
nearby cerca *ser·ka*
nearest más cercano/a ⓜ/ⓕ *mas ser·ka·no/a*
necessary necesario/a ⓜ/ⓕ *ne·se·sa·ryo/a*
neck cuello ⓜ *kwe·yo*
necklace collar ⓜ *ko·yar*
need necesitar *ne·se·see·tar*
needle (sewing) aguja ⓕ *a·goo·ha*
needle (syringe) jeringa ⓕ *he·reen·ga*
negatives negativos ⓜ pl *ne·ga·tee·vos*
neither tampoco *tam·po·ko*
net red ⓕ *red*
network red ⓕ *red*
Netherlands Holanda ⓕ *o·lan·da*
never nunca *noon·ka*
new nuevo/a ⓜ/ⓕ *nwe·vo/a*
New Year Año Nuevo ⓜ *a·nyo nwe·vo*
New Year's Day día ⓜ de Año Nuevo *dee·a de a·nyo nwe·vo*
New Year's Eve fin ⓜ de año *feen de a·nyo*
New Zealand Nueva ⓕ Zelanda *nwe·va se·lan·da*
news noticias ⓕ pl *no·tee·syas*
news stand puesto ⓜ de periódicos *pwes·to de pe·ryo·dee·kos*
newsagency agencia ⓕ de noticias *a·hen·sya de no·tee·syas*
newspaper periódico ⓜ *pe·ryo·dee·ko*
next próximo/a ⓜ/ⓕ *prok·see·mo/a*
next (month) (el mes) que viene *(el mes) ke vye·ne*
next to al lado de *al la·do de*
nice simpático/a ⓜ/ⓕ *seem·pa·tee·ko/a*
nickname apodo ⓜ *a·po·do*
night noche ⓕ *no·che*
no no *no*
noisy ruidoso/a ⓜ/ⓕ *rwee·do·so/a*
none nada *na·da*
non-smoking no fumar *no foo·mar*
noodles fideos ⓜ pl *fee·de·os*
noon mediodía ⓜ *me·dyo·dee·a*
north norte ⓜ *nor·te*
nose nariz ⓕ *na·rees*
notebook cuaderno ⓜ *kwa·der·no*
nothing nada *na·da*
now ahora *a·o·ra*
nuclear energy energía ⓕ nuclear *e·ner·hee·a noo·kle·ar*
nuclear testing pruebas ⓕ pl nucleares *prwe·bas noo·kle·a·res*
nuclear waste residuos ⓜ pl nucleares *re·see·dwos noo·kle·a·res*
number número ⓜ *noo·me·ro*
nun monja ⓕ *mon·ha*
nurse enfermero/a ⓜ/ⓕ *en·fer·me·ro/a*
nuts nueces ⓕ pl *nwe·ses*

O

oats avena ⓕ a·ve·na
ocean océano ⓜ o·se·a·no
off (spoiled) echado/a ⓜ/ⓕ a perder e·cha·do/a a per·der
office oficina ⓕ o·fee·see·na
office worker empleado/a ⓜ/ⓕ de oficina em·ple·a·do/a de o·fee·see·na
offside fuera de lugar fwe·ra de loo·gar
often seguido se·gee·do
oil aceite ⓜ a·say·te
old viejo/a ⓜ/ⓕ vye·ho/a
olive oil aceite ⓜ de oliva a·say·te de o·lee·va
Olympic Games Juegos ⓜ pl Olímpicos hwe·gos o·leem·pee·kos
on en en
once una vez oo·na ves
one-way ticket boleto ⓜ sencillo bo·le·to sen·see·yo
onion cebolla ⓕ se·bo·ya
only sólo so·lo
open abierto/a ⓜ/ⓕ a·byer·to/a
open abrir a·breer
opening hours horario ⓜ o·ra·ryo
opera ópera ⓕ o·pe·ra
operation operación ⓕ o·pe·ra·syon
operator operador/operadora ⓜ/ⓕ o·pe·ra·dor/o·pe·ra·do·ra
opinion opinión ⓕ o·pee·nyon
opposite (location) frente a fren·te a
opposite (opinion) contraria kon·tra·rya
or o o
orange naranja ⓕ na·ran·ha
orange juice jugo ⓜ de naranja hoo·go de na·ran·ha
orchestra orquesta ⓕ or·kes·ta
order (command) orden ⓕ or·den
order (placement) orden ⓜ or·den
order ordenar or·de·nar
ordinary corriente ko·ryen·te
orgasm orgasmo ⓜ or·gas·mo
original original o·ree·hee·nal
other otro/a ⓜ/ⓕ o·tro/a
our nuestro/a ⓜ/ⓕ nwes·tro/a
outside exterior ⓜ ek·ste·ryor
ovarian cyst quiste ⓜ ovárico kees·te o·va·ree·ko
oven horno ⓜ or·no
overcoat abrigo ⓜ a·bree·go
overdose sobredosis ⓕ so·bre·do·sees
overhead projector retroproyector re·tro·pro·yek·tor
owe deber de·ber
owner dueño/a ⓜ/ⓕ dwe·nyo/a
oxygen oxígeno ⓜ ok·see·he·no
oyster ostra ⓜ os.tra
ozone layer capa ⓕ de ozono ka·pa de o·so·no

P

pacemaker marcapasos ⓜ mar·ka·pa·sos
pacifier chupón ⓜ choo·pon
package paquete ⓜ pa·ke·te
packet paquete ⓜ pa·ke·te
padlock candado ⓜ kan·da·do
page página ⓕ pa·hee·na
pain dolor ⓜ do·lor
painful doloroso/a ⓜ/ⓕ do·lo·ro·so/a
painkillers analgésicos ⓜ pl a·nal·he·see·kos
paint pintar peen·tar
painter pintor/pintora ⓜ/ⓕ peen·tor/peen·to·ra
painting pintura ⓕ peen·too·ra
pair (couple) par ⓜ par
palace palacio ⓜ pa·la·syo
pan sartén ⓜ sar·ten
pants pantalones ⓜ pl pan·ta·lo·nes
panty liners pantiprotectores ⓜ pl pan·tee·pro·tek·to·res
pantyhose pantimedias ⓕ pl pan·tee·me·dyas
pap smear papanicolaou ⓜ pa·pa·nee·ko·low
paper papel ⓜ pa·pel
paperwork trámites ⓜ tra·mee·tes

paraplegic parapléjico/a Ⓜ/Ⓕ pa·ra·*ple*·hee·ko/a
parcel paquete Ⓜ pa·*ke*·te
parents padres Ⓜ pl *pa*·dres
park parque Ⓜ *par*·ke
park (car) estacionar es·ta·syo·*nar*
parliament parlamento Ⓜ par·la·*men*·to
parsley perejil Ⓜ pe·re·*heel*
part parte Ⓕ *par*·te
partner (intimate) pareja Ⓕ pa·*re*·ha
part-time medio tiempo *me*·dyo *tyem*·po
party fiesta Ⓕ *fyes*·ta
party (political) partido Ⓜ par·*tee*·do
pass pase Ⓜ *pa*·se
passenger pasajero/a Ⓜ/Ⓕ pa·sa·*he*·ro/a
passport pasaporte Ⓜ pa·sa·*por*·te
passport number número Ⓜ de pasaporte *noo*·me·ro de pa·sa·*por*·te
past pasado Ⓜ pa·*sa*·do
pasta pasta Ⓕ *pas*·ta
pate (food) paté Ⓜ pa·*te*
path sendero Ⓜ sen·*de*·ro
pay pagar pa·*gar*
payment pago Ⓜ *pa*·go
peace paz Ⓕ pas
peach durazno Ⓜ doo·*ras*·no
peak cumbre Ⓕ *koom*·bre
peanuts cacahuates Ⓜ ka·ka·*wa*·tes
pear pera Ⓕ *pe*·ra
peas chícharos Ⓜ pl *chee*·cha·ros
pedal pedal Ⓜ pe·*dal*
pedestrian peatón Ⓜ pe·a·*ton*
pedestrian crossing cruce Ⓜ peatonal *kroo*·se pe·a·to·*nal*
pen pluma Ⓕ *ploo*·ma
pencil lápiz Ⓜ *la*·pees
penis pene Ⓜ *pe*·ne
penknife navaja Ⓕ na·*va*·ha
pensioner jubilado/a Ⓜ/Ⓕ hoo·bee·*la*·do/a
people gente Ⓕ *hen*·te
pepper (bell) pimiento Ⓜ pee·*myen*·to
pepper (spice) pimienta Ⓕ pee·*myen*·ta
per (day) por (día) por (*dee*·a)
percent por ciento por *syen*·to
performance (entertainment) presentación Ⓕ pres·en·ta·*syon*
performance (work) desempeño Ⓜ des·em·*pe*·nyo
perfume perfume Ⓜ per·*foo*·me
period pain cólico Ⓜ menstrual *ko*·lee·ko men·*strwal*
permission permiso Ⓜ per·*mee*·so
permit permiso Ⓜ per·*mee*·so
permit permitir per·mee·*teer*
person persona Ⓕ per·*so*·na
perspire sudar soo·*dar*
petition petición Ⓕ pe·tee·*syon*
petrol gasolina Ⓕ ga·so·*lee*·na
pharmacy farmacia Ⓕ far·*ma*·sya
phone book directorio Ⓜ telefónico dee·rek·*to*·ryo te·le·*fo*·nee·ko
phone box teléfono Ⓜ público te·*le*·fo·no *poo*·blee·ko
photo fotografía Ⓕ fo·to·gra·*fee*·a
photocopier fotocopiadora Ⓕ fo·to·ko·pya·*do*·ra
photographer fotógrafo/a Ⓜ/Ⓕ fo·*to*·gra·fo/a
photography fotografía Ⓕ fo·to·gra·*fee*·a
phrasebook libro Ⓜ de frases *lee*·bro de *fra*·ses
pick-up (truck) pickup pee·*kop* • camioneta ka·myo·*ne*·ta
pick up (lift) levantar le·van·*tar*
pick up (seduce) ligar lee·*gar*
pickaxe pico Ⓜ *pee*·ko
picnic pícnic Ⓜ *peek*·neek
pie pay Ⓜ pay
piece pedazo Ⓜ pe·*da*·so
pig cerdo Ⓜ *ser*·do
pill pastilla Ⓕ pas·*tee*·ya
the Pill la píldora Ⓕ la *peel*·do·ra
pillow almohada Ⓕ al·*mwa*·da
pillowcase funda Ⓕ de almohada *foon*·da de al·*mwa*·da

pineapple piña ⓕ pee·nya
pink rosa ro·sa
pistachio pistache ⓜ pees·ta·che
place lugar ⓜ loo·gar
place of birth lugar ⓜ de nacimiento loo·gar de na·see·myen·to
plane avión ⓜ a·vyon
planet planeta ⓜ pla·ne·ta
plant planta ⓕ plan·ta
plant sembrar sem·brar
plastic plástico ⓜ plas·tee·ko
plate plato ⓜ pla·to
plateau meseta ⓕ me·se·ta
platform plataforma ⓕ pla·ta·for·ma
play obra ⓕ o·bra
play (an instrument) tocar to·kar
play (game/sport) jugar hoo·gar
plug (bath) tapón ⓜ ta·pon
plug (electrical) clavija ⓕ cla·vee·ha
plum ciruela ⓕ seer·we·la
pocket bolsillo ⓜ bol·see·yo
poetry poesía ⓕ po·e·see·a
point apuntar a·poon·tar
point (tip) punto ⓜ poon·to
poisonous venenoso/a ⓜ/ⓕ ve·ne·no·so/a
poker póquer ⓜ po·ker
police policía ⓕ po·lee·see·a
police officer oficial ⓜ de policía o·fee·syal de po·lee·see·a
police station estación ⓕ de policía es·ta·syon de po·lee·see·a
policy política ⓕ po·lee·tee·ka
policy (insurance) póliza ⓕ po·lee·sa
politician político/a ⓜ/ⓕ po·lee·tee·ko/a
politics política ⓕ po·lee·tee·ka
pollen polen ⓜ po·len
polls encuestas ⓕ pl en·kwes·tas
pollution contaminación ⓕ kon·ta·mee·na·syon
pony pony ⓜ po·nee
pool (game) billar ⓜ bee·yar
pool (swimming) alberca ⓕ al·ber·ka
poor pobre po·bre
pope Papa ⓜ pa·pa
popular popular po·poo·lar
pork cerdo ⓜ ser·do
pork sausage chorizo ⓜ cho·ree·so
port puerto ⓜ pwer·to
port (wine) oporto ⓜ o·por·to
possible posible po·see·ble
post code código ⓜ postal ko·dee·go pos·tal
post office oficina ⓕ de correos o·fee·see·na de ko·re·os
postage timbre ⓜ teem·bre
postcard postal ⓕ pos·tal
poste restante lista ⓕ de correos lees·ta de ko·re·os
poster póster ⓜ pos·ter
pot (kitchen) cazuela ⓕ kas·we·la
pot (for plant) maceta ⓕ ma·se·ta
pot (marijuana) mota ⓕ mo·ta
potato papa ⓕ pa·pa
pottery alfarería ⓕ al·fa·re·ree·a
pound (money) libra ⓕ lee·bra
poverty pobreza ⓕ po·bre·sa
power poder ⓜ po·der
prawn camarón ⓜ ka·ma·ron
prayer oración ⓕ o·ra·syon
prayer book libro ⓜ de oraciones lee·bro de o·ra·syo·nes
prefer preferir pre·fe·reer
pregnancy test kit prueba ⓕ de embarazo prwe·ba de em·ba·ra·so
pregnant embarazada em·ba·ra·sa·da
premenstrual tension síndrome ⓜ premenstrual seen·dro·me pre·men·strwal
prepare preparar pre·pa·rar
president presidente/a ⓜ/ⓕ pre·see·den·te/a
pressure presión ⓕ pre·syon
pretty bonito/a ⓜ/ⓕ bo·nee·to/a
prevent prevenir pre·ve·neer
price precio ⓜ pre·syo
priest sacerdote ⓜ sa·ser·do·te
primary school primaria ⓜ pree·ma·rya
prime minister (man) primer ministro ⓜ pree·mer mee·nees·tro

prime minister (woman) primera ministra ⓕ pree·*me*·ra mee·*nees*·tra
printer impresora ⓕ eem·pre·*so*·ra
prison cárcel ⓕ *kar*·sel
prisoner prisionero/a ⓜ/ⓕ pree·syo·*ne*·ro/a
private privado/a ⓜ/ⓕ pree·*va*·do/a
private hospital hospital ⓜ privado os·pee·*tal* pree·*va*·do
produce producir pro·doo·*seer*
profit ganancia ⓜ ga·*nan*·sya
programme programa ⓜ pro·*gra*·ma
projector proyector ⓜ pro·yek·*tor*
promise promesa ⓕ pro·*me*·sa
protect proteger pro·te·*her*
protected protegido/a ⓜ/ⓕ pro·te·*hee*·do/a
protest protesta ⓕ pro·*tes*·ta
protest protestar pro·tes·*tar*
provisions provisiones ⓕ pl pro·vee·*syo*·nes
prune ciruela ⓕ pasa seer·*we*·la *pa*·sa
pub bar ⓜ bar
public telephone teléfono ⓜ público te·*le*·fo·no *poo*·blee·ko
public toilets baños ⓜ pl públicos *ba*·nyos *poo*·blee·kos
pull jalar ha·*lar*
pump bomba ⓕ *bom*·ba
pumpkin calabaza ⓕ ka·la·*ba*·sa
puncture ponchar pon·*char*
punish castigar kas·tee·*gar*
puppy cachorro ⓜ ka·*cho*·ro
pure puro/a ⓜ/ⓕ *poo*·ro/a
purple morado/a ⓜ/ⓕ mo·*ra*·do/a
push empujar em·poo·*har*
put poner po·*ner*

Q

qualifications habilidades ⓕ pl a·bee·lee·*da*·des
quality calidad ⓕ ka·lee·*dad*
quarantine cuarentena ⓕ kwa·ren·*te*·na
quarrel pelea ⓕ pe·*le*·a
quarter cuarto ⓜ *kwar*·to
queen reina ⓕ *ray*·na
question pregunta ⓕ pre·*goon*·ta
question preguntar pre·goon·*tar*
queue fila ⓕ *fee*·la
quick rápido/a ⓜ/ⓕ *ra*·pee·do/a
quiet tranquilo/a ⓜ/ⓕ tran·*kee*·lo/a
quiet tranquilidad ⓕ tran·kee·lee·*dad*
quit renunciar re·noon·*syar*

R

rabbit conejo ⓜ ko·*ne*·ho
race (sport) carrera ⓕ ka·*re*·ra
racetrack pista ⓕ *pees*·ta
racing bike bicicleta ⓕ de carreras bee·see·*kle*·ta de ka·*re*·ras
racquet raqueta ⓕ ra·*ke*·ta
radiator radiador ⓜ ra·dya·*dor*
railway station estación ⓕ de tren es·ta·*syon* de tren
rain lluvia ⓕ *yoo*·vya
raincoat impermeable ⓜ eem·per·me·*a*·ble
rainbow arcoiris ⓜ ar·ko·*ee*·rees
raisin uva ⓕ pasa *oo*·va *pa*·sa
rally rally ⓜ *ra*·lee
rape violar vyo·*lar*
rare raro/a ⓜ/ⓕ *ra*·ro/a
rash irritación ⓕ ee·ree·ta·*syon*
raspberry frambuesa ⓕ fram·*bwe*·sa
rat rata ⓕ *ra*·ta
rate of pay salario ⓜ sa·*la*·ryo
raw crudo/a ⓜ/ⓕ *kroo*·do/a
razor rastrillo ⓜ ras·*tree*·yo
razor blades navajas ⓕ pl de razurar na·*va*·has de ra·soo·*rar*
read leer le·*er*
ready listo/a ⓜ/ⓕ *lees*·to/a
real estate agent agente ⓜ inmobiliario a·*hen*·te een·mo·bee·*lya*·ryo
realise darse cuenta de *dar*·se *kwen*·ta de
realistic realista re·a·*lees*·ta
reason razón ⓕ ra·*son*

receipt recibo ⓜ re·see·bo
receive recibir re·see·beer
recently recientemente re·syen·te·men·te
recognise reconocer re·ko·no·ser
recommend recomendar re·ko·men·dar
recording grabación ⓕ gra·ba·syon
recyclable reciclable re·see·kla·ble
recycle reciclar re·see·klar
red rojo/a ⓜ/ⓕ ro·ho/a
referee árbitro ⓜ ar·bee·tro
reference referencia ⓕ re·fe·ren·sya
refrigerator refrigerador ⓜ re·free·he·ra·dor
refugee refugiado/a ⓜ/ⓕ re·foo·hya·do/a
refund reembolso ⓜ re·em·bol·so
refund reembolsar re·em·bol·sar
refuse negar(se) ne·gar·(se)
registered mail correo ⓜ certificado ko·re·o ser·tee·fee·ka·do
regret lamentar la·men·tar
relationship relación ⓕ re·la·syon
relax relajarse re·la·har·se
relic reliquia ⓕ re·lee·kya
religion religión ⓕ re·lee·hyon
religious religioso/a ⓜ/ⓕ re·lee·hyo·so/a
remember recordar re·kor·dar
remote remoto/a ⓜ/ⓕ re·mo·to/a
remote control control ⓜ remoto kon·trol re·mo·to
rent renta ⓕ ren·ta
rent rentar ren·tar
repair reparar re·pa·rar
repeat repetir re·pe·teer
republic república ⓕ re·poo·blee·ka
reservation reservación ⓕ re·ser·va·syon
reserve reservar re·ser·var
rest descansar des·kan·sar
restaurant restaurante ⓜ res·tow·ran·te
resumé currículum ⓜ koo·ree·koo·loom
retired jubilado/a ⓜ/ⓕ hoo·bee·la·do/a
return volver vol·ver
return ticket boleto ⓜ de viaje redondo bo·le·to de vya·he re·don·do
review crítica ⓕ kree·tee·ka
rhythm ritmo ⓜ reet·mo
rice arroz ⓜ a·ros
rich rico/a ⓜ/ⓕ ree·ko/a
ride paseo ⓜ pa·se·o
ride montar mon·tar
right (correct) correcto/a ⓜ/ⓕ ko·rek·to/a
right (not left) derecha de·re·cha
right-wing de derecha de de·re·cha
ring anillo ⓕ a·nee·yo
ring llamar por teléfono ya·mar por te·le·fo·no
rip-off estafa ⓕ es·ta·fa
risk riesgo ⓜ ryes·go
river río ⓜ ree·o
road camino ⓜ ka·mee·no
rob robar ro·bar
rock roca ⓕ ro·ka
rock (music) rock ⓜ rok
rock climbing escalada ⓕ en roca es·ka·la·da en ro·ka
rock group grupo ⓜ de rock groo·po de rok
rollerblading patinar en línea pa·tee·nar en lee·nya
romantic romántico/a ⓜ/ⓕ ro·man·tee·ko/a
room habitación ⓕ a·bee·ta·syon
room number número ⓜ de habitación noo·me·ro de a·bee·ta·syon
rope cuerda ⓕ kwer·da
round redondo/a ⓜ/ⓕ re·don·do/a
roundabout glorieta ⓕ glo·rye·ta
route ruta ⓕ roo·ta
rowing remo ⓜ re·mo
rubbish basura ⓕ ba·soo·ra
rug alfombra ⓕ al·fom·bra
rugby rugby ⓜ roog·bee
ruins ruinas ⓕ pl rwee·nas

rules reglas ⓕ pl *re*·glas
rum ron ⓜ ron
run correr ko·*rer*
run out of quedarse sin ke·*dar*·se seen

S

sad triste *trees*·te
saddle silla ⓕ de montar *see*·ya de mon·*tar*
safe caja ⓕ fuerte *ka*·ha *fwer*·te
safe seguro/a ⓜ/ⓕ se·*goo*·ro/a
safe sex sexo ⓜ seguro *sek*·so se·*goo*·ro
saint santo/a ⓜ/ⓕ *san*·to/a
salad ensalada ⓕ en·sa·*la*·da
salami salami ⓜ sa·*la*·mee
salary salario ⓜ sa·*la*·ryo
sales tax IVA ⓜ *ee*·va
salmon salmón ⓜ sal·*mon*
salt sal ⓕ sal
same igual ee·*gwal*
sand arena ⓕ a·*re*·na
sandals sandalias ⓕ pl san·*da*·lyas
sanitary napkins toallas ⓕ pl femeninas to·*a*·yas fe·me·*nee*·nas
sauna sauna ⓜ *sow*·na
sausage salchicha ⓕ sal·*chee*·cha
save salvar sal·*var*
save (money) ahorrar a·o·*rar*
say decir de·*seer*
scale (climb) escalar es·ka·*lar*
scarf bufanda ⓕ boo·*fan*·da
school escuela ⓕ es·*kwe*·la
science ciencias ⓕ pl *syen*·syas
scientist científico/a ⓜ/ⓕ syen·*tee*·fee·ko/a
scissors tijeras ⓕ pl tee·*he*·ras
score anotar a·no·*tar*
scoreboard marcador ⓜ mar·ka·*dor*
Scotland Escocia ⓕ es·*ko*·sya
screen pantalla ⓕ pan·*ta*·ya
script guión ⓜ gee·*on*
sculpture escultura ⓕ es·kool·*too*·ra
sea mar ⓜ mar
seasick mareado/a ⓜ/ⓕ ma·re·*a*·do/a
seaside costa ⓕ *kos*·ta
season estación ⓕ es·ta·*syon*
season (in sport) temporada ⓕ tem·po·*ra*·da
seat asiento ⓜ a·*syen*·to
seatbelt cinturón ⓜ de seguridad seen·too·*ron* de se·goo·ree·*dad*
second segundo/a ⓜ/ⓕ se·*goon*·do/a
secondary school secundaria ⓕ se·*goon*·da·rya
second-hand de segunda mano de se·*goon*·da *ma*·no
secretary secretario/a ⓜ/ⓕ se·kre·*ta*·ryo/a
see ver ver
selfish egoísta e·go·*ees*·ta
self-service autoservicio ⓜ ow·to·ser·*vee*·syo
sell vender ven·*der*
send enviar en·*vyar*
sensitive sensible sen·*see*·ble
sensual sensual sen·*swal*
separate separado/a ⓜ/ⓕ se·pa·*ra*·do/a
separate separar se·pa·*rar*
series serie ⓕ *se*·rye
serious serio/a ⓜ/ⓕ *se*·ryo/a
service station gasolinera ⓕ ga·so·lee·*ne*·ra
service charge servicio ⓜ ser·*vee*·syo
set menu comida corrida ⓕ ko·*mee*·da ko·*ree*·da
several varios/as ⓜ/ⓕ *va*·ryos/as
sew coser ko·*ser*
sex sexo ⓜ *sek*·so
sexism sexismo ⓜ sek·*sees*·mo
sexy sexy *sek*·see
shadow sombra ⓕ *som*·bra
shampoo champú ⓜ cham·*poo*
shape forma ⓕ *for*·ma
share (with) compartir kom·par·*teer*
shave rasurar ra·soo·*rar*

shaving cream espuma ⓕ de rasurar es·poo·ma de ra·soo·rar
she élla e·ya
sheep oveja ⓕ o·ve·ha
sheet (bed) sábana ⓕ sa·ba·na
sheet (of paper) hoja ⓕ o·ha
shelf estante ⓜ es·tan·te
ship barco ⓜ bar·ko
ship (send) enviar en·vee·ar
shirt camisa ⓕ ka·mee·sa
shoe shop zapatería ⓕ sa·pa·te·ree·a
shoes zapatos ⓜ pl sa·pa·tos
shoot disparar dees·pa·rar
shop tienda ⓕ tyen·da
shopping centre centro ⓜ comercial sen·tro ko·mer·syal
short (height) bajo/a ⓜ/ⓕ ba·ho/a
short (length) corto/a ⓜ/ⓕ kor·to/a
shortage escasez ⓕ es·ka·ses
shorts shorts ⓜ pl chors
shoulder hombro ⓜ om·bro
shout gritar gree·tar
show espectáculo ⓜ es·pek·ta·koo·lo
show mostrar mos·trar
shower regadera ⓕ re·ga·de·ra
shrine altar ⓜ al·tar
shut cerrado/a ⓜ/ⓕ se·ra·do/a
shut cerrar se·rar
shy tímido/a ⓜ/ⓕ tee·mee·do/a
sick enfermo/a ⓜ/ⓕ en·fer·mo/a
side lado ⓜ la·do
sign señal ⓕ se·nyal
sign firmar feer·mar
signature firma ⓕ feer·ma
silk seda ⓕ se·da
silver plateado/a ⓜ/ⓕ pla·te·a·do/a
silver plata ⓕ pla·ta
SIM card tarjeta ⓕ SIM/chip ⓜ tar·he·ta seem/cheep
similar similar see·mee·lar
simple sencillo/a ⓜ/ⓕ sen·see·yo/a
since (time) desde des·de
sing cantar kan·tar
singer cantante ⓜ&ⓕ kan·tan·te
single soltero/a ⓜ/ⓕ sol·te·ro/a
single room habitación ⓕ individual a·bee·ta·syon een·dee·vee·dwal
singlet camiseta ⓕ ka·mee·se·ta
sister hermana ⓕ er·ma·na
sit sentarse sen·tar·se
size (clothes) talla ⓕ ta·ya
size (general) tamaño ⓜ ta·ma·nyo
skateboarding andar en patineta an·dar en pa·tee·ne·ta
skateboard patineta ⓕ pa·tee·ne·ta
ski esquiar es·kee·ar
skiing esquí ⓜ es·kee
skimmed milk leche ⓕ descremada le·che des·kre·ma·da
skin piel ⓕ pyel
skirt falda ⓕ fal·da
sky cielo ⓜ sye·lo
sleep dormir dor·meer
sleeping bag sleeping ⓜ / bolsa ⓕ de dormir eh·sleep·een/bol·sa de dor·meer
sleeping car coche ⓜ cama ko·che ka·ma
sleeping pills pastillas ⓕ pl para dormir pas·tee·yas pa·ra dor·meer
(be) sleepy tener sueño te·ner swe·nyo
slide transparencia ⓕ trans·pa·ren·sya
slow lento/a ⓜ/ⓕ len·to/a
slowly despacio des·pa·syo
small pequeño/a ⓜ/ⓕ pe·ke·nyo/a
smell olor ⓜ o·lor
smell oler o·ler
smile sonreír son·re·eer
smoke fumar foo·mar
SMS capability capacidad ⓕ de SMS ka·pa·see·dad de e·se e·me e·se
snack botana ⓕ bo·ta·na
snail caracol ⓜ ka·ra·kol
snake serpiente ⓕ ser·pyen·te
snorkelling esnorkelear es·nor·ke·le·ar
snow nieve ⓕ nye·ve
snowboarding snowboarding es·now·bor·deen
soap jabón ⓜ ha·bon
soap opera telenovela ⓕ te·le·no·ve·la
soccer fútbol ⓜ foot·bol

social welfare bienestar social ⓜ *byen·e·star so·syal*
socialist socialista ⓜ&ⓕ *so·sya·lees·ta*
socks calcetines ⓜ pl *kal·se·tee·nes*
soft drink refresco ⓜ *re·fres·ko*
soldier soldado ⓜ *sol·da·do*
some algún *al·goon*
someone alguien *al·gyen*
something algo *al·go*
sometimes de vez en cuando *de ves en kwan·do*
son hijo ⓜ *ee·ho*
song canción ⓕ *kan·syon*
soon pronto *pron·to*
sore adolorido/a ⓜ/ⓕ *a·do·lo·ree·do/a*
soup sopa ⓕ *so·pa*
sour cream crema ⓕ agria *kre·ma a·grya*
south sur ⓜ *soor*
souvenir recuerdo ⓜ *re·kwer·do*
souvenir shop tienda ⓕ de recuerdos *tyen·da de re·kwer·dos*
soy milk leche ⓕ de soya *le·che de so·ya*
soy sauce salsa ⓕ de soya *sal·sa de so·ya*
space espacio ⓜ *es·pa·syo*
Spain España ⓕ *es·pa·nya*
sparkling (liquids) espumoso/a ⓜ/ⓕ *es·poo·mo·so/a*
speak hablar *a·blar*
special especial *es·pe·syal*
specialist especialista ⓜ&ⓕ *es·pe·sya·lees·ta*
speed velocidad ⓕ *ve·lo·see·dad*
speedometer velocímetro ⓜ *ve·lo·see·me·tro*
spermicide espermecida ⓕ *es·per·me·see·da*
spider araña ⓕ *a·ra·nya*
spinach espinaca ⓕ *es·pee·na·ka*
spoon cuchara ⓕ *koo·cha·ra*
sport deportes ⓜ pl *de·por·tes*
sports store tienda ⓕ de deportes *tyen·da de de·por·tes*
sportsperson deportista ⓜ&ⓕ *de·por·tees·ta*
sprain torcedura ⓕ *tor·se·doo·ra*
spring (wire) resorte ⓜ *re·sor·te*
spring (season) primavera ⓕ *pree·ma·ve·ra*
square cuadrado ⓜ *kwa·dra·do*
square (town) zócalo ⓜ *so·ka·lo*
stadium estadio ⓜ *es·ta·dyo*
stage escenario ⓜ *e·se·na·ryo*
stairway escalera ⓕ *es·ka·le·ra*
stamp sello ⓜ *se·yo*
stand-by ticket boleto ⓜ en lista de espera *bo·le·to en lees·ta de es·pe·ra*
stars estrellas ⓕ pl *es·tre·yas*
start comenzar *ko·men·sar*
station estación ⓕ *es·ta·syon*
statue estatua ⓕ *es·ta·twa*
stay (at a hotel) alojarse *a·lo·har·se*
stay (remain) permanecer *per·ma·ne·ser*
stay (somewhere) quedarse *ke·dar·se*
steak (beef) bistec ⓜ *bees·tek*
steal robar *ro·bar*
steep empinado/a ⓜ/ⓕ *em·pee·na·do/a*
step paso ⓜ *pa·so*
stereo estéreo ⓜ *es·te·ryo*
stingy tacaño/a ⓜ/ⓕ *ta·ka·nyo/a*
stock (broth) caldo ⓜ *kal·do*
stockings calcetas ⓕ pl *kal·se·tas*
stomach estómago ⓜ *es·to·ma·go*
stomachache dolor ⓜ de estómago *do·lor de es·to·ma·go*
stone piedra ⓕ *pye·dra*
stoned pacheco/a ⓜ/ⓕ *pa·che·ko/a*
stop parada ⓕ *pa·ra·da*
stop parar *pa·rar*
store tienda ⓕ *tyen·da*
storm tormenta ⓕ *tor·men·ta*
story cuento ⓜ *kwen·to*
stove estufa ⓕ *es·too·fa*
straight derecho/a ⓜ/ⓕ *de·re·cho/a*
strange extraño/a ⓜ/ⓕ *ek·stra·nyo/a*
stranger desconocido/a ⓜ/ⓕ *des·ko·no·see·do/a*

strawberry fresa ⓕ fre·sa
stream arroyo ⓜ a·ro·yo
street calle ⓕ ka·ye
string cuerda ⓕ kwer·da
strong fuerte fwer·te
stubborn terco/a ⓜ/ⓕ ter·ko/a
student estudiante ⓜ&ⓕ es·too·dyan·te
studio estudio ⓜ es·too·dyo
stupid estúpido/a ⓜ/ⓕ es·too·pee·do/a
style estilo ⓜ es·tee·lo
subtitles subtítulos ⓜ pl soob·tee·too·los
suburb afueras ⓕ a·fwe·ras
subway metro ⓜ me·tro
suffer sufrir soo·freer
sugar azúcar ⓜ a·soo·kar
suitcase maleta ⓕ ma·le·ta
summer verano ⓜ ve·ra·no
sun sol ⓜ sol
sunblock bloqueador ⓜ solar blo·ke·a·dor so·lar
sunburn quemadura ⓕ de sol ke·ma·doo·ra de sol
sun-dried tomatoes tomates ⓜ pl deshidratados to·ma·tes des·ee·dra·ta·dos
sunflower oil aceite ⓜ de girasol a·say·te de hee·ra·sol
sunglasses lentes ⓕ pl de sol len·tes de sol
sunny soleado so·le·a·do
sunrise amanecer ⓜ a·ma·ne·ser
sunset puesta ⓕ de sol pwes·ta de sol
supermarket supermercado ⓜ soo·per·mer·ka·do
superstition superstición ⓕ soo·per·stee·syon
supporters aficionados ⓜ&ⓕ pl a·fee·syo·na·dos
surf surfear soor·fe·ar
surface mail correo ⓜ terrestre ko·re·o te·res·tre
surfboard tabla ⓕ de surf ta·bla de soorf
surname apellido ⓜ a·pe·yee·do
surprise sorpresa ⓕ sor·pre·sa
survive sobrevivir so·bre·vee·veer
sweater sueter ⓜ swe·ter
sweet dulce dool·se
sweets (candy) dulces ⓜ pl dool·ses
swim nadar na·dar
swimming pool alberca ⓕ al·ber·ka
swimsuit traje ⓜ de baño tra·he de ba·nyo
synagogue sinagoga ⓕ see·na·go·ga
synthetic sintético/a ⓜ/ⓕ seen·te·tee·ko/a
syringe jeringa ⓕ he·reen·ga

T

table mesa ⓕ me·sa
table tennis ping pong ⓜ peen·pon
tablecloth mantel ⓜ man·tel
tail cola ⓕ ko·la
tailor sastre ⓜ sas·tre
take (away) llevar ye·var
take (the train) tomar (el tren) to·mar (el tren)
take (photos) tomar (fotos) to·mar fo·tos
talk hablar a·blar
tall alto/a ⓜ/ⓕ al·to/a
tampons tampones ⓜ pl tam·po·nes
tanning lotion bronceador ⓜ bron·se·a·dor
tap llave ⓕ yah·ve
tasty sabroso/a ⓜ/ⓕ sa·bro·so/a
tax impuesto ⓜ pl eem·pwes·to
taxi taxi ⓜ tak·see
taxi driver taxista ⓜ&ⓕ tak·sees·ta
taxi stand sitio ⓜ de taxis see·tyo de tak·sees
tea té ⓜ te
teacher maestro/maestra ⓜ/ⓕ ma·es·tro/ma·es·tra
team equipo ⓜ e·kee·po
teaspoon cucharita ⓕ koo·cha·ree·ta

technique técnica ⓕ *tek*·nee·ka
teeth dientes ⓜ pl *dyen*·tes
telegram telegrama ⓜ te·le·*gra*·ma
telephone teléfono ⓜ te·*le*·fo·no
telephone llamar (por teléfono) ya·*mar* (por te·*le*·fo·no)
telephone centre central ⓕ telefónica sen·*tral* te·le·*fo*·nee·ka
telephoto lens teleobjetivo ⓜ te·le·ob·he·*tee*·vo
telescope telescopio ⓜ te·les·*ko*·pyo
television televisión ⓕ te·le·vee·*syon*
tell decir de·*seer*
temperature (fever) fiebre ⓕ *fye*·bre
temperature (weather) temperatura ⓕ tem·pe·ra·*too*·ra
temple templo ⓜ *tem*·plo
tennis tenis ⓜ *te*·nees
tennis court cancha ⓕ de tenis *kan*·cha de *te*·nees
tent tienda ⓕ (de campaña) *tyen*·da (de kam·*pa*·nya)
tent pegs estacas ⓕ pl es·*ta*·kas
terrible terrible te·*ree*·ble
test prueba ⓕ *prwe*·ba
thank dar gracias dar *gra*·syas
theatre teatro ⓜ te·*a*·tro
their su soo
they ellos/ellas ⓜ/ⓕ e·yos/e·yas
thief ladrón/ladrona ⓜ/ⓕ la·*dron*/la·*dro*·na
thin delgado/a ⓜ/ⓕ del·*ga*·do/a
think pensar pen·*sar*
third tercero ter·*se*·ro
(be) thirsty tener sed te·*ner* sed
this éste/ésta ⓜ/ⓕ es·te/es·ta
this (month) este (mes) es·te (mes)
throat garganta ⓕ gar·*gan*·ta
thrush candidiasis oral ⓕ kan·dee·dya·sees o·*ral*
ticket boleto ⓜ bo·*le*·to
ticket collector revisor/revisora ⓜ/ⓕ re·vee·*sor*/re·vee·*sor*·a
ticket machine máquina de boletos ⓕ *ma*·kee·na de bo·*le*·tos
ticket office taquilla ⓕ ta·*kee*·ya
tide marea ⓕ ma·*re*·a
tight apretado/a ⓜ/ⓕ a·pre·*ta*·do/a
time tiempo ⓜ *tyem*·po
time difference diferencia ⓕ de horas dee·fe·*ren*·sya de *o*·ras
timetable horario ⓜ o·*ra*·ryo
tin lata ⓕ *la*·ta
tin opener abrelatas ⓜ a·bre·*la*·tas
tiny pequeño/a ⓜ/ⓕ pe·ke·*nyo*/a
tip (gratuity) propina ⓕ pro·*pee*·na
tired cansado/a ⓜ/ⓕ kan·*sa*·do/a
tissues kleenex ⓜ pl *klee*·neks
toast pan tostado ⓜ pan tos·*ta*·do
toaster tostador ⓜ tos·ta·*dor*
tobacco tabaco ⓜ ta·*ba*·ko
tobacconist tabaquería ⓕ ta·ba·ke·*ree*·a
today hoy oy
toe dedo ⓜ del pie *de*·do del pye
tofu tofú ⓜ to·*foo*
together juntos/as ⓜ/ⓕ *hoon*·tos/as
toilet baño ⓜ *ba*·nyo
toilet paper papel ⓜ higiénico pa·*pel* ee·*hye*·nee·ko
tomato jitomate ⓜ hee-to-*ma*-te
tomato sauce catsup ⓜ *kat*·soop
tomorrow mañana ma·*nya*·na
tomorrow afternoon mañana en la tarde ma·*nya*·na en la *tar*·de
tomorrow evening mañana en la noche ma·*nya*·na en la *no*·che
tomorrow morning mañana en la mañana ma·*nya*·na en la ma·*nya*·na
tonight esta noche es·ta *no*·che
too (expensive) muy (caro/a) ⓜ/ⓕ mooy (*ka*·ro/a)
too much demasiado de·ma·*sya*·do
tooth (back) muela ⓕ *mwe*·la
toothache dolor ⓜ de muelas do·*lor* de *mwe*·las
toothbrush cepillo ⓜ de dientes se·*pee*·yo de *dyen*·tes
toothpaste pasta ⓕ de dientes *pas*·ta de *dyen*·tes

toothpick palillo ⓜ pa·lee·yo
torch linterna ⓕ leen·ter·na
touch tocar to·kar
tour excursión ⓕ ek·skoor·syon
tourist turista ⓜ&ⓕ too·rees·ta
tourist office oficina ⓕ de turismo o·fee·see·na de too·rees·mo
towards hacia a·sya
towel toalla ⓕ to·a·ya
tower torre ⓕ to·re
toxic waste residuos ⓜ pl tóxicos re·see·dwos tok·see·kos
toyshop juguetería ⓕ hoo·ge·te·ree·a
track (footprints) rastro ⓜ ras·tro
track (path) sendero ⓜ sen·de·ro
track (sport) pista ⓕ pees·ta
trade comercio ⓜ ko·mer·syo
traffic tráfico ⓜ tra·fee·ko
traffic lights semáforos ⓜ pl se·ma·fo·ros
trail camino ⓜ ka·mee·no
train tren ⓜ tren
train station estación ⓕ de tren es·ta·syon de tren
tram tranvía ⓜ tran·vee·a
transit lounge sala ⓕ de tránsito sa·la de tran·see·to
translate traducir tra·doo·seer
transport transporte ⓜ trans·por·te
travel viajar vya·har
travel agency agencia ⓕ de viajes a·hen·sya de vya·hes
travel books guías ⓕ pl turísticas gee·as too·rees·tee·kas
travel sickness mareo ⓜ ma·re·o
tree arbol ⓜ ar·bol
trip viaje ⓜ vya·he
trousers pantalones ⓜ pl pan·ta·lo·nes
truck camión ⓜ ka·myon
trust confianza ⓕ kon·fee·an·sa
trust confiar kon·fee·ar
try probar pro·bar
try (attempt) intentar een·ten·tar
T-shirt camiseta ⓕ ka·mee·se·ta
tube (tyre) cámara ⓕ de llanta ka·ma·ra de yan·ta
tuna atún ⓜ a·toon
tune melodía ⓕ me·lo·dee·a
turkey pavo ⓜ pa·vo
turn dar vuelta dar vwel·ta
TV televisión ⓕ te·le·vee·syon
TV series serie ⓕ se·rye
tweezers pinzas ⓕ pl peen·sas
twice dos veces dos ve·ses
twin beds dos camas individuales dos ka·mas een·dee·vee·dwal·es
twins gemelos/as ⓜ/ⓕ pl he·me·los/as
type tipo ⓜ tee·po
type escribir a máquina es·kree·beer a ma·kee·na
typical típico/a ⓜ/ⓕ tee·pee·ko/a
tyre llanta ⓕ yan·ta

U

ultrasound ultrasonido ⓜ ool·tra·so·nee·do
umbrella paraguas ⓜ pa·ra·gwas
umpire árbitro ⓜ ar·bee·tro
uncomfortable incómodo/a ⓜ/ⓕ een·ko·mo·do/a
underpants (men) calzoncillos ⓜ pl kal·son·see·yos
underpants (women) pantaletas ⓕ pl pan·ta·le·tas
understand comprender kom·pren·der
underwear ropa ⓕ interior ro·pa een·te·ryor
unemployed desempleado/a ⓜ/ⓕ des·em·ple·a·do/a
unfair injusto/a ⓜ/ⓕ een·hoos·to/a
uniform uniforme ⓜ oo·nee·for·me
universe universo ⓜ oo·nee·ver·so
university universidad ⓕ oo·nee·ver·see·dad
unleaded sin plomo seen plo·mo
unsafe inseguro/a ⓜ/ⓕ een·se·goo·ro/a

until (June) hasta (junio) *as*·ta (*hoo*·nyo)
unusual raro/a ⓜ/ⓕ *ra*·ro/a
up arriba a·*ree*·ba
uphill cuesta arriba *kwes*·ta a·*ree*·ba
urgent urgente oor·*hen*·te
USA Estados ⓜ pl Unidos (de América) es·*ta*·dos oo·*nee*·dos (de a·*me*·ree·ka)
useful útil *oo*·teel

V

vacant vacante va·*kan*·te
vacation vacaciones ⓕ pl va·ka·*syo*·nes
vaccination vacuna ⓕ va·*koo*·na
vagina vagina ⓕ va·*hee*·na
validate validar va·lee·*dar*
valley valle ⓜ *va*·ye
valuable valioso/a ⓜ/ⓕ va·*lyo*·so/a
value valor ⓜ va·*lor*
van vagoneta ⓕ va·go·*ne*·ta
veal ternera ⓕ ter·*ne*·ra
vegan vegano/a ⓜ/ⓕ veh·*ga*·no/a
vegetable legumbre ⓕ le·*goom*·bre
vegetables verduras ⓕ ver·*doo*·ras
vegetarian vegetariano/a ⓜ/ⓕ ve·he·ta·*rya*·no/a
vein vena ⓕ *ve*·na
venereal disease enfermedad ⓕ venérea en·fer·me·*dad* ve·*ne*·re·a
venue local ⓜ lo·*cal*
very muy mooy
video tape videocassette ⓕ vee·de·o·ka·*set*
view vista ⓕ *vees*·ta
village pueblo ⓜ *pwe*·blo
vine vid ⓕ veed
vinegar vinagre ⓜ vee·*na*·gre
vineyard viñedo ⓜ vee·*nye*·do
virus virus ⓜ *vee*·roos
visa visa ⓕ *vee*·sa
visit visitar vee·see·*tar*
vitamins vitaminas ⓕ pl vee·ta·*mee*·nas
vodka vodka ⓕ *vod*·ka
voice voz ⓕ vos
volume volumen ⓜ vo·*loo*·men
vote votar vo·*tar*

W

wage sueldo ⓜ *swel*·do
wait esperar es·pe·*rar*
waiter mesero/a ⓜ/ⓕ me·*se*·ro/a
waiting room sala ⓕ de espera *sa*·la de es·*pe*·ra
walk caminar ka·mee·*nar*
wall (inside) pared ⓕ pa·*red*
wallet cartera ⓕ kar·*te*·ra
want querer ke·*rer*
war guerra ⓕ *ge*·ra
wardrobe closet ⓜ *klo*·set
warm templado/a ⓜ/ⓕ tem·*pla*·do/a
warn advertir ad·ver·*teer*
wash (oneself) lavarse la·*var*·se
wash (something) lavar la·*var*
wash cloth toallita ⓕ twa·*ee*·ta
washing machine lavadora ⓕ la·va·*do*·ra
watch reloj ⓜ de pulsera re·*loh* de pool·*se*·ra
watch mirar mee·*rar*
water agua ⓕ *a*·gwa
— **boiled water** agua ⓕ hervida *a*·gwa er·*vee*·da
— **still water** agua ⓕsin gas *a*·gwa seen gas
— **tap water** agua ⓕ de la llave *a*·gwa de la *ya*·ve
water bottle botella reutilizable ⓕ bo·*te*·ya re·oo·tee·lee·*sa*·ble
waterfall cascada ⓕ kas·*ka*·da
watermelon sandía ⓕ san·*dee*·a
waterproof impermeable eem·per·me·*a*·ble
waterskiing esquí ⓜ acuático es·*kee* a·*kwa*·tee·ko

wave ola ⓕ o·la
way camino ⓜ ka·mee·no
we nosotros/as ⓜ/ⓕ pl no·so·tros/as
weak débil de·beel
wealthy rico/a ⓜ/ⓕ ree·ko/a
wear llevar ye·var
weather tiempo ⓜ tyem·po
wedding boda ⓕ bo·da
wedding cake pastel ⓜ de bodas pas·tel de bo·das
wedding present regalo ⓜ de bodas re·ga·lo de bo·das
weekend fin ⓜ de semana feen de se·ma·na
weigh pesar pe·sar
weight peso ⓜ pe·so
weights pesas ⓕ pl pe·sas
welcome bienvenida ⓕ byen·ve·nee·da
welcome dar la bienvenida dar la byen·ve·nee·da
welfare bienestar ⓜ byen·es·tar
well (good) bien byen
well (with water) pozo ⓜ po·so
west oeste ⓜ o·es·te
wet mojado/a ⓜ/ⓕ mo·ha·do/a
wetsuit wetsuit ⓜ wet·soot
what qué ke
wheel rueda ⓕ rwe·da
wheelchair silla ⓕ de ruedas see·ya de rwe·das
when cuándo kwan·do
where dónde don·de
white blanco/a ⓜ/ⓕ blan·ko/a
whiteboard pizzarón ⓜ blanco pee·sa·ron blan·ko
who quién kyen
why por qué por ke
wide ancho/a ⓜ/ⓕ an·cho/a
wife esposa ⓕ es·po·sa
win ganar ga·nar
wind viento ⓜ vyen·to
window ventana ⓕ ven·ta·na
window-shopping mirar los aparadores mee·rar los a·pa·ra·do·res
windscreen parabrisas ⓜ pa·ra·bree·sas
windsurfing hacer windsurf a·ser weend·soorf
wine vino ⓜ vee·no
winery bodega ⓕ de vinos bo·de·ga de vee·nos
wings alas ⓕ pl a·las
winner ganador/ganadora ⓜ/ⓕ ga·na·dor/ga·na·do·ra
winter invierno ⓜ een·vyer·no
wire alambre ⓜ a·lam·bre
wish desear de·se·ar
with con kon
within (an hour) dentro de (una hora) den·tro de (oo·na o·ra)
without sin seen
woman mujer ⓕ moo·her
wonderful maravilloso/a ⓜ/ⓕ ma·ra·vee·yo·so/a
wood madera ⓕ ma·de·ra
wool lana ⓕ la·na
word palabra ⓕ pa·la·bra
work trabajo ⓜ tra·ba·ho
work trabajar tra·ba·har
work experience experiencia ⓕ laboral ek·spe·ryen·sya la·bo·ral
work permit permiso ⓜ de trabajo per·mee·so de tra·ba·ho
workout entrenamiento ⓜ en·tre·na·myen·to
workshop taller ⓜ ta·yer
world mundo ⓜ moon·do
World Cup Copa ⓕ Mundial ko·pa moon·dyal
worms lombrices ⓕ pl lom·bree·ses
worried preocupado/a ⓜ/ⓕ pre·o·koo·pa·do/a
worship rezar re·sar
wrist muñeca ⓕ moo·nye·ka
write escribir es·kree·beer
writer escritor/escritora ⓜ/ⓕ es·kree·tor/es·kree·to·ra
wrong equivocado/a ⓜ/ⓕ e·kee·vo·ka·do/a

Y

year año ⓜ a·nyo
yellow amarillo/a ⓜ/ⓕ a·ma·*ree*·yo/a
yes sí see
(not) yet todavía (no) to·da·*vee*·a (no)
yesterday ayer a·*yer*
yoga yoga ⓜ *yo*·ga
yoghurt yogurt ⓜ yo·*goort*
you sg inf tú too
you sg pol Usted oos·*ted*
you pl inf&pol Ustedes oos·*te*·des
young joven *ho*·ven
your inf sg/pl tu/tus too/toos
your pol sg/pl su/sus soo/soos
youth hostel albergue ⓜ juvenil al·*ber*·ge hoo·ve·*neel*

Z

zodiac zodíaco ⓜ so·*dee*·a·ko
zoo zoológico ⓜ so·o·*lo*·hee·ko
zoom lens telefoto ⓜ te·le·*fo*·to

DICTIONARY

Mexican Spanish to English

ESPAÑOL MEXICANO – INGLÉS

Nouns in the dictionary have their gender indicated by ⓜ or ⓕ. If it's a plural noun, you'll also see pl. Where a word that could be either a noun or a verb has no gender indicated, it's a verb. For all words relating to local food, see the **menu decoder** (p189).

A

a bordo a *bor*·do aboard
abajo a·*ba*·ho below • down
abeja ⓕ a·*be*·ha bee
abierto/a ⓜ/ⓕ a·*byer*·to/a open
abogado/a ⓜ/ⓕ a·bo·*ga*·do/a lawyer
aborto ⓜ a·*bor*·to abortion
— natural na·too·*ral* miscarriage
abrazar ⓜ a·bra·*sar* cuddle • hug
abrazo ⓜ a·*bra*·so hug
abrelatas ⓜ a·bre·*la*·tas can opener • tin opener
abrigo ⓜ a·*bree*·go overcoat
abrir a·*broor* open
abuela ⓕ a·*bwe*·la grandmother
abuelo ⓜ a·*bwe*·lo grandfather
aburrido/a a·boo·*ree*·do/a bored • boring
acabar a·ka·*bar* end
acampar a·kam·*par* camp
acantilado ⓜ a·kan·tee·*la*·do cliff
accidente ⓜ ak·see·*den*·te accident
aceptar a·sep·*tar* accept
acondicionador ⓜ a·kon·dee·syo·na·*dor* conditioner
acoso ⓜ a·*ko*·so harassment
acta ⓕ **de nacimiento** *ak*·ta de na·see·*myen*·to birth certificate
acupuntura ⓕ a·koo·poon·*too*·ra acupuncture
adaptador ⓜ a·dap·ta·*dor* adaptor
adentro a·*den*·tro inside
adiós a·*dyos* goodbye
adivinar a·dee·vee·*nar* guess
administración ⓕ ad·mee·nees·tra·*syon* administration
admitir ad·mee·*teer* admit • allow
adolorido/a ⓜ/ⓕ a·do·lo·*ree*·do/a sore
aduana ⓕ a·*dwa*·na customs
adulto/a ⓜ/ⓕ a·*dool*·to/a adult
advertir ad·ver·*teer* warn
aerolínea ⓕ a·e·ro·*lee*·ne·a airline
aeropuerto ⓜ a·e·ro·*pwer*·to airport
aficionados ⓜ&ⓕ pl a·fee·syo·*na*·dos supporters
afortunado/a ⓜ/ⓕ a·for·too·*na*·do/a lucky

agencia ⓕ **de noticias** a·hen·sya de no·tee·syas newsagency
agencia ⓕ **de viajes** a·hen·sya de vya·hes travel agency
agenda ⓕ a·hen·da diary
agente ⓜ **inmobiliario** a·hen·te een·mo·bee·lya·ryo real estate agent
agotar a·go·tar exhaust
agresivo/a ⓜ/ⓕ a·gre·see·vo/a aggressive
agricultura ⓕ a·gree·kool·too·ra agriculture
agua ⓕ a·gwa water
aguja ⓕ a·goo·ha needle (sewing)
ahora a·o·ra now
ahorrar a·o·rar save (money)
aire ⓜ ai·re air
— acondicionado a·kon·dee·syo·na·do air-conditioning
ajedrez ⓜ a·he·dres chess
ajo ⓜ a·ho garlic
al lado de al la·do de next to
alacena ⓕ a·la·se·na cupboard
alambre ⓜ a·lam·bre wire
alas ⓕ pl a·las wings
alba ⓕ al·ba dawn
alberca ⓕ al·ber·ka swimming pool
albergue ⓜ **juvenil** al·ber·ge hoo·ve·neel youth hostel
alcalde ⓜ&ⓕ al·kal·de mayor
Alemania ⓕ a·le·ma·nya Germany
alergia ⓕ a·ler·hya allergy
— al polen al po·len hay fever
aletas pl ⓕ a·le·tas flippers
alfarería ⓕ al·fa·re·ree·a pottery
alfombra ⓕ al·fom·bra rug
algo al·go something
algodón ⓜ al·go·don cotton
alguien al·gyen someone
algún al·goon some
alguno/a ⓜ/ⓕ sg al·goo·no/a any
algunos/as ⓜ/ⓕ pl al·goo·nos/as some
alimentar a·lee·men·tar feed
alimento ⓜ **para bebé** a·lee·men·to pa·ra be·be baby food
almohada ⓕ al·mwa·da pillow
almuerzo ⓜ al·mwer·so lunch
alojamiento ⓜ a·lo·ha·myen·to accommodation
alojarse a·lo·har·se stay (somewhere)
alpinismo ⓜ al·pee·nees·mo mountaineering
altar ⓜ al·tar altar
altar ⓜ al·tar shrine
alto/a ⓜ/ⓕ al·to/a high • tall
altura ⓕ al·too·ra altitude
alucinar a·loo·see·nar hallucinate
ama ⓕ **de casa** a·ma de ka·sa homemaker
amable a·ma·ble kind
amanecer ⓜ a·ma·ne·ser dawn • sunrise
amante ⓜ&ⓕ a·man·te lover
amar a·mar love
amarillo/a ⓜ/ⓕ a·ma·ree·yo/a yellow
amigo/a ⓜ/ⓕ a·mee·go/a friend
ampolla ⓕ am·po·ya blister
analgésicos ⓜ pl a·nal·he·see·kos painkillers
análisis ⓜ **de sangre** a·na·lee·sees de san·gre blood test
anarquista ⓜ&ⓕ a·nar·kees·ta anarchist
ancho/a ⓜ/ⓕ an·cho/a wide
andar an·dar go • walk
— en bicicleta en bee·see·kle·ta cycle
— en patineta en pa·tee·ne·ta skate-boarding
anillo ⓕ a·nee·yo ring
animal ⓜ a·nee·mal animal
anotar a·no·tar score
antier an·tyer day before yesterday
anteojos ⓜ pl an·te·o·hos glasses
antibióticos ⓜ pl an·tee·byo·tee·kos antibiotics
anticonceptivos ⓜ pl an·tee·kon·sep·tee·vos contraceptives
antigüedad ⓕ an·tee·gwe·dad antique
antiguo/a ⓜ/ⓕ an·tee·gwo/a ancient

antiséptico ⓜ an·tee·*sep*·tee·ko antiseptic
antología ⓕ an·to·lo·*hee*·a anthology
anuncio ⓜ a·*noon*·syo advertisement
año ⓜ *a*·nyo year
apellido ⓜ a·pe·*yee*·do family name
apenado/a ⓜ/ⓕ a·pe·*na*·do/a embarrassed
apéndice ⓜ a·*pen*·dee·se appendix
apodo ⓜ a·*po*·do nickname
aprender a·pren·*der* learn
apretado/a ⓜ/ⓕ a·pre·*ta*·do/a tight
aptitudes ⓕ pl ap·tee·*too*·des natural talents • skills
apuesta ⓕ a·*pwes*·ta bet
apuntar a·poon·*tar* point
aquí a·*kee* here
araña ⓕ a·*ra*·nya spider
árbitro ⓜ *ar*·bee·tro umpire • referee
árbol ⓜ *ar*·bol tree
arcoiris ⓜ ar·co·*ee*·rees rainbow
área ⓕ **para acampar** *a*·re·a *pa*·ra a·kam·*par* campsite
arena ⓕ a·*re*·na sand
aretes ⓜ pl a·*re*·tes earrings
arqueológico/a ⓜ/ⓕ ar·ke·o·*lo*·hee·ko/a archaeological
archeólogo/a ⓜ/ⓕ ar·ke·o·lo·go/a archeologist
arquitecto/a ⓜ/ⓕ ar·kee·*tek*·to/a architect
arquitectura ⓕ ar·kee·tek·*too*·ra architecture
arriba a·*ree*·ba above • up
arroyo ⓜ a·*ro*·yo stream
arte ⓜ *ar*·te art
artes ⓜ pl **marciales** *ar*·tes mar·*sya*·les martial arts
artesanía ⓕ ar·te·sa·*nee*·a handicraft
artista ⓜ&ⓕ ar·*tees*·ta artist
— callejero/a ⓜ/ⓕ ka·ye·*he*·ro/a busker
asiento ⓜ a·*syen*·to seat
— de seguridad para bebés de se·goo·ree·*dad* *pa*·ra be·*bes* child seat
asma ⓜ *as*·ma asthma
aspirina ⓕ as·pee·*ree*·na aspirin
asqueroso/a ⓜ/ⓕ as·ke·*ro*·so/a foul
atletismo ⓜ at·le·*tees*·mo athletics
atmósfera ⓕ at·*mos*·fe·ra atmosphere
audífono ⓜ ow·*dee*·fo·no hearing aid
audioguía ⓕ ow·dyo·*gee*·a guide (audio)
autobús ⓜ ow·to·*boos* bus (city)
autoservicio ⓜ ow·to·ser·*vee*·syo self-service
avenida ⓕ a·ve·*nee*·da avenue
avión ⓜ a·*vyon* plane
ayer a·*yer* yesterday
ayudar a·yoo·*dar* help
azteca as·*te*·ka Aztec
azul a·*sool* blue

B

bailar bai·*lar* dance
baile ⓜ *bai*·le dance • dancing
bajo/a ⓜ/ⓕ *ba*·ho/a low • short (height)
balcón ⓜ bal·*kon* balcony
básquetbol/básquet ⓜ *bahs*·ket·bol/ *bahs*·ket basketball
bálsamo ⓜ **labial** *bal*·sa·mo la·*byal* lip balm
banco ⓜ *ban*·ko bank
bandera ⓕ ban·*de*·ra flag
baño ⓜ *ba*·nyo toilet • bathroom
baños ⓜ pl **públicos** *ba*·nyos *poo*·blee·kos public toilet
banqueta ⓕ ban·*ke*·ta footpath • sidewalk
bar ⓜ bar bar • pub
— con música en vivo kon *moo*·see·ka en *vee*·vo bar (with live music)
barato/a ⓜ/ⓕ ba·*ra*·to/a cheap
barbero ⓜ bar·*beh*·ro barber
barco ⓜ *bar*·ko ship
barrio ⓜ *bar*·yo neighbourhood

basura ⓕ *ba·soo·ra* rubbish
batería ⓕ *ba·te·ree·a* drums • battery (car)
bautizo ⓜ *bow·tee·so* baptism
bebé ⓜ *be·be* baby
bebida ⓕ *be·bee·da* drink
becerro ⓜ *be·se·ro* calf
besar *be·sar* kiss
beso ⓜ *be·so* kiss
biblioteca ⓕ *bee·blyo·te·ka* library
bicho ⓜ *bee·cho* bug (insect)
bici ⓕ *bee·see* bike
bicicleta ⓕ *bee·see·kle·ta* bicycle
— de carreras *de ka·re·ras* racing bike
— de montaña *de mon·ta·nya* mountain bike
bien *byen* well
bienestar ⓜ *byen·es·tar* welfare
bienestar social ⓜ *byen·e·star so·syal* social welfare
bienvenida ⓕ *byen·ve·nee·da* welcome
billetes ⓜ pl *bee·ye·tes* banknotes
biodegradable *byo·de·gra·da·ble* biodegradable
biografía ⓕ *byo·gra·fee·a* biography
blanco *blan·ko* white
bloqueado/a ⓜ/ⓕ *blo·ke·a·do/a* blocked
bloqueador ⓜ **solar** *blo·ke·a·dor so·lar* sunblock
boca ⓕ *bo·ka* mouth
bocado ⓜ *bo·ka·do* bite (food)
boda ⓕ *bo·da* wedding
bodega ⓕ **de vinos** *bo·de·ga de vee·nos* winery
bol ⓜ *bol* bowl
bolas ⓕ pl **de algodón** *bo·las de al·go·don* cotton balls
boleto ⓜ *bo·le·to* ticket
— de viaje redondo *de vya·he re·don·do* return ticket
— en lista de espera *en lees·ta de es·pe·ra* standby ticket
— sencillo *sen·see·yo* one-way ticket
bolsa ⓕ *bol·sa* bag • handbag
— de dormir *de dor·meer* sleeping bag
bolsillo ⓜ *bol·see·yo* pocket
bomba ⓕ *bom·ba* pump • bomb
bondadoso/a ⓜ/ⓕ *bon·da·do·so/a* caring
bonito/a ⓜ/ⓕ *bo·nee·to/a* pretty
borracho/a ⓜ/ⓕ *bo·ra·cho/a* drunk
bosque ⓜ *bos·ke* forest
botana ⓕ *bo·ta·na* snack
botas ⓕ pl *bo·tas* boots
— de montaña *de mon·ta·nya* hiking boots
bote ⓜ *bo·te* boat
botella ⓕ *bo·te·ya* bottle
botella reutilizable ⓕ *bo·te·ya re·oo·tee·lee·sa·ble* water bottle
botiquín de primeros auxilios ⓜ *bo·tee·keen de pree·me·ros awk·see·lyos* first-aid kit
botones ⓜ pl *bo·to·nes* buttons
boxeo ⓜ *bok·se·o* boxing
brazo ⓜ *bra·so* arm
brillante *bree·yan·te* brilliant
broma ⓕ *bro·ma* joke
bromear *bro·me·ar* joke
bronceador ⓜ *bron·se·a·dor* tanning lotion
bronquitis ⓕ *bron·kee·tees* bronchitis
brújula ⓕ *broo·hoo·la* compass
buceo ⓜ *boo·se·o* diving
budista ⓜ&ⓕ *boo·dees·ta* Buddhist
bueno/a ⓜ/ⓕ *bwe·no/a* good
bufanda ⓕ *boo·fan·da* scarf
bulto ⓜ *bool·to* lump
burlarse de *boor·lar·se de* make fun of
burro ⓜ *boo·ro* donkey
buscar *boos·kar* look for
buzón ⓜ *boo·son* mailbox

C

caballo ⓜ *ka·ba·yo* horse
cabeza ⓕ *ka·be·sa* head
cable ⓜ *ka·ble* cable

cables ⓜ pl **pasacorriente** *ka·bles pa·sa·ko·ryen·tes* jumper leads
cabra ⓕ *ka·bra* goat
cachorro ⓜ *ka·cho·ro* puppy
cada *ka·da* each
cadena ⓕ **de bici** *ka·de·na de bee·see* bike chain
café ⓜ *ka·fe* coffee • cafe
caída ⓕ *ka·ee·da* fall (tumble)
caja ⓕ *ka·ha* box • cash register
— fuerte *fwer·te* safe
cajero/a ⓜ/ⓕ *ka·he·ro/a* cashier
cajero ⓜ **automático** *ka·he·ro ow·to·ma·tee·ko* ATM
calcetines ⓜ pl *kal·se·tee·nes* socks
calculadora ⓕ *kal·koo·la·do·ra* calculator
caldo ⓜ *kal·do* stock (soup)
calefacción ⓕ **central** *ka·le·fak·syon sen·tral* central heating
calendario ⓜ *ka·len·da·ryo* calendar
calentador ⓜ *ka·len·ta·dor* heater
calidad ⓕ *ka·lee·dad* quality
caliente *ka·lyen·te* hot
calle ⓕ *ka·ye* street
calor ⓜ *ka·lor* heat
cama ⓕ *ka·ma* bed
— matrimonial *ma·tree·mo·nyal* double bed
cámara ⓕ **de llanta** *ka·ma·ra de yan·ta* tube (tyre)
cámara ⓕ *ka·ma·ra* camera
cambiar *kam·byar* change • exchange (money)
— un cheque *oon che·ke* cash a cheque
cambio ⓜ *kam·byo* exchange • change (money) • loose change
— de moneda *de mo·ne·da* currency exchange
caminar *ka·mee·nar* walk
camino ⓜ *ka·mee·no* road • trail • way • path
camión ⓜ *ka·myon* intercity bus • truck
camioneta ⓕ *ka·myo·ne·ta* pickup • ute
camisa ⓕ *ka·mee·sa* shirt
camiseta ⓕ *ka·mee·se·ta* singlet • T-shirt
campo ⓜ *kam·po* field • countryside
— de golf *de golf* golf course
canasta ⓕ *ka·nas·ta* basket
cancelar *kan·se·lar* cancel
cancha ⓕ **de tenis** *kan·cha de te·nees* tennis court
canción ⓕ *kan·syon* song
candado ⓜ *kan·da·do* padlock
candidiasis oral ⓕ *kan·dee·dya·sees o·ral* thrush
cansado/a ⓜ/ⓕ *kan·sa·do/a* tired
cantante ⓜ&ⓕ *kan·tan·te* singer
cantar *kan·tar* sing
capa ⓕ *ka·pa* cloak
— de ozono *de o·so·no* ozone layer
cara ⓕ *ka·ra* face
caracol ⓜ *ka·ra·kol* snail
caravana ⓕ *ka·ra·va·na* caravan
cárcel ⓕ *kar·sel* prison • jail
cardiopatía ⓕ *kar·dyo·pa·tee·a* heart condition
carne ⓕ *kar·ne* meat
carnicería ⓕ *kar·nee·se·ree·a* butcher's shop
caro/a ⓜ/ⓕ *ka·ro/a* expensive
carpintero ⓜ *kar·peen·te·ro* carpenter
carrera ⓕ *ka·re·ra* race (sport) • university studies
carretera ⓕ *ka·re·te·ra* motorway • highway
carta ⓕ *kar·ta* letter • menu
cartas ⓕ pl *kar·tas* playing cards
cartón ⓜ *kar·ton* cardboard • carton
casa ⓕ *ka·sa* house
— de cambio *de kam·byo* foreign exchange office
casarse *ka·sar·se* marry
cascada ⓕ *kas·ka·da* waterfall
casco ⓜ *kas·ko* helmet
casi *ka·see* almost

casilleros ⓜ pl ka·see·ye·ros luggage lockers
castigar kas·tee·gar punish
castillo ⓜ kas·tee·yo castle
catedral ⓕ ka·te·dral cathedral
católico/a ⓜ/ⓕ ka·to·lee·ko/a Catholic
caza ⓕ ka·sa hunting
cazuela ⓕ ka·swe·la pot (kitchen)
cejas ⓕ pl se·has eyebrows
celebración ⓕ se·le·bra·syon celebration
celebrar se·le·brar celebrate (an event)
celoso/a ⓜ/ⓕ se·lo·so/a jealous
cementerio ⓜ se·men·te·ryo cemetery
cena ⓕ se·na dinner
cenicero ⓜ se·nee·se·ro ashtray
centavo ⓜ sen·ta·vo cent
centímetro ⓜ sen·tee·me·tro centimetre
central ⓕ **telefónica** sen·tral te·le·fo·nee·ka telephone centre
centro ⓜ sen·tro centre
— comercial ko·mer·syal shopping centre
— de la ciudad de la syoo·dad city centre
Centroamérica ⓕ sen·tro·a·me·ree·ka Central America
cepillo ⓜ se·pee·yo hairbrush
— de dientes de dyen·tes toothbrush
cerámica ⓕ se·ra·mee·ka ceramic
cerca ⓕ ser·ka fence
cerca ser·ka near • nearby
cerillos ⓜ pl se·ree·yos matches
cerrado/a ⓜ/ⓕ se·ra·do/a closed • shut
— con llave kon ya·ve locked
cerradura ⓕ se·ra·doo·ra lock
cerrar se·rar close • lock • shut
certificado ⓜ ser·tee·fee·ka·do certificate • registered (mail)
cerveza ⓕ ser·ve·sa beer
chaleco ⓜ **salvavidas** cha·le·ko sal·va·vee·das life jacket
chamarra ⓕ cha·ma·ra jacket
champán ⓜ cham·pan champagne
chapulines ⓜ pl cha·poo·lee·nes grasshoppers
cheque ⓜ che·ke cheque • check (bank)
chichis ⓕ pl inf chee·chees breasts
chicle ⓜ chee·kle chewing gum
chica ⓕ chee·ka girl
chico ⓜ chee·ko boy
chico/a ⓜ/ⓕ chee·ko/a small
chimenea ⓕ chee·me·ne·a fireplace
chip ⓜ cheep SIM card
choque ⓜ cho·ke crash
chupón ⓜ choo·pon dummy • pacifier
cibercafé ⓜ see·ber·ka·fe internet cafe
ciclismo ⓜ see·klees·mo cycling
ciclista ⓜ&ⓕ see·klees·ta cyclist
ciclovía ⓕ see·klo·vee·a bike path
ciego/a ⓜ/ⓕ sye·go/a blind
cielo ⓜ sye·lo sky
ciencias ⓕ pl syen·syas science
científico/a ⓜ/ⓕ syen·tee·fee·ko/a scientist
cigarro ⓜ see·ga·ro cigarette
cine ⓜ see·ne cinema
cinturón ⓜ **de seguridad** seen·too·ron de se·goo·ree·dad seatbelt
circo ⓜ seer·ko circus
cita ⓕ see·ta appointment • date
ciudad ⓕ syoo·dad city
ciudadanía ⓕ syoo·da·da·nee·a citizenship
clase ⓕ **ejecutiva** kla·se e·he·koo·tee·va business class
clase ⓕ **turística** kla·se too·rees·tee·ka economy class
clásico/a ⓜ/ⓕ kla·see·ko/a classical
clavija ⓕ cla·vee·ha plug (electrical)

clavos ⓜ pl de olor *kla*·vos de o·*lor* cloves
cliente/a ⓜ/ⓕ klee·*en*·te/a client
cobija ⓕ ko·*bee*·ha blanket
cocaína ⓕ ko·ka·*ee*·na cocaine
coche ⓜ *ko*·che car
— cama *ka*·ma sleeping car
cocina ⓕ ko·*see*·na kitchen
cocinar ko·see·*nar* cook
cocinero ⓜ ko·see·*ne*·ro cook
codeína ⓕ ko·de·*ee*·na codeine
código ⓜ postal *ko*·dee·go pos·*tal* post code
congelar kon·he·*lar* freeze
cola ⓕ *ko*·la bottom • queue • tail
colchón ⓜ kol·*chon* mattress
colega ⓜ&ⓕ ko·*le*·ga colleague
cólico ⓜ menstrual *ko*·lee·ko men·*strwal* period pain
colina ⓕ ko·*lee*·na hill
collar ⓜ ko·*yar* necklace
colonia ⓜ ko·*lo*·nya neighbourhood
color ⓜ ko·*lor* colour
combustible ⓜ kom·boos·*tee*·ble fuel
comedia ⓕ ko·*me*·dya comedy
comenzar ko·men·*sar* begin • start
comer ko·*mer* eat
comerciante ⓜ&ⓕ ko·mer·*syan*·te business person
comercio ⓜ ko·*mer*·syo trade
comezón ⓜ ko·me·*son* itch
comida ⓕ ko·*mee*·da food
cómo *ko*·mo how
cómodo/a ⓜ/ⓕ *ko*·mo·do/a comfortable
compañero/a ⓜ/ⓕ kom·pa·*nye*·ro/a companion
compañía ⓕ kom·pa·*nyee*·a company
compartir kom·par·*teer* share (with)
comprar kom·*prar* buy
comprender kom·pren·*der* understand
compromiso ⓜ kom·pro·*mee*·so commitment
computadora ⓕ kom·poo·ta·*do*·ra computer
— laptop *lap*·top laptop
— portátil por·*ta*·teel laptop
comunión ⓕ ko·moo·*nyon* communion
comunista ⓜ&ⓕ ko·moo·*nees*·ta communist
con kon with
concierto ⓜ kon·*syer*·to concert
condones ⓜ pl kon·*do*·nes condoms
conducir kon·doo·*seer* drive
conectar ko·nek·*tar* plug
conejo ⓜ ko·*ne*·ho rabbit
conexión ⓕ ko·nek·*syon* connection
confesión ⓕ kon·fe·*syon* confession
confianza ⓕ kon·fee·*an*·sa trust
confiar kon·fee·*ar* trust
confirmar kon·feer·*mar* confirm
conocer ko·no·*ser* know (someone)
consejo ⓜ kon·*se*·ho advice
conservador(a) ⓜ/ⓕ kon·ser·va·*dor*/kon·ser·va·*do*·ra conservative
consigna ⓕ kon·*seeg*·na left luggage
construir kon·stroo·*eer* build
consulado ⓜ kon·soo·*la*·do consulate
contaminación ⓕ kon·ta·mee·na·*syon* pollution
contar kon·*tar* count
contestadora ⓕ kon·tes·ta·*do*·ra answering machine
contrato ⓜ kon·*tra*·to contract
control ⓜ kon·*trol* checkpoint
— remoto re·*mo*·to remote control
convento ⓜ kon·*ven*·to convent
copa ⓕ *ko*·pa wineglass
corazón ⓜ ko·ra·*son* heart
cordillera ⓕ kor·dee·*ye*·ra mountain range
correcto/a ⓜ/ⓕ ko·*rek*·to/a right (correct)

correo ⓜ ko·re·o mail
— aéreo a·e·re·o airmail
— certificado ser·tee·fee·ka·do registered mail
— expresso ek·spre·so express mail
— terrestre te·res·tre surface mail
correr ko·rer run
corrida (de toros) ⓕ ko·ree·da (de to·ros) bullfight
corriente ⓕ ko·ryen·te current (electricity)
corriente ko·ryen·te ordinary
corrupto/a ⓜ/ⓕ ko·roop·to/a corrupt
cortar kor·tar cut
cortauñas ⓜ kor·ta·oo·nyas nail clippers
corte ⓜ **de pelo** kor·te de pe·lo haircut
corto/a ⓜ/ⓕ kor·to/a short (length)
cosecha ⓕ ko·se·cha crop
coser ko·ser sew
costa ⓕ kos·ta coast • seaside
costar kos·tar cost
costo ⓜ kos·to cost
cover ⓜ ko·ver cover charge
crecer kre·ser grow
crema ⓕ kre·ma cream
— hidratante ee·dra·tan·te moisturiser
cristiano/a ⓜ/ⓕ krees·tya·no/a Christian • person
crítica ⓕ kree·tee·ka review
crudo/a ⓜ/ⓕ kroo·do/a raw • hungover
cuaderno ⓜ kwa·der·no notebook
cuadrado ⓜ kwa·dra·do square (shape)
cuando kwan·do when
cuanto kwan·to how much
cuarentena ⓕ kwa·ren·te·na quarantine
cuarto ⓜ kwar·to quarter • room
cubeta ⓕ koo·be·ta bucket
cubiertos ⓜ pl koo·byer·tos cutlery
cucaracha ⓕ koo·ka·ra·cha cockroach
cuchara ⓕ koo·cha·ra spoon
cucharita ⓕ koo·cha·ree·ta teaspoon
cuchillo ⓜ koo·chee·yo knife
cuenta ⓕ kwen·ta bill (account)
— bancaria ban·ka·rya bank account
cuento ⓜ kwen·to story
cuerda ⓕ kwer·da rope • string
cuero ⓜ kwe·ro leather
cuerpo ⓜ kwer·po body
cuesta abajo kwes·ta a·ba·ho downhill
cuesta arriba kwes·ta a·ree·ba uphill
cuevas ⓕ pl kwe·vas caves
cuidar kwee·dar look after • mind
cuidar de kwee·dar de care for
culo ⓜ koo·lo bum (ass)
culpable kool·pa·ble guilty
cumbre ⓕ koom·bre peak
cumpleaños ⓜ koom·ple·a·nyos birthday
cupón ⓜ koo·pon coupon
curitas ⓕ pl koo·ree·tas plasters • Band-Aids
currículum ⓜ koo·ree·koo·loom CV • resumé

D

dados ⓜ pl da·dos dice
dar dar give
— gracias gra·syas thank
— la bienvenida la byen·ve·nee·da welcome
— vuelta vwel·ta turn
dar mordida dar mor·dee·da bribe
darse cuenta de dar·se kwen·ta de realise
de de of • from
— (cuatro) estrellas (kwa·tro) es·tre·yas (four-)star
— derecha de·re·cha right-wing
— izquierda ees·kyer·da left-wing
— segunda mano se·goon·da ma·no second-hand

— vez en cuando ves en *kwan*·do sometimes
deber de·*ber* owe
débil *de*·beel weak
decidir de·see·*deer* decide
decir de·*seer* say • tell
dedo ⓜ *de*·do finger
— del pie del pye toe
defectuoso/a ⓜ/ⓕ de·fek·*two*·so/a faulty
deforestación ⓕ de·fo·res·ta·*syon* deforestation
dejar de·*har* quit
delgado/a ⓜ/ⓕ del·*ga*·do/a thin
delirante de·lee·*ran*·te delirious
demasiado de·ma·*sya*·do too (much)
democracia ⓕ de·mo·*kra*·sya democracy
demora ⓕ de·*mo*·ra delay
dentista ⓜ den·*tees*·ta dentist
dentro de (una hora) *den*·tro de (*oo*·na *o*·ra) within (an hour)
deportes ⓜ pl de·*por*·tes sport
deportista ⓜ&ⓕ de·por·*tees*·ta sportsperson
depósito ⓜ de·*po*·see·to deposit (bank) • convenience liquor store
derecha de·*re*·cha right (not left)
derecho de·*re*·cho straight
derechos ⓜ pl rights
— civiles see·*vee*·les civil rights
— humanos oo·*ma*·nos human rights
desayuno ⓜ de·sa·*yoo*·no breakfast
descansar des·kan·*sar* rest
intermedio ⓜ een·ter·*me*·dyo intermission
descendiente ⓜ de·sen·*dyen*·te descendant
descomponerse des·kom·po·*ner*·se break down
desconocido/a ⓜ/ⓕ des·ko·no·*see*·do/a stranger
descubrir des·koo·*breer* discover
descuento ⓜ des·*kwen*·to discount
desde *des*·de since (time)
desear de·se·*ar* wish
desechable de·se·*cha*·ble disposable
desempeño ⓜ des·em·*pe*·nyo performance (work)
desempleado/a ⓜ/ⓕ des·em·*ple*·a·do/a unemployed
desierto ⓜ de·*syer*·to desert
desodorante ⓜ de·so·do·*ran*·te deodorant
despacio des·*pa*·syo slowly
despedida ⓕ des·pe·*dee*·da farewell
despertador ⓜ des·per·ta·*dor* alarm clock
después de des·*pwes* de after
destapador ⓜ des·ta·pa·*dor* bottle opener
destino ⓜ des·*tee*·no destination
destruir des·troo·*eer* destroy
detallado/a ⓜ/ⓕ de·ta·*ya*·do/a itemised
detalle ⓜ de·*ta*·ye detail
detener de·te·*ner* stop • arrest
detrás de de·*tras* de behind • at the back
día ⓜ *dee*·a day
— de campo de *kam*·po daytrip in the outdoors
— festivo fes·*tee*·vo holiday
diafragma ⓜ dee·a·*frag*·ma diaphragm
diariamente dya·rya·*men*·te daily
diarrea ⓕ dee·a·*re*·a diarrhoea
dibujar dee·boo·*har* draw
diccionario ⓜ deek·syo·*na*·ryo dictionary
dientes ⓜ pl *dyen*·tes teeth
dieta ⓜ *dye*·ta diet
diferencia ⓕ **de horas** dee·fe·*ren*·sya de *o*·ras time difference
diferente dee·fe·*ren*·te different
difícil dee·*fee*·seel difficult
dinero ⓜ dee·*ne*·ro money
— en efectivo en e·fek·*tee*·vo cash
dios ⓜ dyos god
diosa ⓕ *dyo*·sa goddess
dirección ⓕ dee·rek·*syon* address • direction
directo/a ⓜ/ⓕ dee·*rek*·to/a direct

director(a) ⓜ/ⓕ dee·rek·*tor*/ dee·rek·*to*·ra director • manager
directorio ⓜ **telefónico** dee·rek·*to*·ryo te·le·*fo*·nee·ko phone book
discapacitado/a ⓜ/ⓕ dees·ka·pa·see·*ta*·do/a disabled
disco ⓜ *dees*·ko nightclub • record (music) • disk
discriminación ⓕ dees·kree·mee·na·*syon* discrimination
discutir dees·koo·*teer* argue
diseño ⓜ dee·*se*·nyo design
disparar dees·pa·*rar* shoot
DIU ⓜ dee·ee·oo IUD
diversión ⓕ dee·ver·*syon* fun
divertido/a ⓜ/ⓕ dee·ver·*tee*·do/a funny
divertirse dee·ver·*teer*·se enjoy oneself • have fun
divorciado/a ⓜ/ⓕ dee·vor·*sya*·do/a divorced
doble *do*·ble double
docena ⓕ do·*se*·na dozen
doctor(a) ⓜ/ⓕ dok·*tor*/dok·*to*·ra doctor
documentación ⓕ do·koo·men·ta·*syon* check-in • paperwork
documental ⓜ do·koo·men·*tal* documentary
dolor ⓜ do·*lor* pain
— de cabeza de ka·*be*·sa headache
— de estómago de es·*to*·ma·go stomachache
— de muelas de *mwe*·las toothache
doloroso/a ⓜ/ⓕ do·lo·*ro*·so/a painful
donde *don*·de where
dormir dor·*meer* sleep
dos camas individuales dos *ka*·mas een·dee·vee·*dwal*·es twin beds
dos veces dos *ve*·ses twice
droga ⓕ *dro*·ga drug
drogadicción ⓕ dro·ga·deek·*syon* drug addiction
drogas ⓕ pl *dro*·gas drugs (illegal)
dueño/a ⓜ/ⓕ *dwe*·nyo/a owner
duro/a ⓜ/ⓕ *doo*·ro/a hard

E

edad ⓕ e·*dad* age
edificio ⓜ e·dee·*fee*·syo building
educación ⓕ e·doo·ka·*syon* education
egoísta e·go·*ees*·ta selfish
ejemplo ⓜ e·*hem*·plo example
él el he
elecciones ⓕ pl e·lek·*syo*·nes elections
electricidad ⓕ e·lek·tree·see·*dad* electricity
elegir e·le·*heer* choose
elevador ⓜ e·le·va·*dor* lift • elevator
ella *e*·ya she
ellos/ellas ⓜ/ⓕ *e*·yos/*e*·yas they
embajada ⓕ em·ba·*ha*·da embassy
embajador(a) ⓜ/ⓕ em·ba·ha·*dor*/ em·ba·ha·*do*·ra ambassador
embarazada em·ba·ra·*sa*·da pregnant
embarcar em·bar·*kar* board (ship, etc)
embrague ⓜ em·*bra*·ge clutch
emergencia ⓕ e·mer·*hen*·sya emergency
emocional e·mo·syo·*nal* emotional
empinado/a ⓜ/ⓕ em·pee·*na*·do/a steep
empleado/a ⓜ&ⓕ em·ple·*a*·do/a employee
— de oficina de o·fee·*see*·na office worker
empujar em·poo·*har* push
en en on
— casa *ka*·sa (at) home
— el extranjero el ek·stran·*he*·ro abroad
encaje ⓜ en·*ka*·he lace
encantador/a ⓜ/ⓕ en·kan·ta·*dor*/ en·kan·ta·*do*·ra charming
encendedor ⓜ en·sen·de·*dor* cigarette lighter

encontrar en·kon·*trar* find • meet
encuestas ⓕ pl en·*kwes*·tas polls • surveys
energía ⓕ **nuclear** e·ner·*hee*·a noo·kle·*ar* nuclear energy
enfermedad ⓕ en·fer·me·*dad* disease
— venérea ve·*ne*·re·a venereal disease
enfermero/a ⓜ/ⓕ en·fer·*me*·ro/a nurse
enfermo/a ⓜ/ⓕ en·*fer*·mo/a sick • ill
enfrente de en·*fren*·te de in front of
enojado/a ⓜ/ⓕ e·no·*ha*·do/a angry
enorme e·*nor*·me huge
enseñar en·se·*nyar* teach • show
entrar en·*trar* enter
entre *en*·tre between • among
entrega ⓕ **de equipaje** en·*tre*·ga de e·kee·*pa*·he baggage claim
entregar en·tre·*gar* deliver
entrenador(a) ⓜ/ⓕ en·tre·na·*dor*/en·tre·na·*do*·ra coach
entrenamiento ⓜ en·tre·na·*myen*·to workout
entrevista ⓕ en·tre·*vees*·ta interview
enviar en·*vyar* send
epilepsia ⓕ e·pee·*lep*·sya epilepsy
equipaje ⓜ e·kee·*pa*·he luggage • baggage
equipo ⓜ e·*kee*·po team • equipment
— de buceo de boo·*se*·o diving equipment
— estéreo ⓜ es·*te*·ryo stereo
equitación ⓕ e·kee·ta·*syon* horse riding
equivocado/a ⓜ/ⓕ e·kee·vo·*ka*·do/a wrong (mistaken)
error ⓜ e·*ror* mistake
escalada ⓕ **en roca** es·ka·*la*·da en *ro*·ka rock climbing
escalar es·ka·*lar* climb
escalera ⓕ es·ka·*le*·ra stairway
escaleras ⓕ pl **eléctricas** es·ka·*le*·ras e·*lek*·tree·kas escalator
escape ⓜ es·*ka*·pe exhaust pipe
escarcha ⓕ es·*kar*·cha frost
escasez ⓕ es·ka·*ses* shortage
escenario ⓜ e·se·*na*·ryo stage
escribir es·kree·*beer* write
— a máquina a *ma*·kee·na type
escritor(a) ⓜ/ⓕ es·kree·*tor*/es·kree·*to*·ra writer
escuchar es·koo·*char* listen
escuela ⓕ es·*kwe*·la school
escultura ⓕ es·kool·*too*·ra sculpture
esa ⓕ *e*·sa that
ese ⓜ *e*·se that
esgrima ⓕ es·*gree*·ma fencing (sport)
esnorkelear es·nor·ke·le·*ar* snorkelling
espacio ⓜ es·*pa*·syo space
espalda ⓕ es·*pal*·da back (body)
España ⓕ es·*pa*·nya Spain
especial es·pe·*syal* special
especialista ⓜ&ⓕ es·pe·sya·*lees*·ta specialist
especies ⓕ pl **en peligro de extinción** es·*pe*·syes en pe·*lee*·gro de ek·steen·*syon* endangered species
espectáculo ⓜ es·pek·*ta*·koo·lo show
espejo ⓜ es·*pe*·ho mirror
esperar es·pe·*rar* wait
esposa ⓕ es·*po*·sa wife
esposo ⓜ es·*po*·so husband
espuma ⓕ **de rasurar** es·*poo*·ma de ra·soo·*rar* shaving cream
espumoso/a ⓜ/ⓕ es·poo·*mo*·so/a sparkling (liquids) • bubbly
esquí ⓜ es·*kee* skiing
— acuático a·*kwa*·tee·ko waterskiing
esquiar es·kee·*ar* ski
esquina ⓕ es·*kee*·na corner
estacas ⓕ pl es·*ta*·kas tent pegs
estación ⓕ es·ta·*syon* station • season
— de autobuses de ow·to·*boo*·ses bus station
— del metro es·ta·*syon* del *me*·tro metro station

— de policía de po·lee·see·a police station
— de tren de tren railway station • train station
estacionamiento ⓜ es·ta·syo·na·myen·to car park
estacionar es·ta·syo·nar park (car)
estadio ⓜ es·ta·dyo stadium
estado ⓜ **civil** es·ta·do see·veel marital status
Estados ⓜ pl **Unidos (de América)** es·ta·dos oo·nee·dos (de a·me·ree·ka) USA
estafa ⓕ es·ta·fa rip-off
estante ⓜ es·tan·te shelf
estar es·tar be
— de acuerdo de a·kwer·do agree
estatua ⓕ es·ta·twa statue
este es·te east
éste/ésta ⓜ/ⓕ es·te/es·ta this
estilo ⓜ es·tee·lo style
ésto es·to this one
estómago ⓜ es·to·ma·go stomach
estrella ⓕ es·tre·ya star
estreñimiento ⓜ es·tre·nyee·myen·to constipation
estudiante ⓜ&ⓕ es·too·dyan·te student
estudio ⓜ es·too·dyo studio
estufa ⓕ es·too·fa stove
estúpido/a ⓜ/ⓕ es·too·pee·do/a stupid
etiqueta ⓕ **de equipaje** e·tee·ke·ta de e·kee·pa·he luggage tag
eutanasia ⓕ e·oo·ta·na·sya euthanasia
eventual e·ven·twal casual • temporary • possible
excelente ek·se·len·te excellent
excluído/a ⓜ/ⓕ ek·skloo·ee·do/a excluded
excursión ⓕ ek·skoor·syon tour
senderismo ⓜ sen·de·rees·mo hiking
experiencia ⓕ ek·spe·ryen·sya experience
— laboral la·bo·ral work experience
exponer ek·spo·ner exhibit
exposición ⓕ ek·spo·see·syon exhibition
expreso ek·spre·so express
exterior ⓜ ek·ste·ryor outside
extrañar ek·stra·nyar miss (feel absence)
extranjero/a ⓜ/ⓕ ek·stran·he·ro/a foreign
extraño/a ⓜ/ⓕ ek·stra·nyo/a strange

F

fábrica ⓕ fa·bree·ka factory
fácil fa·seel easy
factura ⓕ **del coche** fak·too·ra del ko·che car owner's title
falda ⓕ fal·da skirt
falta ⓕ fal·ta fault
familia ⓕ fa·mee·lya family
famoso/a ⓜ/ⓕ fa·mo·so/a famous
farmacéutico/a ⓜ/ⓕ far·ma·sew·tee·ko chemist (person)
farmacia ⓕ far·ma·sya pharmacy • chemist (shop)
faros ⓜ pl fa·ros headlights
fecha ⓕ fe·cha date (time)
— de nacimiento de na·see·myen·to date of birth
feliz fe·lees happy
ferretería ⓕ fe·re·te·ree·a hardware store
ficción ⓕ feek·syon fiction
fiebre ⓕ fye·bre fever
fiesta ⓕ fyes·ta party
fin ⓜ feen end
— de semana de se·ma·na weekend
firma ⓕ feer·ma signature
firmar feer·mar sign
flor ⓕ flor flower
florista ⓜ&ⓕ flo·rees·ta florist
foco ⓜ fo·ko light bulb
folklórico/a ⓜ/ⓕ fol·klo·ree·ko/a folk
folleto ⓜ fo·ye·to brochure
forma ⓕ for·ma shape
fotografía ⓕ fo·to·gra·fee·a photo • photography

fotógrafo/a ⓜ/ⓕ fo·to·gra·fo/a photographer
fotómetro ⓜ fo·to·me·tro light meter
frágil fra·heel fragile
Francia ⓕ fran·sya France
franela ⓕ fra·ne·la flannel
freír fre·eer fry
frenos ⓜ pl fre·nos brakes
frente a fren·te a opposite
frío/a ⓜ/ⓕ free·o/a cold
frontera ⓕ fron·te·ra border
fruta ⓕ froo·ta fruit
fuego ⓜ fwe·go fire
fuera de lugar fwe·ra de loo·gar offside
fuerte fwer·te strong
fumar foo·mar smoke
funda ⓕ **de almohada** foon·da de al·mwa·da pillowcase
funeral ⓜ foo·ne·ral funeral
fútbol ⓜ foot·bol football • soccer
futuro ⓜ foo·too·ro future

G

galería ⓕ **de arte** ga·le·ree·a de ar·te art gallery
ganador(a) ⓜ/ⓕ ga·na·dor/ga·na·do·ra winner
ganancia ⓜ ga·nan·sya profit
ganar ga·nar win • earn
garganta ⓕ gar·gan·ta throat
gasolina ⓕ ga·so·lee·na petrol • gas
gasolinera ⓕ ga·so·lee·ne·ra service station
gatito/a ⓜ/ⓕ ga·tee·to/a kitten
gato/a ⓜ/ⓕ ga·to/a cat
gay gay gay
gelatina ⓕ he·la·tee·na gelatin
gemelos/as ⓜ/ⓕ pl he·me·los/as twins
general he·ne·ral general
gente ⓕ hen·te people
gimnasia ⓕ heem·na·sya gymnastics
ginebra ⓕ hee·ne·bra gin
ginecólogo/a ⓜ/ⓕ hee·ne·ko·lo·go/a gynaecologist
glorieta ⓕ glo·rye·ta roundabout
gobierno ⓜ go·byer·no government
goggles ⓜ pl go·gles goggles
goma ⓕ go·ma hangover • eraser
gordo/a ⓜ/ⓕ gor·do/a fat
gotas ⓕ pl **para los ojos** go·tas pa·ra los o·hos eye drops
grabación ⓕ gra·ba·syon recording
gramo ⓜ gra·mo gram
grande gran·de big • large
granja ⓕ gran·ha farm
granjero/a ⓜ/ⓕ gran·he·ro/a farmer
grasa gra·sa fat (meat) • grease
gripe ⓕ gree·pe influenza
gris grees grey
gritar gree·tar shout
grupo ⓜ groo·po band
— sanguíneo san·gee·ne·o blood group
guantes ⓜ pl gwan·tes gloves
guapo/a ⓜ/ⓕ gwa·po/a gorgeous
guardarropa ⓜ gwar·da·ro·pa cloakroom
guerra ⓕ ge·ra war
güey ⓜ gway mate • pal (colloquial)
guía ⓜ&ⓕ gee·a guide (person)
guía ⓕ gee·a guidebook
— del ocio del o·syo entertainment guide
— turística too·rees·tee·ka guidebook
guion ⓜ gee·on script
guitarra ⓕ gee·ta·ra guitar
gusanos ⓜ pl **de maguey** goo·sa·nos de ma·gay cactus worms
gustar goos·tar like

H

habitación ⓕ a·bee·ta·syon room • bedroom
— doble do·ble double room

— individual een·dee·vee·*dwal* single room
hablar a·*blar* speak • talk
hacer a·*ser* do • make
hacer senderismo/a a·ser sen·de·rees·mo hike
hachís ⓜ ha·*shees* hash
hacia a·sya towards
hamaca ⓕ a·*ma*·ka hammock
hambre ⓕ *am*·bre hunger
harina ⓕ a·*ree*·na flour
hasta (junio) *as*·ta (*hoo*·nyo) until (June)
hecho/a ⓜ/ⓕ e·cho/a made
— a mano a *ma*·no handmade
— de (algodón) de (al·go·*don*) made of (cotton)
heladería ⓕ e·la·de·*ree*·a ice-cream parlour
helado ⓜ e·*la*·do ice cream
herida ⓕ e·*ree*·da injury
hermana ⓕ er·*ma*·na sister
hermano ⓜ er·*ma*·no brother
hermoso/a ⓜ/ⓕ er·*mo*·so/a beautiful
heroína ⓕ e·ro·*ee*·na heroin
hielo ⓜ *ye*·lo ice
hierbas ⓕ pl *yer*·bas herbs
hígado ⓜ *ee*·ga·do liver
hija ⓕ *ee*·ha daughter
hijo ⓜ *ee*·ho son
hijos ⓜ pl *ee*·hos children
hilo ⓜ **dental** *ee*·lo den·*tal* dental floss
hindú een·*doo* Hindu
hipódromo ⓜ ee·*po*·dro·mo racetrack (horses)
histórico/a ⓜ/ⓕ ees·*to*·ree·ko/a historical
hoja ⓕ *o*·ha leaf • sheet (of paper)
Holanda ⓕ o·*lan*·da Netherlands
hombre ⓜ *om*·bre man
hombro ⓜ *om*·bro shoulder
hora ⓕ *o*·ra time • hour
horario ⓜ **de servicio** o·*ra*·ryo de ser·*vee*·syo timetable • opening hours
hormiga ⓕ or·*mee*·ga ant
horno ⓜ *or*·no oven
— de microondas de mee·kro·*on*·das microwave oven
horóscopo ⓜ o·*ros*·ko·po horoscope
hospital ⓜ os·pee·*tal* hospital
— privado pree·*va*·do private hospital
hotel ⓜ o·*tel* hotel
hotelería ⓕ o·te·le·*ree*·a hospitality
hoy oy today
hueso ⓜ *we*·so bone
humanidades ⓕ pl oo·ma·nee·*da*·des humanities

I

identificación ⓕ ee·den·tee·fee·ka·*syon* identification
idiomas ⓜ pl ee·*dyo*·mas languages
idiota ⓜ&ⓕ ee·*dyo*·ta idiot
iglesia ⓕ ee·*gle*·sya church
igual ee·*gwal* same
igualdad ⓕ ee·gwal·*dad* equality
— de oportunidades de o·por·too·nee·*da*·des equal opportunity
imbécil ⓜ&ⓕ eem·*be*·seel fool
impermeable ⓜ eem·per·me·a·ble raincoat
impermeable eem·per·me·a·ble waterproof
importante eem·por·*tan*·te important
impuesto ⓜ eem·*pwes*·to tax
— sobre la renta (ISR) so·bre la *ren*·ta (ee·ese·ere) income tax
incendio ⓜ een·*sen*·dyo fire
incluído/a ⓜ/ⓕ een·kloo·ee·do/a included
incómodo/a ⓜ/ⓕ een·*ko*·mo·do/a uncomfortable
indicador ⓜ een·dee·ka·*dor* indicator
indigestión ⓕ een·dee·hes·*tyon* indigestion
industria ⓕ een·*doos*·trya industry
infección ⓕ een·fek·*syon* infection
inflamación ⓕ een·fla·ma·*syon*

inflammation
informática ⓕ een·for·*ma*·tee·ka IT
informativo ⓜ een·for·ma·*tee*·vo current affairs
ingeniería ⓕ een·he·nye·*ree*·a engineering
ingeniero/a ⓜ/ⓕ een·he·*nye*·ro/a engineer
Inglaterra ⓕ een·gla·*te*·ra England
inglés ⓜ een·*gles* English (language)
ingrediente ⓜ een·gre·*dyen*·te ingredient
injusto/a ⓜ/ⓕ een·*hoos*·to/a unfair
inmigración ⓕ een·mee·gra·*syon* immigration
inocente ee·no·*sen*·te innocent
inseguro/a ⓜ/ⓕ een·se·*goo*·ro/a unsafe
instructor(a) ⓜ/ⓕ een·strook·*tor*/eens·trook·*to*·ra instructor
intentar een·ten·*tar* try (attempt)
interesante een·te·re·*san*·te interesting
internacional een·ter·na·syo·*nal* international
intérprete ⓜ&ⓕ een·*ter*·pre·te interpreter
inundación ⓕ ee·noon·da·*syon* flooding
invierno ⓜ een·*vyer*·no winter
invitar een·vee·*tar* invite
inyección ⓕ een·yek·*syon* injection
inyectar een·yek·*tar* inject
ir eer go
— de compras de *kom*·pras go shopping
— de excursión de ek·skoor·*syon* tour
irritación ⓕ ee·ree·ta·*syon* irritation • rash
isla ⓕ *ees*·la island
itinerario ⓜ ee·tee·ne·*ra*·ryo itinerary
IVA ⓜ *ee*·va sales tax
izquierda ⓕ ees·*kyer*·da left

J

jabón ⓜ ha·*bon* soap
jalar ha·*lar* pull
Japón ⓜ ha·*pon* Japan
jarabe (para la tos) ⓜ ha·ra·be (*pa*·ra la tos) cough medicine
jardín ⓜ har·*deen* garden
— botánico bo·*ta*·nee·ko botanic garden
— de niños de *nee*·nyos kindergarten
jarra ⓕ *ha*·ra jar
jefe/a ⓜ/ⓕ *he*·fe/a employer • manager
jeringa ⓕ he·*reen*·ga syringe
joven *ho*·ven young
joyería ⓕ ho·ye·*ree*·a jewellery
jubilado/a ⓜ/ⓕ hoo·bee·*la*·do/a retired • retiree
judío/a ⓜ/ⓕ hoo·*dee*·o/a Jewish
juego ⓜ **de computadora** *hwe*·go de kom·poo·ta·*do*·ra computer game
juez ⓜ&ⓕ hwes judge
jugar hoo·*gar* play (sport/games)
— a las cartas a las *kar*·tas play (cards)
jugo ⓜ *hoo*·go juice
juguetería ⓕ hoo·ge·te·*ree*·a toyshop
juntos/as ⓜ/ⓕ *hoon*·tos/as together

L

labios ⓜ pl *la*·byos lips
lado ⓜ *la*·do side
ladrón ⓜ la·*dron* thief
lagartija ⓕ la·gar·*tee*·ha lizard • pushup
lago ⓜ *la*·go lake
lamentar la·men·*tar* regret
lana ⓕ *la*·na wool
lancha ⓕ **de motor** *lan*·cha de mo·*tor* motorboat
lápiz ⓜ *la*·pees pencil
— labial *la*·byal lipstick
larga distancia *lar*·ga dees·*tan*·sya long-distance
largo/a ⓜ/ⓕ *lar*·go/a long
lastimar las·tee·*mar* hurt
lata ⓕ *la*·ta can • tin
lavadora ⓕ la·va·*do*·ra washing machine

lavandería ⓕ la·van·de·ree·a laundry • laundrette
lavar la·var wash (something)
lavarse la·var·se wash (oneself)
leche ⓕ le·che milk
leer le·er read
legal le·gal legal
legislación ⓕ le·hees·la·syon legislation
legumbre ⓕ le·goom·bre vegetable • legume
lejos le·hos far
leña ⓕ le·nya firewood
lente ⓜ len·te lens
lentes ⓜ&ⓕ pl len·tes glasses
— de sol de sol sunglasses
lento/a ⓜ/ⓕ len·to/a slow
ley ⓕ lay law
LGBTI+ eh·leh·heh·beh·teh·ee·mas LGBTIQ+
libra ⓕ lee·bra pound (money)
libre lee·bre free (not bound)
librería ⓕ lee·bre·ree·a bookshop
libro ⓜ lee·bro book
— de frases de fra·ses phrasebook
— de oraciones de o·ra·syo·nes prayer book
licencia ⓕ **de manejo** lee·sen·sya de ma·ne·ho driving licence
licenciatura ⓕ lee·sen·sya·too·ra undergraduate degree
licorería ⓕ lee·ko·re·rya liquor store
líder ⓜ&ⓕ lee·der leader
ligar lee·gar chat up • pick up
ligero/a ⓜ/ⓕ lee·he·ro/a light (of weight)
límite ⓜ **de equipaje** lee·mee·te de e·kee·pa·he baggage allowance
limosnero/a ⓜ/ⓕ lee·mos·ne·ro/a beggar
limpio/a ⓜ/ⓕ leem·pyo/a clean
línea ⓕ lee·ne·a line
linterna ⓕ leen·ter·na torch • flashlight
listo/a ⓜ/ⓕ lees·to/a ready
llamada ⓕ **por cobrar** ya·ma·da por ko·brar collect call
llamar ya·mar call
— por teléfono por te·le·fo·no telephone • ring
llanta ⓕ yan·ta tyre
llave ⓕ ya·ve key • faucet • tap
llegadas ⓕ pl ye·ga·das arrivals
llegar ye·gar arrive
llenar ye·nar fill
lleno/a ⓜ/ⓕ ye·no/a booked out • crowded • full (place/thing)
llevar ye·var carry • take (away) • wear
lluvia ⓕ yoo·vya rain
local lo·kal local
loción ⓕ **para después del afeitado** lo·syon pa·ra des·pwes del a·fay·ta·do aftershave
loco/a ⓜ/ⓕ lo·ko/a crazy
lodo ⓜ lo·do mud
lombrices ⓕ pl lom·bree·ses worms
lubricante ⓜ loo·bree·kan·te lubricant
luces ⓕ pl loo·ses lights
luchar loo·char fight
lugar ⓜ loo·gar place
— de nacimiento de na·see·myen·to place of birth
lujo ⓜ loo·ho luxury
luna ⓕ loo·na moon
— de miel de myel honeymoon
— llena ye·na full moon
luz ⓕ loos light

M

maceta ⓕ ma·se·ta pot (for plant)
madera ⓕ ma·de·ra wood
madre ⓕ ma·dre mother
maestro/a ⓜ/ⓕ ma·es·tro/a teacher
mago/a ⓜ/ⓕ ma·go/a magician
maleta ⓕ ma·le·ta suitcase
malo/a ⓜ/ⓕ ma·lo/a bad
mamá ⓕ ma·ma mum
mamograma ⓜ ma·mo·gra·ma mammogram

mañana ⓕ ma·*nya*·na morning
mañana ma·*nya*·na tomorrow
— en la mañana en la ma·*nya*·na tomorrow morning
— en la noche en la *no*·che tomorrow evening
— en la tarde en la *tar*·de tomorrow afternoon
mandíbula ⓕ man·*dee*·boo·la jaw
manifestación ⓕ ma·nee·fes·ta·*syon* demonstration (protest)
mano ⓕ *ma*·no hand
manteca ⓕ man·*te*·ka lard
mantel ⓜ man·*tel* tablecloth
manubrio ⓜ ma·*noo*·bryo handlebar
mapa ⓜ *ma*·pa map
maquillaje ⓜ ma·kee·*ya*·he make-up
máquina ⓕ *ma*·kee·na machine
— de tabaco de ta·*ba*·ko cigarette machine
máquina ⓕ **de boletos** *ma*·kee·na de bo·*le*·tos ticket machine
mar ⓜ mar sea
maravilloso/a ⓜ/ⓕ ma·ra·vee·*yo*·so/a wonderful
marcación ⓕ **directa** mar·ka·*syon* dee·*rek*·ta direct-dial
marcador ⓜ mar·ka·*dor* scoreboard
marcapasos ⓜ mar·ka·*pa*·sos pacemaker
marea ⓕ ma·*re*·a tide
mareado/a ⓜ/ⓕ ma·re·a·do/a dizzy • seasick
mareo ⓜ ma·*re*·o travel sickness
mariposa ⓕ ma·ree·*po*·sa butterfly
martillo ⓜ mar·*tee*·yo hammer
más mas more
— cercano/a ⓜ/ⓕ mas ser·*ka*·no/a nearest
masaje ⓜ ma·*sa*·he massage
masajista ⓜ&ⓕ ma·sa·*hees*·ta masseur/masseuse
matar ma·*tar* kill
matrícula ⓕ ma·*tree*·koo·la car registration
matrimonio ⓜ ma·tree·*mo*·nyo marriage
mecánico/a ⓜ/ⓕ me·*ka*·nee·ko/a mechanic
medianoche ⓕ me·dya·*no*·che midnight
medicina ⓕ me·dee·*see*·na medicine
medio ambiente ⓜ *me*·dyo am·*byen*·te environment
medio litro *me*·dyo *lee*·tro half a litre
medio/a ⓜ/ⓕ *me*·dyo/a half
mediodía ⓜ me·dyo·*dee*·a noon
medios ⓜ pl **de comunicación** *me*·dyos de ko·moo·nee·ka·*syon* media
mejor me·*hor* better • best
melodía ⓕ me·lo·*dee*·a tune
menos *me*·nos less
mensaje ⓜ men·*sa*·he message
menstruación ⓕ men·strwa·*syon* menstruation
mentiroso/a ⓜ/ⓕ men·tee·*ro*·so/a liar
comida corrida ⓕ ko·*mee*·da ko·*ree*·da set menu
mercado ⓜ mer·*ka*·do market
mes ⓜ mes month
mesa ⓕ *me*·sa table
mesero/a ⓜ/ⓕ me·*se*·ro/a waiter
meseta ⓕ me·*se*·ta plateau
meter ⓜ me·*ter* put
— un gol oon gol kick a goal
metro ⓜ *me*·tro metre • subway
mezclar mes·*klar* mix
mezquita ⓕ mes·*kee*·ta mosque
mi mee my
miembro ⓜ *myem*·bro member
migraña ⓕ mee·*gra*·nya migraine
milímetro ⓜ mee·*lee*·me·tro millimetre
militar ⓜ mee·lee·*tar* military
millón ⓜ mee·*yon* million
minuto ⓜ mee·*noo*·to minute
mirador ⓜ mee·ra·*dor* lookout
mirar mee·*rar* look • watch
— los aparadores los a·pa·ra·*do*·res window-shopping
misa ⓕ *mee*·sa mass

mochila ⓕ mo·*chee*·la backpack • knapsack
mojado/a ⓜ/ⓕ mo·*ha*·do/a wet
monasterio ⓜ mo·nas·*te*·ryo monastery
monedas ⓕ pl mo·*ne*·das coins
monja ⓕ *mon*·ha nun
mononucleosis ⓜ mo·no·nyoo·klee·*oh*·sees glandular fever
montaña ⓕ mon·*ta*·nya mountain
montar mon·*tar* ride
monumento ⓜ mo·noo·*men*·to monument
morado/a ⓜ/ⓕ mo·*ra*·do/a purple
mordedura ⓕ mor·de·*doo*·ra bite (dog)
moretón ⓜ mo·re·*ton* bruise
morir mo·*reer* die
mosquitero ⓜ mos·kee·*te*·ro mosquito net
mosquito ⓜ mos·*kee*·to mosquito
mostrador ⓜ mos·tra·*dor* counter
mostrar mos·*trar* show
mota ⓕ *mo*·ta pot (marijuana)
motocicleta ⓕ mo·to·see·*kle*·ta motorcycle
motor ⓜ mo·*tor* engine
muchos/as ⓜ/ⓕ pl *moo*·chos/as many
mudo/a ⓜ/ⓕ *moo*·do/a mute
muebles ⓜ pl *mwe*·bles furniture
muela ⓕ *mwe*·la tooth (back)
muerto/a ⓜ/ⓕ *mwer*·to/a dead
mujer ⓕ moo·*her* woman
multa ⓕ *mool*·ta fine
mundo ⓜ *moon*·do world
muñeca ⓕ moo·*nye*·ka doll • wrist
murallas ⓕ pl moo·*ra*·yas city walls
músculo ⓜ *moos*·koo·lo muscle
museo ⓜ moo·*se*·o museum
música ⓕ *moo*·see·ka music
músico ⓜ&ⓕ *moo*·see·ko musician
musulmán/musulmana ⓜ/ⓕ moo·sool·*man*/moo·sool·*ma*·na Muslim
muy mooy very

N

nacionalidad ⓕ na·syo·na·lee·*dad* nationality
nada *na*·da none • nothing
nadar na·*dar* swim
naranja na·*ran*·ha orange (colour)
nariz ⓕ na·*rees* nose
naturaleza ⓕ na·too·ra·*le*·sa nature
naturopatía ⓕ na·too·ro·pa·*tee*·a naturopathy
náuseas ⓕ pl **del embarazo** *now*·se·as del em·ba·*ra*·so morning sickness
navaja ⓕ na·*va*·ha penknife
navajas ⓕ pl **de rasurar** na·*va*·has de ra·soo·*rar* razor blades
neblinoso ne·blee·*no*·so foggy
necesario/a ⓜ/ⓕ ne·se·*sa*·ryo/a necessary
necesitar ne·se·see·*tar* need
negar ne·*gar* deny
negar(se) ne·*gar*·(se) refuse
negativos ⓜ pl ne·ga·*tee*·vos negatives (film)
negocios ⓜ pl ne·*go*·syos business
negro/a ⓜ/ⓕ *ne*·gro/a black
nieto/a ⓜ/ⓕ *nye*·to/a grandchild
nieve ⓕ *nye*·ve snow
niñera ⓕ nee·*nye*·ra babysitter
niño/a ⓜ/ⓕ *nee*·nyo/a child
niños ⓜ&ⓕ pl *nee*·nyos children
no fumar no foo·*mar* non-smoking
noche ⓕ *no*·che evening
nombre ⓜ *nom*·bre name • first name
— primer pree·*mer* first name
norte ⓜ *nor*·te north
nosotros/as ⓜ/ⓕ pl no·*so*·tros/as we
noticias ⓕ pl no·*tee*·syas news
novia ⓕ *no*·vya girlfriend
novio ⓜ *no*·vyo boyfriend
nube ⓕ *noo*·be cloud
nublado noo·*bla*·do cloudy
nuestro/a ⓜ/ⓕ *nwes*·tro/a our
Nueva ⓕ **Zelanda** *nwe*·va se·*lan*·da New Zealand

nuevo/a Ⓜ/Ⓕ nwe·vo/a new
número Ⓜ noo·me·ro number
— de habitación de a·bee·ta·syon room number
— de pasaporte de pa·sa·por·te passport number
— de placa de pla·ka licence plate number
nunca noon·ka never

O

o o or
obra Ⓕ o·bra play
obrero/a Ⓜ/Ⓕ o·bre·ro/a labourer • manual worker
océano Ⓜ o·se·a·no ocean
ocupado/a Ⓜ/Ⓕ o·koo·pa·do/a busy
oeste Ⓜ o·es·te west
oficina Ⓕ o·fee·see·na office
— de correos de ko·re·os post office
— de turismo de too·rees·mo tourist office
— de objetos perdidos de ob·he·tos per·dee·dos lost property office
oír o·eer hear
ojo Ⓜ o·ho eye
ola Ⓕ o·la wave
oler o·ler smell
olor Ⓜ o·lor smell
olvidar ol·vee·dar forget
operación Ⓕ o·pe·ra·syon operation
operador(a) Ⓜ/Ⓕ o·pe·ra·dor/o·pe·ra·do·ra operator
opinión Ⓕ o·pee·nyon opinion
oportunidad Ⓕ o·por·too·nee·dad chance • possibility
oración Ⓕ o·ra·syon prayer
orden Ⓜ or·den order (placement)
orden Ⓕ or·den order (command)
ordenar or·de·nar order
oreja Ⓕ o·re·ha ear
orgasmo Ⓜ or·gas·mo orgasm
original o·ree·hee·nal original
orquesta Ⓕ or·kes·ta orchestra
oscuro/a Ⓜ/Ⓕ os·koo·ro/a dark
otoño Ⓜ o·to·nyo autumn • fall
otra vez o·tra ves again
otro/a Ⓜ/Ⓕ o·tro/a other
oveja Ⓕ o·ve·ha sheep
oxígeno Ⓜ ok·see·he·no oxygen

P

pacheco/a Ⓜ/Ⓕ pa·che·ko/a stoned • high
padre Ⓜ pa·dre father
padres Ⓜ pl pa·dres parents
padrísimo/a Ⓜ/Ⓕ pa·dree·see·mo/a great
pagar pa·gar pay
página Ⓕ pa·hee·na page
pago Ⓜ pa·go payment
país Ⓜ pa·ees country
pájaro Ⓜ pa·ha·ro bird
palabra Ⓕ pa·la·bra word
palacio Ⓜ pa·la·syo palace
palillo Ⓜ pa·lee·yo toothpick
pan Ⓜ pan bread
panadería Ⓕ pa·na·de·ree·a bakery
pantaletas Ⓕ pl pan·ta·le·tas underpants (women)
pantalla Ⓕ pan·ta·ya screen
pantalones Ⓜ pl pan·ta·lo·nes trousers • pants
— de mezclilla de mes·klee·ya jeans
pantimedias Ⓕ pl pan·tee·me·dyas pantyhose • stockings
pantiprotectores Ⓜ pl pan·tee·pro·tek·to·res panty liners
pañal Ⓜ pa·nyal nappy • diaper
papá Ⓜ pa·pa dad
papanicolaou Ⓜ pa·pa·nee·ko·low pap smear
papel Ⓜ pa·pel paper
— de fumar de foo·mar cigarette papers
— higiénico ee·hye·nee·ko toilet paper
paquete Ⓜ pa·ke·te package • packet
para pa·ra for

— siempre *syem*·pre forever
parabrisas ⓜ pa·ra·*bree*·sas windscreen
parada ⓕ pa·*ra*·da stop
— de autobuses de ow·to·*boo*·ses bus stop
paraguas ⓜ pa·*ra*·gwas umbrella
parapléjico/a ⓜ/ⓕ pa·ra·*ple*·hee·ko/a paraplegic
parar pa·*rar* stop
pared ⓕ pa·*red* wall (inside)
pareja ⓕ pa·*re*·ha partner
parlamento ⓜ par·la·*men*·to parliament
paro ⓜ *pa*·ro dole
parque ⓜ *par*·ke park
— nacional na·syo·*nal* national park
parte ⓕ *par*·te part
partido ⓜ par·*tee*·do match (sport) • party (political)
pasado ⓜ pa·*sa*·do past
pasado mañana pa·*sa*·do ma·*nya*·na day after tomorrow
pasajero ⓜ pa·sa·*he*·ro passenger
pasaporte ⓜ pa·sa·*por*·te passport
pase ⓜ *pa*·se pass
— de abordar de a·bor·*dar* boarding pass
paseo ⓜ pa·*se*·o ride
paso ⓜ *pa*·so step
pasta ⓕ **de dientes** *pas*·ta de *dyen*·tes toothpaste
pastel ⓜ pas·*tel* cake
— de bodas de *bo*·das wedding cake
— de cumpleaños de koom·ple·*a*·nyos birthday cake
pastelería ⓕ pas·te·le·*ree*·a cake shop
pastillas ⓕ pl pas·*tee*·yas pills
— antipalúdicas an·tee·pa·*loo*·dee·kas antimalarial tablets
— de menta de *men*·ta mints
— para dormir *pa*·ra dor·*meer* sleeping pills
pasto ⓜ *pas*·to grass
patear pa·te·*ar* kick
patinar en línea pa·tee·nar en *lee*·nya rollerblading
patineta ⓕ pa·tee·*ne*·ta skateboard
pato ⓜ *pa*·to duck
pavo ⓜ *pa*·vo turkey
pay ⓜ pay pie
paz ⓕ pas peace
peatón ⓜ pe·a·*ton* pedestrian
pecho ⓜ *pe*·cho chest
pedazo ⓜ pe·*da*·so piece
pedir pe·*deer* ask (for something)
— aventón a·ven·*ton* hitchhike
— prestado pres·*ta*·do borrow
pedo ⓜ *pe*·do fart
peinar pay·*nar* comb
peine ⓜ *pay*·ne comb
pelea ⓕ pe·*le*·a fight • quarrel
película ⓕ pe·*lee*·koo·la film • movie
— en color en ko·*lor* colour film
peligroso/a ⓜ/ⓕ pe·lee·*gro*·so/a dangerous
pelo ⓜ *pe*·lo hair
pelota ⓕ pe·*lo*·ta ball
peluquero/a ⓜ/ⓕ pe·loo·*ke*·ro/a hairdresser
pene ⓜ *pe*·ne penis
pensar pen·*sar* think
pensión ⓕ pen·*syon* boarding house
pequeño/a ⓜ/ⓕ pe·*ke*·nyo/a small • tiny
perder per·*der* lose
perdido/a ⓜ/ⓕ per·*dee*·do/a lost
perdonar per·do·*nar* forgive
perfume ⓜ per·*foo*·me perfume
periódico ⓜ pe·*ryo*·dee·ko newspaper
periodista ⓜ&ⓕ pe·ryo·*dees*·ta journalist
permiso ⓜ per·*mee*·so permission • permit
— de trabajo de tra·*ba*·ho work permit
permitir per·mee·*teer* allow • permit
pero *pe*·ro but
perro/a ⓜ/ⓕ *pe*·ro/a dog
perro ⓜ **guía** *pe*·ro *gee*·a guide dog
persona ⓕ per·*so*·na person
pesado/a ⓜ/ⓕ pe·*sa*·do/a heavy

pesar pe·*sar* weigh
pesas ⓕ pl *pe*·sas weights
pesca ⓕ *pes*·ka fishing
pescadería ⓕ pes·ka·de·*ree*·a fish shop
peso ⓜ *pe*·so weight • peso (Mexican currency)
petate ⓜ pe·*ta*·te mat
petición ⓕ pe·tee·*syon* petition
pez ⓜ pes fish
picadura ⓕ pee·ka·*doo*·ra bite (insect)
pícnic ⓜ *peek*·neek picnic
pico ⓜ *pee*·ko pickaxe
pie ⓜ pye foot
piedra ⓕ *pye*·dra stone
piel ⓕ pyel skin
pierna ⓕ *pyer*·na leg
pila ⓕ *pee*·la battery (small)
píldora ⓕ *peel*·do·ra the Pill
pintar peen·*tar* paint
pintor(a) ⓜ/ⓕ peen·*tor*/peen·*to*·ra painter
pintura ⓕ peen·*too*·ra painting
pinzas ⓕ pl *peen*·sas tweezers
piojos ⓜ pl *pyo*·hos lice
piolet ⓜ pyo·*le* ice axe
piso ⓜ *pee*·so floor
pista ⓕ *pees*·ta racetrack (runners)
plancha ⓕ *plan*·cha iron (for clothing)
planeta ⓜ pla·*ne*·ta planet
plano/a ⓜ/ⓕ *pla*·no/a flat
planta ⓕ *plan*·ta plant
plástico ⓜ *plas*·tee·ko plastic
plata ⓕ *pla*·ta silver • money (slang)
plataforma ⓕ pla·ta·*for*·ma platform
plateado/a ⓜ/ⓕ pla·te·a·do/a silver • silver-coloured
plato ⓜ *pla*·to plate
playa ⓕ *pla*·ya beach
playera ⓕ pla·*ye*·ra T-shirt
plaza ⓕ *pla*·sa square
— de toros de *to*·ros bullring
pluma ⓕ *ploo*·ma pen
pobre *po*·bre poor
pobreza ⓕ po·*bre*·sa poverty
pocos/as ⓜ/ⓕ pl *po*·kos/as few

poder ⓜ po·*der* power
poder po·*der* (to be) able • can
poesía ⓕ po·e·*see*·a poetry
polen ⓜ *po*·len pollen
policía ⓕ po·lee·*see*·a police
política ⓕ po·*lee*·tee·ka politics • policy
político/a ⓜ/ⓕ po·*lee*·tee·ko/a politician
póliza ⓕ *po*·lee·sa policy (insurance)
ponchar pon·*char* puncture
poner po·*ner* put
popular po·poo·*lar* popular
póquer ⓜ *po*·ker poker
por (día) por (*dee*·a) per (day)
por ciento por *syen*·to percent
por qué por *ke* why
por vía ⓕ **aérea** por *vee*·a a·e·re·a by airmail
porque *por*·ke because
portafolios ⓜ por·ta·*fo*·lyos briefcase
portero/a ⓜ/ⓕ por·*te*·ro/a goalkeeper • doorman
posible po·*see*·ble possible
postal ⓕ pos·*tal* postcard
pozo ⓜ *po*·so well
precio ⓜ *pre*·syo price
— de entrada de en·*tra*·da admission price
preferir pre·fe·*reer* prefer
pregunta ⓕ pre·*goon*·ta question
preguntar pre·goon·*tar* ask (a question)
preocupado/a ⓜ/ⓕ pre·o·koo·*pa*·do/a worried
preocuparse por pre·o·koo·*par*·se por care about something • worry
preparar pre·pa·*rar* prepare
presentación ⓕ pres·en·ta·*syon* performance (entertainment)
presidente/a ⓜ/ⓕ pre·see·*den*·te/a president
presión ⓕ pre·*syon* pressure
— arterial ar·te·*ryal* blood pressure
prevenir pre·ve·*neer* prevent
primavera ⓕ pree·ma·*ve*·ra spring (season)

primer ministro ⓜ *pree·mer mee·nees·tro* prime minister
primera ministra ⓕ *pree·me·ra mee·nees·tra* prime minister
primera clase *pree·me·ra kla·se* first class
primero/a ⓜ/ⓕ *pree·me·ro/a* first
principal *preen·see·pal* main
prisa *pree·sa* in a hurry
prisionero/a ⓜ/ⓕ *pree·syo·ne·ro/a* prisoner
privado/a ⓜ/ⓕ *pree·va·do/a* private
probadores ⓜ pl *pro·ba·do·res* changing room
probar *pro·bar* try
producir *pro·doo·seer* produce
productos ⓜ pl **congelados** *pro·dook·tos kon·he·la·dos* frozen foods
profundo/a ⓜ/ⓕ *pro·foon·do/a* deep
programa ⓜ *pro·gra·ma* programme
promesa ⓕ *pro·me·sa* promise
prometida ⓕ *pro·me·tee·da* fiancée
prometido ⓜ *pro·me·tee·do* fiancé
pronto *pron·to* soon
propietaria ⓕ *pro·pye·ta·rya* landlady
propietario ⓜ *pro·pye·ta·ryo* landlord
propina ⓕ *pro·pee·na* tip (gratuity)
prórroga ⓕ *pro·ro·ga* extension (visa)
proteger *pro·te·her* protect
protegido/a ⓜ/ⓕ *pro·te·hee·do/a* protected
protesta ⓕ *pro·tes·ta* protest
protestar *pro·tes·tar* protest
provisiones ⓕ pl *pro·vee·syo·nes* provisions
proyector ⓜ *pro·yek·tor* projector
prueba ⓕ *prwe·ba* test
— de embarazo *de em·ba·ra·so* pregnancy test kit
pruebas ⓕ pl **nucleares** *prwe·bas noo·kle·a·res* nuclear testing
pueblo ⓜ *pwe·blo* village
puente ⓜ *pwen·te* bridge
puerta ⓕ *pwer·ta* door
puerto ⓜ *pwer·to* harbour • port
puesta ⓕ **de sol** *pwes·ta de sol* sunset
puesto ⓜ **de periódicos** *pwes·to de pe·ryo·dee·kos* news stand
pulga ⓕ *pool·ga* flea
pulmones ⓜ pl *pool·mo·nes* lungs
punto ⓜ *poon·to* point
pupilentes ⓜ *poo·pee·len·tes* contact lenses
puro ⓜ *poo·ro* cigar
puro/a ⓜ/ⓕ *poo·ro/a* pure

Q

qué *ke* what
quedarse *ke·dar·se* stay (remain)
— sin *seen* run out of
quehacer ⓜ *ke·a·ser* housework
quejarse *ke·har·se* complain
quemadura ⓕ *ke·ma·doo·ra* burn
— de sol *de sol* sunburn
quemar *ke·mar* burn
querer *ke·rer* want
quién *kyen* who
quincena ⓕ *keen·se·na* fortnight
quiste ⓜ **ovárico** *kees·te o·va·ree·ko* ovarian cyst
quizás *kee·sas* perhaps

R

radiador ⓜ *ra·dya·dor* radiator
rápido/a ⓜ/ⓕ *ra·pee·do/a* fast • quick
raqueta ⓕ *ra·ke·ta* racquet
raro/a ⓜ/ⓕ *ra·ro/a* rare • strange • unusual
rastrillo ⓜ *ras·tree·yo* razor
rastro ⓜ *ras·tro* track (footprints)
rasurarse *ra·soo·rar·se* shave
rata ⓕ *ra·ta* rat
ratón ⓜ *ra·ton* mouse
raza ⓕ *ra·sa* race (people)
razón ⓕ *ra·son* reason • right
realista *re·a·lees·ta* realistic
recámara ⓕ *re·ka·ma·ra* bedroom

recibir re·see·*beer* receive
recibo ⓜ re·*see*·bo receipt
reciclable re·see·*kla*·ble recyclable
reciclar re·see·*klar* recycle
recientemente re·syen·te·*men*·te recently
recolección ⓕ **de fruta** re·ko·lek·*syon* de *froo*·ta fruit picking
recomendar re·ko·men·*dar* recommend
reconocer re·ko·no·*ser* recognise
recordar re·kor·*dar* remember
recorrido ⓜ **guiado** re·ko·*ree*·do gee·*a*·do guided tour
recostarse re·kos·*tar*·se lie (not stand)
recuerdo ⓜ re·*kwer*·do souvenir
red ⓕ red net
redondo/a ⓜ/ⓕ re·*don*·do/a round
reembolsar re·em·bol·*sar* refund
reembolso ⓜ re·em·*bol*·so refund
referencia ⓕ re·fe·*ren*·sya reference
refresco ⓜ re·*fres*·ko soft drink
refrigerador ⓜ re·free·he·ra·*dor* refrigerator
refugiado/a ⓜ/ⓕ re·foo·*hya*·do/a refugee
regadera ⓕ re·ga·*de*·ra shower
regalar re·ga·*lar* give a gift
regalo ⓜ re·*ga*·lo gift
— de bodas de *bo*·das wedding present
reglas ⓕ pl *re*·glas rules
reina ⓕ *ray*·na queen
reír re·*eer* laugh
relación ⓕ re·la·*syon* relationship
relajarse re·la·*har*·se relax
religión ⓕ re·lee·*hyon* religion
religioso/a ⓜ/ⓕ re·lee·*hyo*·so/a religious
reliquia ⓕ re·*lee*·kya relic
reloj ⓜ re·*loh* clock
— de pulsera de pool·*se*·ra watch
remo ⓜ *re*·mo rowing
remoto/a ⓜ/ⓕ re·*mo*·to/a remote
renta ⓕ *ren*·ta rent
— de coches de *ko*·ches car hire
rentar ren·*tar* hire • rent
reparar re·pa·*rar* repair
repartir re·par·*teer* deal (cards) • distribute
repelente ⓜ **contra mosquitos** re·pe·*len*·te *kon*·tra mos·*kee*·tos mosquito repellent
repetir re·pe·*teer* repeat
república ⓕ re·*poo*·blee·ka republic
reservación ⓕ re·ser·va·*syon* reservation
reservar re·ser·*var* book • reserve
resfriado ⓜ res·free·*a*·do cold (illness)
residuos ⓜ pl **tóxicos** re·*see*·dwos *tok*·see·kos toxic waste
residuos ⓜ pl **nucleares** re·*see*·dwos noo·kle·*a*·res nuclear waste
resorte ⓜ re·*sor*·te spring (wire)
respaldo ⓜ res·*pal*·do back (of chair)
respirar res·pee·*rar* breathe
respuesta ⓕ res·*pwes*·ta answer
restaurante ⓜ res·tow·*ran*·te restaurant
revisar re·vee·*sar* check
revisor(a) ⓜ/ⓕ re·vee·*sor*/re·vee·*sor*·a ticket collector • inspector
revista ⓕ re·*vees*·ta magazine
rey ⓜ ray king
rezar re·*sar* pray • worship
rico/a ⓜ/ⓕ *ree*·ko/a rich • wealthy
riesgo ⓜ *ryes*·go risk
río ⓜ *ree*·o river
ritmo ⓜ *reet*·mo rhythm
robar ro·*bar* rob • steal
roca ⓕ *ro*·ka rock
rodilla ⓕ ro·*dee*·ya knee
rojo/a ⓜ/ⓕ *ro*·ho/a red
romántico/a ⓜ/ⓕ ro·*man*·tee·ko/a romantic
romper rom·*per* break
ron ron rum
ropa ⓕ *ro*·pa clothing
— de cama de *ka*·ma bedding
— interior een·te·*ryor* underwear
rosa *ro*·sa pink
rosadura ⓕ ro·sa·*doo*·ra nappy/

diaper rash
roto/a ⓜ/ⓕ ro·to/a broken
rueda ⓕ rwe·da wheel
ruidoso/a ⓜ/ⓕ rwee·do·so/a loud • noisy
ruinas ⓕ pl rwee·nas ruins
ruta ⓕ roo·ta route

S

sábana ⓕ sa·ba·na sheet (bed)
saber sa·ber know (something)
sabroso/a ⓜ/ⓕ sa·bro·so/a tasty
sacerdote ⓜ sa·ser·do·te priest
sala ⓕ **de espera** sa·la de es·pe·ra waiting room
sala ⓕ **de tránsito** sa·la de tran·see·to transit lounge
salario ⓜ sa·la·ryo pay rate • salary
saldo ⓜ sal·do balance (account)
salida ⓕ sa·lee·da exit • departure
saliente ⓜ sa·lyen·te ledge
salir sa·leer exit
salir con sa·leer kon date (a person) • go out with
salir de sa·leer de depart
salón ⓜ **de belleza** sa·lon de be·ye·sa beauty salon
saltar sal·tar jump
salud ⓕ sa·lood health
salvar sal·var save
sandalias ⓕ pl san·da·lyas sandals
sangrar san·grar bleed
sangre ⓕ san·gre blood
santo/a ⓜ/ⓕ san·to/a saint
sarampión ⓜ sa·ram·pyon measles
sartén ⓜ sar·ten frying pan • pan
sastre ⓜ sas·tre tailor
secar se·kar dry
secretario/a ⓜ/ⓕ se·kre·ta·ryo/a secretary
sed ⓕ sed thirst
seda ⓕ se·da silk
seguido se·gee·do often
seguir se·geer follow
segundo ⓜ se·goon·do second (time)
segundo/a ⓜ/ⓕ se·goon·do/a second (place)
seguro ⓜ se·goo·ro insurance
seguro/a ⓜ/ⓕ se·goo·ro/a safe
sello ⓜ se·yo stamp
semáforos ⓜ pl se·ma·fo·ros traffic lights
sembrar sem·brar plant
semidirecto/a ⓜ/ⓕ se·mee·dee·rek·to/a non-direct
señal ⓕ se·nyal sign
sencillo/a ⓜ/ⓕ sen·see·yo/a simple
sendero ⓜ sen·de·ro path
sendero de montaña ⓜ sen·de·ro de mon·ta·nya mountain path
senderos ⓜ pl sen·de·ros hiking route
senos ⓜ pl se·nos breasts
sensibilidad ⓕ sen·see·bee·lee·dad film speed
sensible sen·see·ble sensitive
sensual sen·swal sensual
sentarse sen·tar·se sit
sentimientos ⓜ pl sen·tee·myen·tos feelings
sentir sen·teer feel
separado/a ⓜ/ⓕ se·pa·ra·do/a separate
separar se·pa·rar separate
ser ser be
serie ⓕ se·rye series • TV series
serio/a ⓜ/ⓕ se·ryo/a serious
seropositivo/a ⓜ/ⓕ se·ro·po·see·tee·vo/a HIV positive
serpiente ⓕ ser·pyen·te snake
servicio ⓜ **militar** ser·vee·syo mee·lee·tar military service
servicio de niñera ⓜ ser·vee·cyo de nee·nye·ra childminding service • creche
servilleta ⓕ ser·vee·ye·ta napkin
sexismo ⓜ sek·sees·mo sexism
sexo ⓜ sek·so sex
— seguro se·goo·ro safe sex
si see if
sí see yes
SIDA ⓜ see·da AIDS

siempre *syem*·pre always
silla ⓕ *see*·ya chair
— de montar de mon·*tar* saddle
— de ruedas de *rwe*·das wheelchair
similar see·mee·*lar* similar
simpático/a ⓜ/ⓕ seem·*pa*·tee·ko/a nice
sin seen without
— hogar o·*gar* homeless
— plomo *plo*·mo unleaded
sinagoga ⓕ see·na·*go*·ga synagogue
síndrome ⓜ **premenstrual** *seen*·dro·me pre·men·*strwal* premenstrual tension
sintético/a ⓜ/ⓕ seen·*te*·tee·ko/a synthetic
sitio ⓜ **de taxis** *see*·tyo de *tak*·sees taxi stand
sleeping ⓜ eh·*sleep*·een sleeping bag
sobornar so·bor·*nar* bribe
soborno ⓜ so·*bor*·no bribe
sobre ⓜ *so*·bre envelope
sobre *so*·bre about
sobredosis ⓕ so·bre·*do*·sees overdose
sobrevivir so·bre·vee·*veer* survive
socialista ⓜ&ⓕ so·sya·*lees*·ta socialist
sol ⓜ sol sun
soldado ⓜ&ⓕ sol·*da*·do soldier
soleado so·le·*a*·do sunny
sólo *so*·lo only
solo/a ⓜ/ⓕ *so*·lo/a alone
soltero/a ⓜ/ⓕ sol·*te*·ro/a single (person)
sombra ⓕ *som*·bra shadow
sombrero ⓜ som·*bre*·ro hat
soñar so·*nyar* dream
sonreír son·re·*eer* smile
sordo/a ⓜ/ⓕ *sor*·do/a deaf
sorpresa ⓕ sor·*pre*·sa surprise
su soo his • her • their • your pol
subtítulos ⓜ pl soob·*tee*·too·los subtitles
sucio/a ⓜ/ⓕ *soo*·syo/a dirty
sucursal ⓕ soo·koor·*sal* branch office
sudar soo·*dar* perspire
suegra ⓕ *swe*·gra mother-in-law
suegro ⓜ *swe*·gro father-in-law
sueldo ⓜ *swel*·do wage
suelto/a ⓜ/ⓕ *swel*·to/a loose
suerte ⓕ *swer*·te luck
suertudo/a ⓜ/ⓕ swer·*too*·do/a lucky
sueter ⓜ *swe*·ter jumper • sweater
suficiente soo·fee·*syen*·te enough
sufrir soo·*freer* suffer
supermercado ⓜ soo·per·mer·*ka*·do supermarket
superstición ⓕ soo·per·stee·*syon* superstition
sur ⓜ soor south
surfear soor·fe·*ar* surf

T

tabaco ⓜ ta·*ba*·ko tobacco
tabaquería ⓕ ta·ba·ke·*ree*·a tobacconist
tabla ⓕ **de surf** *ta*·bla de soorf surfboard
tablero ⓜ **de ajedrez** ta·*ble*·ro de a·he·*dres* chess board
tacaño/a ⓜ/ⓕ ta·*ka*·nyo/a stingy
tal vez tal ves maybe
talco ⓜ **para bébe** *tal*·ko *pa*·ra be·be baby powder
talla ⓕ *ta*·ya size (clothes)
taller ⓜ ta·*yer* workshop
tamaño ⓜ ta·*ma*·nyo size
también tam·*byen* also
tampoco tam·*po*·ko neither
tampones ⓜ pl tam·*po*·nes tampons
tapón ⓜ ta·*pon* bath plug
tanga ⓕ *tan*·ga g-string
tapones ⓜ pl **para los oídos** ta·*po*·nes *pa*·ra los o·*ee*·dos earplugs
taquilla ⓕ ta·*koo*·ya ticket office
tarde ⓕ *tar*·de afternoon
tarde *tar*·de late
tarifa de uso ⓕ **de aeropuerto (TUA)** ta·*ree*·fa de·*oo*·so de a·e·ro·*pwer*·to (*too*·a) airport tax

T MEXICAN SPANISH – ENGLISH

tarjeta ⓕ **de crédito** tar·he·ta de kre·dee·to credit card
taza ⓕ ta·sa cup
té ⓜ te tea
teatro ⓜ te·a·tro theatre
teclado ⓜ te·kla·do keyboard
técnica ⓕ tek·nee·ka technique
tela ⓕ te·la fabric
tele ⓕ te·le TV
teleférico ⓜ te·le·fe·ree·ko cable car
teléfono ⓜ te·le·fo·no telephone
— celular se·loo·lar mobile/cell phone
— público poo·blee·ko phone box • public telephone
telegrama ⓜ te·le·gra·ma telegram
telenovela ⓕ te·le·no·ve·la soap opera
teleobjetivo ⓜ te·le·ob·he·tee·vo telephoto lens
telescopio ⓜ te·les·ko·pyo telescope
televisión ⓕ te·le·vee·syon television
temperatura ⓕ tem·pe·ra·too·ra temperature (weather)
templado/a ⓜ/ⓕ tem·pla·do/a warm
templo ⓜ tem·plo temple
temporada ⓕ tem·po·ra·da season (in sport)
temprano tem·pra·no early
tendedero ⓜ ten·de·de·ro clothes line
tenedor ⓜ te·ne·dor fork
tener te·ner have
— gripa gree·pa have a cold
— hambre am·bre (be) hungry
— sed sed (be) thirsty
— sueño swe·nyo (be) sleepy
tercio ⓜ ter·syo third
terco/a ⓜ/ⓕ ter·ko/a stubborn
terminar ter·mee·nar finish • end
terremoto ⓜ te·re·mo·to earthquake
terrible te·ree·ble terrible
tía ⓕ tee·a aunt
tiempo ⓜ tyem·po time • weather
— completo kom·ple·to full-time
tienda ⓕ tyen·da shop • convenience store
— de abarrotes de a·ba·ro·tes convenience store • grocery store
— de campaña de kam·pa·nya tent
— de camping de kam·peen camping store
— de deportes de de·por·tes sports store
— de electrónica de el·ek·tron·ica electrical store
— de fotografía de fo·to·gra·fee·a camera shop
— de recuerdos de re·kwer·dos souvenir shop
— de ropa de ro·pa clothing store
— departamental de·par·ta·men·tal department store
Tierra ⓕ tye·ra Earth
tierra ⓕ tye·ra land
tijeras ⓕ pl tee·he·ras scissors
tímido/a ⓜ/ⓕ tee·mee·do/a shy
tina ⓕ tee·na bathtub
típico/a ⓜ/ⓕ tee·pee·ko/a typical
tipo ⓜ tee·po type
— de cambio de kam·byo exchange rate
título ⓜ tee·too·lo degree • deed
toalla ⓕ to·a·ya towel
toallas ⓕ pl **femeninas** to·a·yas fe·me·nee·nas sanitary napkins
toallita ⓕ twa·ee·ta wash cloth
toallita ⓕ **facial** to·a·yee·ta fa·syal face cloth
tobillo ⓜ to·bee·yo ankle
tocar to·kar touch • play (instrument)
todavía (no) to·da·vee·a (no) (not) yet
todo/a ⓜ/ⓕ to·do/a all • everything
todos/as ⓜ/ⓕ to·dos/as all (of them)
tomar to·mar drink • take (the train)
— fotos fo·tos take photographs
tono de marcar ⓜ toh·no de mar·kar dial tone
torcedura ⓕ tor·se·doo·ra sprain
tormenta ⓕ tor·men·ta storm
toro ⓜ to·ro bull
torre ⓕ to·re tower
tos ⓕ tos cough

tostador ⓜ tos·ta·*dor* toaster
trabajar tra·ba·*har* work
trabajo ⓜ tra·*ba*·ho job • work
— de limpieza de leem·*pye*·sa cleaning
— eventual e·ven·*twal* casual work • temporary work
traducir tra·doo·*seer* translate
traer tra·*er* bring
traficante ⓜ&ⓕ **de drogas** tra·fee·*kan*·te de *dro*·gas drug dealer
tráfico ⓜ *tra*·fee·ko traffic
traje ⓜ **de baño** *tra*·he de *ba*·nyo bathing suit • swimsuit
trámites ⓜ *tra*·mee·tes paperwork
tramposo/a ⓜ/ⓕ tram·*po*·so/a cheat
tranquilidad ⓕ tran·kee·lee·*dad* quiet
tranquilo/a ⓜ/ⓕ tran·*kee*·lo/a quiet
transparencia ⓕ trans·pa·*ren*·sya slide
transporte ⓜ trans·*por*·te transport
tranvía ⓜ tran·*vee*·a tram
tren ⓜ tren train
triste *trees*·te sad
calzoncillos ⓜ pl kal·son·*see*·yos underpants (men)
tu sg inf too your
tú sg inf too you
tumba ⓕ *toom*·ba grave
turista ⓜ&ⓕ too·*rees*·ta tourist

U

ultrasonido ⓜ ool·tra·so·*nee*·do ultrasound
una vez *oo*·na ves once
uniforme ⓜ oo·nee·*for*·me uniform
universidad ⓕ oo·nee·ver·see·*dad* university • college
universo ⓜ oo·nee·*ver*·so universe
urgente oor·*hen*·te urgent
Usted sg pol oos·*ted* you
Ustedes pl pol oos·*te*·des you
útil *oo*·teel useful

V

vaca ⓕ *va*·ka cow
vacaciones ⓕ pl va·ka·*syo*·nes holidays • vacation
vacante va·*kan*·te vacant
vacío/a ⓜ/ⓕ va·*see*·o/a empty
vacuna ⓕ va·*koo*·na vaccination
vagina ⓕ va·*hee*·na vagina
vagón ⓜ **restaurante** va·*gon* res·tow·*ran*·te dining car
vagoneta ⓕ va·go·*ne*·ta van
validar va·lee·*dar* validate
valiente va·*lyen*·te brave
valioso/a ⓜ/ⓕ va·*lyo*·so/a valuable
valle ⓜ *va*·ye valley
valor ⓜ va·*lor* value
varios/as ⓜ/ⓕ *va*·ryos/as several
vaso ⓜ *va*·so glass
vegano/a ⓜ/ⓕ veh·*ga*·no/a vegan
vegetariano/a ⓜ/ⓕ ve·he·ta·*rya*·no/a vegetarian
vela ⓕ *ve*·la candle
velocidad ⓕ ve·lo·see·*dad* speed
velocímetro ⓜ ve·lo·*see*·me·tro speedometer
velódromo ⓜ ve·*lo*·dro·mo racetrack (bicycles)
vena ⓕ *ve*·na vein
vendaje ⓜ ven·*da*·he bandage
vendedor(a) ⓜ/ⓕ **de flores** ven·de·*dor*/ven·de·*do*·ra de *flo*·res flower seller
vender ven·*der* sell
venenoso/a ⓜ/ⓕ ve·ne·*no*·so/a poisonous
venir ve·*neer* come
ventana ⓕ ven·*ta*·na window
ventilador ⓜ ven·tee·la·*dor* fan (machine)
ver ver see
verano ⓜ ve·*ra*·no summer
verde *ver*·de green
verdulería ⓕ ver·doo·le·*ree*·a greengrocery

verduras ⓕ ver·*doo*·ras vegetables
vestíbulo ⓜ ves·*tee*·boo·lo foyer
vestido ⓜ ves·*tee*·do dress
viajar vya·*har* travel
viaje ⓜ *vya*·he trip
vid ⓕ veed vine
vida ⓕ *vee*·da life
viejo/a ⓜ/ⓕ *vye*·ho/a old
viento ⓜ *vyen*·to wind
viñedo ⓜ vee·*nye*·do vineyard
vino ⓜ *vee*·no wine
violar vyo·*lar* rape
virus ⓜ *vee*·roos virus
visa ⓕ *vee*·sa visa
visitar vee·see·*tar* visit
vista ⓕ *vees*·ta view
vitaminas ⓕ pl vee·ta·*mee*·nas vitamins
víveres ⓜ pl *vee*·ve·res food supplies
vivir vee·*veer* live
volar vo·*lar* fly
volumen ⓜ vo·*loo*·men volume
volver vol·*ver* return
votar vo·*tar* vote
voz ⓕ vos voice
vuelo ⓜ **doméstico** *vwe*·lo do·*mes*·tee·ko domestic flight

Y

y ee and
ya ya already
yerbero/a ⓜ/ⓕ yer·*be*·ro/a herbalist
yo yo I

Z

zapatería ⓕ sa·pa·te·*ree*·a shoe shop
zapatos ⓜ pl sa·*pa*·tos shoes
zócalo ⓜ *so*·ka·lo main square
zodíaco ⓜ so·*dee*·a·ko zodiac
zoológico ⓜ so·o·*lo*·hee·ko zoo

INDEX

ÍNDICE

For topics that are covered in several sections of this book, we've indicated the most relevant page number in bold.

A

B

C

D

E

F

G

H

I

J

K

L

M

N

O

P

Q

R

S

T

U

V

W

X

Y

10 Ways TO START A SENTENCE

When's (the next flight)?	¿Cuándo sale (el próximo vuelo)?	*kwan*·do sa·le (el *prok*·see·mo *vwe*·lo)
Where's the (station)?	¿Dónde está (la estación)?	*don*·de es·*ta* (la es·ta·*syon*)
Where can I (buy a ticket)?	¿Dónde puedo (comprar un boleto)?	*don*·de *pwe*·do (kom·*prar* oon bo·*le*·to)
How much is (a room)?	¿Cuánto cuesta (una habitación)?	*kwan*·to *kwes*·ta (*oo*·na a·bee·ta·*syon*)
Do you have (a map)?	¿Tiene (un mapa)?	*tye*·ne (oon *ma*·pa)
Is there (a toilet)?	¿Hay (baño)?	ai (*ba*·nyo)
I'd like (to hire a car).	Quisiera (rentar un coche).	kee·*sye*·ra (ren·*tar* oon *ko*·che)
Can I (enter)?	¿Se puede (entrar)?	se *pwe*·de (en·*trar*)
Could you please (help me)?	¿Puede (ayudarme), por favor?	*pwe*·de (a·yoo·*dar*·me) por fa·*vor*
Do I have to (get a visa)?	¿Necesito (obtener una visa)?	ne·se·*see*·to (ob·te·*ner* *oo*·na *vee*·sa)